Smart Talent Management

Smart Talent Management

Building Knowledge Assets for Competitive Advantage

Edited by

Vlad Vaiman

FH Joanneum University of Applied Sciences, Austria

Charles M. Vance

Loyola Marymount University, USA

Edward Elgar

Cheltenham, UK • Northampton, MA, USA

Published by
Edward Elgar Publishing Limited
The Lypiatts
15 Lansdown Road
Cheltenham
Glos GL50 2JA
UK

Edward Elgar Publishing, Inc.
William Pratt House
9 Dewey Court
Northampton
Massachusetts 01060
USA

Paperback edition 2010
Paperback edition reprinted 2015

A catalogue record for this book
is available from the British Library

Library of Congress Cataloguing in Publication Data
Smart talent management : building knowledge assets for competitive
advantage / edited by Vlad Vaiman and Charles Vance.
    p. cm.
    Includes bibliographical references and index.
1. Knowledge management. 2. Intellectual capital. 3. Employee selection.
4. Personnel management. I. Vaiman, Vlad, 1971– II. Vance, Charles, 1952–
    HD30.2.S624 2008
    658.4′038—dc22

                                                           2008000458

MIX
Paper from
responsible sources
FSC
www.fsc.org   FSC® C013604

ISBN   978 1 84720 513 1 (cased)
        978 1 84980 071 6 (paperback)

Printed and bound in Great Britain by the CPI Group (UK) Ltd

Contents

List of figures   vii
List of tables and boxes   viii
List of contributors   ix

1 Smart talent management: on the powerful amalgamation
   of talent management and knowledge management   1
   Charles M. Vance and Vlad Vaiman

PART 1   HR PLANNING AND STAFFING

2 Critical considerations of talent management and knowledge
   management for effective HR planning   19
   Patrick F. Schutz and Donald A. Carpenter
3 Talent staffing systems for effective knowledge management   33
   Mark L. Lengnick-Hall and Leticia S. Andrade
4 Attracting and retaining Generation Y knowledge worker
   talent   66
   Siri Terjesen and Regina-Viola Frey

PART 2   TRAINING AND COACHING

5 The role of social networks in managing organizational
   talent, knowledge and employee learning   93
   Rob F. Poell and Ferd J. Van der Krogt
6 The power of career counseling for enhanced talent and
   knowledge management   119
   Ans De Vos and Nele Soens
7 Accelerated development of organizational talent   139
   Konstantin Korotov

PART 3   PERFORMANCE MANAGEMENT

8 Reward and recognition concepts that support talent and
   knowledge management initiatives   161
   Nancy A. Inskeep and Bettie Hall

9 Talent management, performance management, and the management of organizational knowledge: the case for a congruent relationship   176
   Patrick F. Schutz and Donald A. Carpenter

PART 4 ORGANIZATIONAL LEARNING AND DEVELOPMENT

10 Talent management and the global learning organization   195
    Dennis Briscoe
11 Social capital: bridging the link between talent management and knowledge management   217
    Rhonda Jones
12 Certifying knowledge and skills is critical for talent management   234
    Jim M. Graber and William J. Rothwell

Index   263

Figures

3.1	Employee flows	39
4.1	Working age (15–64) population: % change expected 2005 to 2025	67
4.2	Extrinsic and intrinsic incentives	79
5.1	Process cycle	98
5.2	Relationships between the work network, work process, and work structure	101
5.3	Four ideal-typical work-network structures along three dimensions	104
5.4	Learning-program creation	106
5.5	Four ideal-typical learning-network structures and their climates	107
6.1	An integrative model for career counseling within organizations	127
9.1	Independent systems	184
9.2	Partially integrated systems	185
9.3	Fully integrated, loosely coupled systems	185
9.4	Fully integrated, tightly coupled systems	186
9.5	Comparison of performance appraisal systems	187
11.1	Nonaka's SECI process	221
11.2	Formula for competitive advantage for all organizations	224
12.1	ALR data collection template	249
12.2	Introduction section of completed template	251
12.3	Learning objectives section of template	252
12.4	Developmental opportunities section of template	252
12.5	Knowledge and skill section of template	252
12.6	Review questions section of template	253

Tables and boxes

TABLES

3.1	Issues in integrating knowledge management and talent staffing systems	60
4.1	Mean ratings of organizational attributes by importance	73
4.2	Mean ratings and differences in perceptions	75
4.3	Relationship between attractiveness and likelihood to apply	77
4.4	Retention tools	81
5.1	Relationships expected between work-network structures and work structures	102
5.2	Relationships expected between learning-network structures and learning programs	111
10.1	Sample elements of intangible capital	201
12.1	Elements of CT^5	241
12.2	How CT^5 was implemented at ALR	246
12.3	How CT^5 was implemented at PDC	255

BOXES

12.1	ALR's Phase 1 steps	247
12.2	Organizational readiness dimensions assessed at ALR	247

Contributors

Leticia S. Andrade is a doctoral student in the Organization and Management PhD program at the University of Texas at San Antonio. She has an article forthcoming in *Emergence: Complexity and Organization* on conflict in organizations. Her current research interests include: strategic human resource management, organizational unlearning, managing human capital in dynamic environments, and the effects of employment discrimination on victims.

Dennis Briscoe is Professor of International Human Resource Management and former Associate Director of the John M. Ahlers Center for International Business at the University of San Diego. His PhD is in Management from Michigan State University and his BBA and MBA are from Washington State University. Dr. Briscoe has published six books, including *International Human Resource Management*, 2nd edition, with Randall Schuler (the 3rd edition, with Dr. Lisbeth Claus, is due in early 2008), *Industrial Relations Around the World*, and over 60 articles. He has about 20 years' experience as a manager and human resource manager, has founded or helped to found a number of organizations, both for-profit and not-for-profit, and has served on a number of boards. Dr. Briscoe has worked and lived in 15 countries and traveled fairly extensively in about 70. Dr. Briscoe taught at the University of San Diego for 28 years (he retired in June 2007) and speaks around the world on topics related to the new world of business and careers. He is a member of the Academy of International Business, the Academy of Management, Society for Industrial and Organizational Psychology (SIOP), and Society for Human Resource Management (SHRM) Global Forum and is recognized globally as an authority on international human resource management. Dr. Briscoe speaks and consults on organizational learning and knowledge management, global executive development, cross-cultural communication and management, and project leadership. When Dr. Briscoe is not busy with his academic activities, he is actively engaged in volunteer work, with organizations such as Habitat for Humanity.

Donald A. Carpenter is Professor of Computer Information Systems (CIS) in the Department of Business at Mesa State College in Grand Junction, Colorado. Previously he taught at Pikes Peak Community College, University of Colorado at Colorado Springs, and University of Nebraska at Kearney, where he was Chairperson of the Department of Computer Science and Information Systems for 15 years. He holds a BS from Kearney State College, an MBA from the University of Colorado at Colorado Springs, and a PhD from the University of Nebraska-Lincoln. Prior to starting his now 27-year teaching career, he accumulated ten years' experience in the information technology industry. Teaching and research interests are in CIS education, decision support systems, information requirements determination, enterprise requirements planning, and meaningfulness of IS work. He has published in the *Journal of Computer Information Systems, Journal of Computer Science Education, International Journal of Decision Support Systems* and others. He is a regular contributor to the Decision Sciences Institute's various proceedings both as author and reviewer and presently serves as President of the Board of Directors of the Mountain Plains Management Association.

Ans De Vos is Associate Professor at the HRM Department of Vlerick Leuven Gent Management School. She holds a Master's in Psychology and in Personnel Management, and obtained her doctoral degree on the topic of psychological contract formation. She is currently responsible for the Career Management Research Centre within Vlerick, in which research on career development and career management is conducted in close collaboration with the business world. Her research interests include psychological contracts, organizational support for career development, and individual career management. Current research projects include the career expectations and experiences of graduates making the transition from school to work, best practices in competency management, and the importance of individual proactivity for career development.

Regina-Viola Frey is a PhD student at Heilbronn Business School in Germany. She recently completed her Honors thesis on recruitment. Regina-Viola has held positions in human resources with a number of German multinational companies.

Jim M. Graber is an organizational psychologist with 30+ years of experience working with private and public sector organizations interested in improving their talent and performance management. Jim's expertise is in organizational psychology, particularly competency modeling, career development, workforce and succession planning, performance management, employee assessments, and employee certification. He has spearheaded the development of *focus*™ software, a comprehensive talent and performance management solution used worldwide. He has also leads the talent management consulting practice for Business Decisions, Inc., Chicago. Research and development of new, improved solutions and services is always a part of Jim's work. Currently, Jim is working on new products in the areas of rigorous employee development/certification ('grow your own talent' approaches that really work); a 'competency store' that will provide a standard, updated competency library and related tools to users worldwide; comprehensive workforce planning; online behavioral interviewing; and role-based job profiling. Jim has taught at the undergraduate and graduate levels at three universities. He has presented at numerous professional conferences and has contributed to a number of professional journals and books. He earned his Bachelor's degree from the University of Michigan and his PhD in Psychology from Claremont Graduate University.

Bettie Hall, MEd, is an educational consultant with more than 20 years of experience assisting organizations to implement information technology systems that meet the needs of the people who use them. She has published and presented her work on topics ranging from how to choose technologies that address adult learning styles to creating reward systems that motivate people to do their best. She is currently completing her Doctorate of Education with a specialization in Knowledge Technologies, and has helped launch HI Results Consulting with a goal of using educational research findings to improve business results.

Nancy A. Inskeep is a consultant who has led projects and implemented key business strategies for more than 25 years in financial services, telecommunications, and retail environments. She has served as project leader in the selection and implementation of human resources, investment, materials management, and customer services, as well as vendor relationship management and financial analysis. Nancy holds a JD, an MEd, and an MBA. She is PMP-certified and has published on topics involving law, project management, and HRIS. She has been the principal consultant of Organization & Guidance Consulting and recently co-founded HI Results Consulting.

Rhonda Jones is a Collegiate Associate Professor and Program Director for the graduate Human Resource (HR) specialization at the University of Maryland University College. She also provides management, organizational development, and HR consulting services to public agencies and small businesses to help strategically align human capital initiatives with each organization's mission, vision, and objectives. Dr. Jones has taught in-person and online courses in the United States, Hong Kong, and Singapore, and presented at several academic and professional conferences. She has earned a BA in Psychology, an MBA, and a Doctorate of Education (EdD) in HR Development. In addition, Dr. Jones holds the Senior Professional in Human Resources (SPHR) and the International Public Management

Association for Human Resources Certified Professional (IPMA-HR CP) designations, and is a member of the Academy of Management (AOM), the Academy of Human Resource Development (AHRD), the Society for Human Resource Management (SHRM), and the International Public Management Association for Human Resources (IPMA-HR).

Konstantin Korotov is Assistant Professor of Leadership and Organizational Behavior at the European School of Management and Technology (ESMT) (Berlin). He received a PhD in Management from INSEAD Business School. In addition to his academic work, he has over 14 years of practical management development experience in various parts of the world. Konstantin's current research is on leadership development, identity dynamics, and executive coaching. His recent work is reflected in *Coach and Couch: The Psychology of Making Better Leaders*, a book co-edited with Manfred Kets de Vries and Elizabeth Florent-Treacy (Palgrave, 2007), as well as in academic and practitioner articles on leadership development in Europe, and teaching materials for participants in leadership development executive programs. As an expert on leadership and management in Russia and post-Soviet economies, Konstantin also conducts research on leadership styles of business elite and emerging leaders in the region. With Manfred Kets de Vries and associates he co-authored *The New Russian Business Leaders* (Edward Elgar, 2004), as well as academic and practitioner-oriented articles and case studies on leadership, leadership development, and careers in Russia. Previously, Konstantin has held the positions of Director of Professional Development for Ernst & Young (CIS), consultant for the Center for Business Skills Development (CBSD) (Moscow), and researcher at New York University.

Mark L. Lengnick-Hall is Professor of Management in the College of Business at the University of Texas at San Antonio. He received his PhD in Organizational Behavior and Human Resource Management from Purdue University, Indiana. His work has been published in many journals, including *Academy of Management Review, Academy of Management Executive, Personnel Psychology, Human Resource Management Review*, and *Human Resource Management*. He has co-authored four books, the most recent being *Hidden Talent: How Leading Companies Hire, Retain, and Benefit from People with Disabilities* (Praeger, 2007). Dr. Lengnick-Hall was the recipient of the HR Educator of the Year award presented by the HR Southwest Conference in 2003, and has received national recognition for his research in strategic human resource management. His current research interests include the employment of people with disabilities, strategic human resource management, human resource management in the knowledge economy, and the implementation of information technology in organizations.

Rob F. Poell, PhD, is Professor of Human Resource Development in the Department of Human Resource Studies at Tilburg University in the Netherlands. He received his BEd (with distinction), MEd, and PhD from the Radboud University Nijmegen in the Netherlands. His main interest is in workplace learning, especially the different organizing strategies employed by workers, managers, and HR professionals in workplace learning. He has also published on work-related learning projects, new roles of HRD professionals, learning networks, on-the-job learning styles, HRD policies of organizations, the learning paths of individual employees, social capital, coaching, combining formal and informal learning, amongst others. Rob is General Editor of the journal *Human Resource Development International* and was elected to the Board of Directors for the international Academy of Human Resource Development twice. He publishes regularly in *Management Learning, Adult Education Quarterly, Applied Psychology International Review, International Journal of Human Resource Management, Human Resource Development Quarterly, Human Resource Development International, Human Resource Development Review, Personnel Review*, amongst others. His teaching focuses on HRD, HRM, and qualitative research methods.

William J. Rothwell, PhD, SPHR (Senior Professional in Human Resources), is President of Rothwell and Associates, Inc., a full-service consulting firm that offers services in succession planning and management. He is also Professor of Human Resource Development on the University Park campus of the Pennsylvania State University. As a consultant, he has worked with over 30 multinational corporations. As an academic, he heads up the leading graduate program in HRD in the United States. Before arriving at Penn State, he was previously Assistant Vice President and Management Development Director for the Franklin Life Insurance Co., a wholly owned subsidiary of a Fortune 48 corporation. Before that, he was Training Director for the Illinois Office of the Auditor General. Dr. Rothwell was National Thought Leader for a Linkage-DDI sponsored study of 18 multinational corporations in 2001 that examined corporate best practices in succession planning and management. His bestselling book *Effective Succession Planning: Ensuring Leadership Continuity and Building Talent from Within*, 3rd edition (Amacom, 2005) is regarded by some as the 'corporate bible' on succession management practices.

Patrick F. Schutz holds a PhD in Education and Human Resource Studies from Colorado State University, an MS in Economics and Human Resource Management from the University of Utah, and a BS degree from Eastern Michigan University. He is an Assistant Professor of Business

Administration and Management at Mesa State College in Grand Junction, Colorado. He holds the credential of Senior Professional in Human Resources (SPHR) from the Human Resource Certification Institute (HRCI) and is a member of the Phi Kappa Phi scholastic honor society. Dr. Schutz has nearly 30 years of direct management experience in both the private and public sectors. Human resource management is his passion and for many years he has shuttled between direct management responsibilities and classroom teaching of management theory. These days, he is a full-time professor and researcher in the fields of human resource management and organizational behavior. His current research is primarily directed toward seeking a greater understanding of the relationship between employee performance evaluation systems and overall organizational performance.

Nele Soens is a PhD researcher at the HRM Department of the Vlerick Leuven Gent Management School. She holds a Master's degree in Commercial Engineering (University of Antwerp). She has conducted research in the area of career management, labor market and career mobility, and comparative international HRM. Currently she is working on her PhD as an ICM (Intercollegiate Center for Doctoral Studies in Management, Belgium) fellow studying the mediating role of line managers and employees in the linkage between human resource management and firm performance.

Siri Terjesen is an Assistant Professor in the Department of Management at Indiana University. Concurrently, she is a Visiting Research Fellow at the Max Planck Institute of Economics in Jena, Germany. Previously, she was a Lecturer at the London School of Economics and Political Science and a Senior Lecturer at the Brisbane Graduate School of Business at Queensland University of Technology. She has published in several journals, including *Strategic Management Journal, Small Business Economics, Journal of Business Ethics, Entrepreneurship Theory & Practice* and *Venture Capital* and is co-author (with Anne Huff, Steve Floyd, and Hugh Sherman) of *Strategic Management* (Wiley, 2008). She is on the board of the National Policy Research Council (NPRC), USA.

Vlad Vaiman is currently a Professor of International Management at FH Joanneum University of Applied Sciences in Graz, Austria, and, as of 1 August 2008, an Associate Professor of International Business at Reykjavik University in Iceland. He holds a Doctorate in Business Administration from the University of St. Gallen in Switzerland. His academic experience includes teaching undergraduate, graduate, and executive courses in top universities around the world, including Helsinki School of Economics,

University of Graz, Oslo University College, California Lutheran University, Danube University of Krems, Management Center Innsbruck, and Reykjavik University. His research interests include issues of both organizational behavior and international management and, particularly, matters of cultural differences and their influences on leadership, motivation, and talent management in multinational companies. He is also an active member of the International Association of Management Consultants and its Canadian chapter.

Ferd J. Van der Krogt is an Associate Professor at Radboud University Nijmegen (Netherlands). He is interested in theory and research about the organization of HRD processes in organizations. He developed the 'learning network theory.'

Charles M. Vance is a Professor of Management at Loyola Marymount University (Los Angeles). He has delivered numerous presentations at academic and practitioner association meetings, and has published widely in journals such as *Journal of World Business*, *Academy of Management Learning and Education*, *Training and Development Journal*, *Journal of Business Ethics*, *Journal of Management Development*, *Management International Review*, and *Human Relations*. Professor Vance has focused his teaching, consulting, and research within many different organizations in the United States and abroad on training and management development, organization change and development, international management, and human resource management. In 2005 and 2006 Professor Vance held US Fulbright teaching and research appointments in Austria and China. He is the author/editor of *Managing a Global Workforce* (M.E. Sharpe, 2006) and *Mastering Management Education* (Sage, 1993).

1. Smart talent management: on the powerful amalgamation of talent management and knowledge management

Charles M. Vance and Vlad Vaiman

One innovation that forever changed our world was the discovery of the dramatically new strength of materials obtained from the admixture of carbon and iron—resulting in steel. Both elements alone have their limitations in terms of material strength, but their unique characteristics in combination resulted in tremendous power that enabled the construction of our industrialized and post-industrialized worlds. We believe that in much the same way the useful concepts of talent management (TM) and knowledge management (KM) can be combined to form a powerful conceptual amalgamation contributing to an organization's success in our competitive global marketplace. For want of a more precise and scientific label, we call this combination simply 'smart talent management.' We hope that this book will prompt further examination of the benefits of this combined focus on talent and knowledge management, including the development of useful definitions. But in this early stage we define our concept of smart talent management as the combined use of the distinctly different concepts of knowledge management and talent management to resolve human performance problems and to achieve organizational objectives.

Our little play on words refers *not* to the effective management of only the top performers (i.e., the smart employees), but to the effective/smart integration of knowledge management (i.e., the 'smarts') into the paradigm. Smart talent management means the smart or effective management of all human resources, who embody an organization's knowledge capital and capability in generating, acquiring, storing, transferring, and applying knowledge in support of company goals and objectives (competitive advantage). 'Smart' also corresponds to our emphasis of the strategic role of knowledge management in today's organizations, and particularly within the human resource management (HRM) function. Our further use of 'knowledge assets' in our book's title provides an explicit reference to the essential role of knowledge management tied to the human factor, building upon the past use of 'human capital' as a strategic tool for competitive advantage.

Thus, the purpose of our book is to present a valuable fusion of two important areas of emphasis for current research and practice in human resource management: talent management and knowledge management. The significance of knowledge management to competitive advantage and organizational success in our rapidly changing global knowledge-based economy is immense—the generation/acquisition of ideas and knowledge, their internal transfer and application throughout the organization, cross-border transfer of knowledge, and so on—have all become an integral and important part of contemporary management, both domestic and international. But what many knowledge management scholars have missed in their predominantly theoretical perspective is the fact that effective knowledge management in practice is largely dependent upon human talent management, and especially upon such practical components as recruitment of talent, training, knowledge sharing, coaching and mentoring, performance management, succession planning, development of global leadership competencies, global alignment, and rewards management. As Illegems and Verbeke (2004) have noted, past HRM research generally fails to consider the new challenges that HRM faces in knowledge-intensive and knowledge-competitive organizations. And in its special issue call for research to address the interaction of strategic HRM practices and knowledge processes in firms, the leading HRM journal *Human Resource Management* recently stated: 'From theoretical, empirical and managerial perspectives, the key issue is to understand how the deployment of specific HRM practices may best facilitate knowledge creation, transformation, transfer/ sharing, and harvesting/application.'

On the other hand, existing publications on talent management are predominantly practitioner-oriented without a strong conceptual foundation that knowledge management can provide. They tend to focus directly on major practices in attracting, selecting, engaging, developing, and retaining employees, yet they largely fail to adequately recognize human talent as repositories of potentially valuable knowledge—both tacit and explicit. This shortcoming of current perspectives in human resource and talent management was evident in a recent remark by an HRM practitioner colleague of a large biotechnology firm that is undergoing some downsizing through mostly voluntary terminations (including her own). She indicated that a lot of valuable knowledge was unfortunately leaving the company due to inadequate attention to effective knowledge management.

TALENT MANAGEMENT: STRENGTHS AND LIMITATIONS

With our somewhat novel conceptual admixture in 'smart talent management,' this text takes a fresh look at human talent in organizations, with employees at all levels representing potentially key agents of knowledge management in acquiring, transferring, and applying important knowledge for competitive advantage. Like 'human capital' and the more generic 'human resource management,' talent management is grounded in resource-based theory of organizations (Barney, 1991; 1995), where organizations can gain competitive advantage to the extent that their assets and resources with which they compete and pursue organizational objectives are valuable, rare, and difficult to imitate. Organizations that are able to attract human talent consistently and effectively, as well as develop and update, deploy where needed, obtain commitment to organization goals, elicit ideas for ongoing improvement, and retain this talent will fare well in the long term in the global marketplace compared with other organizations that neglect such attention to human talent.

We believe that the term 'talent management' is an improvement upon other preceding common terms such as human resource management and even human capital. Although both of these terms are improvements upon the former 'personnel' moniker by lending a positive sense of employees as assets or resources for the organization, they still refer to some 'thing' that organizations use and expend—a fairly negative meaning from a humanistic perspective that reduces the human being to a material inventory level. Of course, as Fournies (1999) has pointed out, managers often look at their mechanical/physical material resources as something worthy of and needing continuous monitoring, caring for, upgrading, and investing in. Perhaps if managers really looked at their people as the potentially vital human resources that they really are, they would at least give equal consideration to their employees as to their valuable machines and physical resources. Nevertheless, talent management as a powerful image and attitude-shaping term can take managers even further beyond the terms 'human resources' and 'human capital' in valuing, utilizing, and benefiting from employees. Far more than the terms 'resources' and 'capital,' the word 'talent' conveys a sense of the important prerequisites of value, rarity, and inimitability—and in an inherently humanistic way—that contribute to an organization's competitive advantage.

Although some writers might limit the term 'talent' to some kind of natural capability or learned skill that benefits an organization, and upon extension refer to talent as only those in the organization possessing these valued characteristics, in this book we generally refer to talent as all of the employed people within an organization who may differ dramatically in levels of knowledge, skill, and ability. Certainly there are strategic points and positions of core competencies where the quality or degree of human talent within an organization is more critical than in other positions and locations within the organization. Nevertheless, especially in conjunction with knowledge management, in this book an organization's talent (employees) at all levels represent potential sources of valuable knowledge through their multiple points of external knowledge access and insight acquisition, internal idea/knowledge generation, and knowledge transfer and application.

We learn from the Sapir-Whorf theory of cultural anthropology that our thoughts, attitudes, and subsequent actions are very much affected by the language we use. New language and terminology can serve as keys to unlock the doors into new passageways of managerial approaches leading to performance improvement. What are some powerful semantic benefits of the use of the term 'talent management' over personnel or human resource management? We believe there are several. First, based on the language of the entertainment industry, the term 'talent' can serve as a powerful metaphor, evoking the image of a talented actor whose role in a motion picture or play is critical to the success of the production. The human talent in entertainment productions really make it happen. For those who are familiar with Western culture, can you really imagine the classic movie *Gone With The Wind* with any actors other than Clark Gable and Vivien Leigh playing the roles of Rhett Butler and Scarlett O'Hara? Or Sir Laurence Olivier, for another example, had a powerfully unique and unforgettable impact on his many works on the stage and screen. It is due to the careful skills of a fine director-manager to identify potential, and to help guide and shape the performance of this talent that brings off a smashing success and memorable performance. Even when the acting talent is as of yet 'undiscovered' to the general public, as was Audrey Hepburn in *Roman Holiday*, the perceptive and skillful director-manager recognizes this talent—even in rough form—and patiently works with and develops this talent to its stardom potential. As directors of human talent in their organizations, managers and supervisors bear the same challenge and opportunity of identifying the human talent in their midst, and in developing and managing this talent toward optimal performance and ultimate company productivity. But they must first sense the immense value of this human talent to their workplace productions, and how their concern and attention for this talent is essential.

Second, as in the above entertainment metaphor, talent management is more consistent with our more flexible trend in today's global marketplace in sourcing and utilizing human talent as the need arises—on a contingent basis. On a global scale there is a burgeoning growth in contingent employee staffing in the use of temporary, part-time, contracted, leased, outsourced, and consulting services. In a major film production, you typically schedule an actor for the hours or days in which scenes need to be shot—not for the duration of the shooting of the entire movie. In fact, perhaps a more accurate way to think of actors today is as 'temps,' especially those not playing a leading role in the entire film production. Thus, as increasingly is the case with our more porous and open organizational boundaries, talent can also be represented by the workers of suppliers, vendors, contingent arrangements (e.g., temps), and outsourced services/manufacturing firms who contribute to our business viability. Although our book will focus primarily upon internal human resources as the talent, organizations should consider the needs of all workers who contribute to the success of their operations.

Third, the term 'human resource management' typically conjures up the image of staff professionals—the HR department of specialists that is often seen as only adding cost to the organization and reminding management of legal restrictions and what management can't do. Unlike the HR functional specialist or professional that we typically equate with 'HR manager,' the talent manager is more easily seen as a general manager or supervisor who regularly works closely with human talent to achieve organizational performance objectives. Talent management emphasizes in our minds what all managers need to be concerned about and actively involved in— the identification, development, management, and retention of valuable human talent. HR specialists and professionals can provide essential input and guidance, but managers and supervisors bear an essential role in ultimately implementing the HR agenda. Thus, by fully embracing the concept of effective talent management, all supervisors and managers of people within the organization more fully adopt the role of human resource practitioners (not HR specialists or HR professionals), who are directly dealing with people challenges and opportunities on a regular basis.

Finally, the term talent provides an added meaning of preciousness and distinct value to a human resource that should be invested in, cared for, shaped, developed—but certainly not taken for granted or squandered. The obtuse and inane (but all too real) manager caricatured by Scott Adams in his 'Dilbert' comic strip often considers contingent workers, such as interns and temporary employees, as expendable resources that can be 'deposited in a dumpster' or otherwise easily discarded once their perceived value to the organization is 'used up.' But this minimal level of respect and appreciation for an organization's human talent, which results in inadequate attention to the development and organization-wide utilization of vital human resource management practices, can never build a long-term strategy of competitive advantage, let alone compete well with such a reputation in the war of attracting and retaining strong human talent (Michaels, Handfield-Jones, & Axelrod, 2001; Tulgan, 2002).

Unfortunately, notwithstanding the above important strengths of the use of the talent management designation over human capital or the more traditional human resource management, or the even more dated 'personnel,' much of the current TM literature seems only to be 'warmed over' old HRM and dressed in a catchy phrase. Much of this work appears to differ little from the previous generation of works under the label of HRM and the management of human capital. In their thoughtful critical review of recently published works and the growing interest in talent management, Lewis and Heckman (2006: 140) state:

> It is apparent from the above that the term 'talent management' has no clear meaning. It is used in too many ways and is often a means to highlight the 'strategic' importance of an HR specialty (recruiting, selection, development, etc.) without adding to the theory or practice of that specialty . . . Perhaps it serves the purpose of re-branding HR practices to keep them seemingly new and fresh, but it does not advance our understanding of the strategic and effective management of talent.

Certainly a new 'spin' on an old concept can provide a refreshing change, as well as an opportunity to renew and recommit efforts for organizational improvement. But if talent management is to make a significantly new contribution beyond simply providing a rather superficial 'new and improved' label to essentially the same HR practices, it must hold a more clear link with strategic human resource management (Boudreau & Ramstad, 2005; Wright & Haggerty, 2005).

KNOWLEDGE MANAGEMENT: STRENGTHS AND LIMITATIONS

Besides the distinctly different emphases that we place on the term 'talent,' our addition of the conceptual discipline of knowledge management to the picture takes talent management to a more strategic level, where the human talent at all levels represent important sources, transmitters, and implementers of knowledge essential to competitive advantage. Consistent with the maxim 'knowledge is power,' the competitive advantages of organizations are derived from core competencies and 'know-how' that are developed within them over time (Prahalad & Hamel, 1990). This collective knowledge is held explicitly within the set of documented policies, practices, directions, instructions, and so on, and implicitly or tacitly within developed routines of organizational life, as well as the conscious and unconscious experience base of employees at all levels (Polanyi, 1966; Nonaka & Takeuchi, 1995).

To a significant extent, employees embody the knowledge in use within the organization. According to the knowledge-based view of the firm (Grant, 1996), this employee know-how that greatly contributes to a firm's human core competencies potentially provides a strategic resource to assist the firm in adapting and competing in its market environments (Haesli & Boxall, 2005). Clearly, when all employee talent (including both regular and contingent employees) are seen as current and potential sources and purveyors of knowledge and know-how for beneficial application within the firm, the perceived role of human resource management policies and practices to attract, develop, motivate, facilitate knowledge exchange interactions among, and retain this talent grows dramatically in importance. Unfortunately, in many organizations there is a lack of consistency and coordination among the HR functions such as staffing, training, appraisal, and compensation (Guest, 1987; Lam & Schaubroeck, 1998). Besides increasing the perceived importance of HR policies and practices to the organization, knowledge management also provides a common, unifying purpose and link to integrate and coordinate these policies and practices more effectively within the various HR functions.

Despite the valuable potential contributions of knowledge management, there are potential shortcomings that limit its value and utility in improving organizational performance. Many efforts in knowledge management have focused on hardware and software database applications (e.g., expert systems) with apparently little regard for human dimensions affecting both the entry and retrieval of experience-based knowledge and information, which can become even more problematic due to cultural differences within our global organizations (Paik & Choi, 2005). Much work that does focus on human organizational issues in knowledge management remains at a rather abstract, theoretical, and fairly macro level, with little reference to specific HR policies, practices, and procedures for guiding and bringing knowledge management to the micro level of local firm operations (Cohen & Levinthal, 1990; Gupta & Govindarajan, 2000; Bhagat et al., 2002).

Nonaka and Takeuchi (1995) have presented the concept of the 'knowledge spiral,' which examines four modes of knowledge transformations, involving knowledge creation and transfer between tacit knowledge (i.e., know-how or experience-based knowledge that is difficult to document) and explicit knowledge (i.e., more easily communicated or shared) at different levels within the firm. Hansen, Nohria, and Tierney (1999) provide a simpler way of envisioning links between knowledge management and the human dimension by distinguishing major approaches of knowledge management: the 'personalization' and 'codification' of knowledge. In the personalization approach, tacit or experience-based knowledge remains closely tied to the individuals who create or discover it from external sources, and transmit this knowledge primarily through person-to-person contact. In contrast, the codification approach attempts to make knowledge more explicit and facilitate its transfer through entry onto databases and into operations manuals and employee training plans for wider company dissemination. The application of the personalization knowledge management approach appears to work most favorably in unique, novel situations, while the codification approach works best in situations involving fairly predictable conditions and routine organizational practices. However, despite their contributions to theory development, these research efforts in knowledge management still fail to make a close link to specific HR functional practices for guiding local operations—such as in specific staffing, training and development, and various communications efforts and activities for creating and moving both explicit and tacit knowledge through the organization. There is still limited understanding of specific ways in which knowledge management and human resource practices may interact to support competitive advantage (Storey & Quintas, 2001; Currie & Kerrin, 2003; Haesli & Boxall, 2005).

Another limitation of knowledge management and related management of knowledge workers is the predominant focus on cerebral and cognitive, intellectual processes—what we call the cognitive domain (Bloom, 1956). There appears to be little attention directed at learning and skill development in areas critical for individual, group, and organizational performance within the affective (e.g., feelings, emotions) and psycho-motor (e.g., skills) domains (Krathwohl, Bloom, & Masia, 1964; Harrow, 1972). Although discussions about implicit or tacit knowledge can relate to the largely unconscious and internalized knowledge aspects of the psycho-motor domain, they tend to lack sufficient detail about how this form of knowledge can be effectively developed.

Considerable work in emotional intelligence, creativity, and nonlinear thinking also points to the need to look beyond strictly cognitive dimensions of rational data-gathering and logical analysis of knowledge and information for achieving and maintaining high levels of performance (Csikszentmihalyi, 1996; Sadler-Smith & Shefy, 2004; Vance et al., 2007). In a departure from the nearly complete focus on the cognitive domain, past work analyzing the learning benefits of knowledge-sharing groups (both within and across organizations) has identified important forms of learning in the affective domain, such as increased confidence in problem-solving, reduced anxiety caused by feelings of isolation, or an increased awareness of and accompanying sense of urgency in addressing a potential future problem (Vance, 1990; Vance et al., 1991).

VALUE OF THE TALENT/KNOWLEDGE MANAGEMENT HYBRIDIZATION

A combined conceptualization of talent management and knowledge management in smart talent management considers that which employees can bring of value to the organization as extending far beyond only the cognitive domain. The power of the concept of talent includes its relevance to other essential domains of human development and performance besides an individual's store of rational information and cerebral knowledge. The concept of talent held by an experienced employee provides a more vivid picture and strengthens the meaning of deep, hard to articulate, tacit knowledge, directing it closer to the influence of specific HR practices in identifying, surfacing and capturing, and spreading this tacit knowledge talent within the organization. The concept of talent also reaches into the affective domain, such as with emotional intelligence and the ability to read and manage one's own feelings in a constructive fashion, and to influence others in doing the same (Goleman, 1995; 1998).

We can see very successful global organizations today operating with the combined TM/KM model. One such organization is igus, GmbH of Germany, a leading manufacturer of energy chain systems that support industrial automation and robotics. The active involvement of all managers at all levels in HR practices combining talent management and knowledge management is quickly apparent in a visit to the headquarters manufacturing facility in Cologne. As symbolized by the lower case letters in its name, igus promotes a strong culture of humility, continuous learning, empowerment, and equality. This culture is apparent on its website (www.igus.de), which states that: 'nearly every team member acts as an independent manager from the start.' With 26 branches in 21 countries, the company heavily invests in training and talent development worldwide. Its open office space and furniture design supports an egalitarian atmosphere and facilitates the sharing of information. Everyone can contact anyone else in the company directly. A good example of this combined TM/KM smart talent management model in action, which here merges an empowerment approach with knowledge management, is the igus common maxim: 'First decide, then inform.'

As another good example, the multinational giant Procter & Gamble has been extremely successful in attracting, developing, and retaining its managerial talent worldwide. P&G's combined TM/KM effectiveness in disseminating key knowledge, skills, and abilities throughout its worldwide operations has resulted in the distinct competitive advantage of decision-makers who share a common mindset and alignment that supports an integrated and coordinated global business strategy. This TM/KM merger affecting specific HR practice is evident in the work of P&G's East Asia regional senior HR executive, Hide Aida, in what he calls 'knowledge-based leadership.' The purpose of P&G's knowledge-based leadership approach is to enable all employees to perform at their peak by ultimately providing opportunities to make decisions in their area of responsibilities. In implementing knowledge-based leadership, employees participate in various forms of training and development to master their three critical areas of knowledge/understanding: (1) the specific technical expertise involved in their work, (2) successful P&G business strategies and approaches, and (3) the Procter & Gamble PVP model that makes up the core fabric of their culture: *purposes* (e.g., company mission), *values* (e.g., core personal and interpersonal values held by each employee such as integrity, trust, passion for winning, ownership), and *principles* of business practice linked to company success (e.g., 'mutual interdependency is a way of life,' 'innovation is the cornerstone of our success'). Once employees demonstrate that they have gained sufficient knowledge and demonstrable understanding (including internalized commitment—learning in the affective domain) in these three primary areas, they are fully empowered to make decisions on their own to accomplish their work performance objectives.

The TM/KM model hybrid merges the strengths of each individual approach, yet in combination is also able to surmount the limitations of each. From the above discussion we can summarize the distinct strengths of the combined TM/KM model in smart talent management:

1. With its merger with knowledge management, talent management becomes more than just a catchy, new phrase and is clearly raised to a strategic level of vital consideration.
2. Knowledge management provides a common purpose and focus to help unify and integrate HR functional efforts and activities, and broaden the link with HR and organizational strategy.
3. The term 'talent' has a potent meaning that conveys the current or potential value of each employee within the organization—including contingent employees.
4. The TM/KM model has sound theoretical grounding, yet is positioned within the realm of specific HR functional practices, where all managers and supervisors perceive they have an important, central role.
5. The view of talent extends knowledge management beyond primarily a conscious cognitive dimension to include deeper tacit and affective dimensions.

The intent of this book is to present the TM/KM conceptual hybrid, smart talent management, as a valuable multi-faceted direction for managerial action in key HR functional disciplines, leading to organizational improvement and enhanced competitiveness. However, the idea of building a stronger connection between knowledge management and key HR practices is still in its infancy. We hope that our selection of papers will serve to enhance our understanding of this potentially powerful union and spur further theoretical and applied developments.

OVERVIEW OF THIS BOOK

The four parts of this book will examine (1) HR planning and staffing, (2) training/coaching, (3) performance management, and (4) organizational learning and development. The first part of the book, devoted to HR planning and staffing, opens with a chapter by Patrick Schutz and Donald Carpenter on effective planning of human resources. In this chapter the authors examine in more detail the central positions that both talent management and knowledge management play in effective HR planning. They also investigate important conditions and practices that should be present to enhance the impact of both talent management and knowledge management on HR planning, and ultimately on effective strategic management in organizations.

The next chapter in this first part, by Mark Lengnick-Hall and Leticia Andrade, is dedicated to talent staffing systems necessary for effective knowledge management. The main purpose of this chapter is to integrate talent staffing systems as an essential HR function with knowledge management. In particular, the authors show that a combination of traditional HRM policies, programs, and practices, along with some new perspectives and approaches, can be used to help organizations develop staffing systems that manage people and knowledge effectively.

The authors of the last chapter in this first part, Siri Terjesen and Regina-Viola Frey, concentrate their efforts on the essentials of attracting and retaining Generation Y knowledge worker talent. In particular, this chapter is concerned with effective attraction and retention positions, policies, and programs for Generation Y employees, that is, those born between 1977 and 1994. The two aforementioned components of HR planning are extremely important to an organization's talent management and knowledge management processes. Attraction is important for establishing the pool from which individuals can be hired, while retention efforts are devoted to keeping these knowledge-carrying individuals engaged in their careers.

Our second part of this book, dedicated to training and coaching, begins with a chapter by Rob Poell and Ferd Van der Krogt on the role of social networks in managing organizational talent, knowledge, and employee learning. The chapter presents an interesting perspective on organizations as social networks of actors, which can help explain how employees (the talent pool of the organization) create individual learning paths, and what constraints and opportunities they encounter in doing so. The chapter illustrates how individual employees' opportunities to engage in development are strongly dependent on the social networks from which they operate in the organization. The authors attract our attention to two such networks, which they call, respectively, the work network and the learning network. Besides providing learning-relevant experiences on which individual learning paths are based and influencing how individuals make meaning of these experiences, these two networks also affect the opportunities for talent and knowledge management.

In the next chapter, 'The power of career counseling for enhanced talent and knowledge management,' Ans De Vos and Nele Soens describe the process of career counseling as a means of matching individual and organizational needs; integrate counseling within the broader career and performance management system; examine the involvement of HR professionals, line management and individual employees; and outline some critical success factors involving overall knowledge and talent management.

The following chapter in the second part, written by Konstantin Korotov, is dedicated to accelerated development of organizational talent. According to the author, organizations in many parts of the world are experimenting with ways to speed up the development of their management and employee talent in response to current and anticipated pressures from the global marketplace. They aim to equip organizational members with the skills, knowledge, attitudes, and behavioral patterns necessary for success in their future roles and tasks. Also, in preparation for an expected promotion of an executive, knowledge needs to be transferred to his or her potential replacement, and the latter needs support in preparation for the new job. Thus, concludes the author, in effective accelerated development and broader succession planning and implementation efforts one can see an essential link between talent management and knowledge management.

In the third part of the book, which focuses on performance management, the first chapter by Nancy Inskeep and Bettie Hall is called 'Reward and recognition concepts that support talent and knowledge management initiatives.' They begin by asking several important questions such as 'How can I make working attractive when even people in well-paying jobs want to leave them?' and 'How can I attract, retain, motivate, recognize, and reward a diverse workforce that is geographically scattered and working in the electronically connected e-world?' One of the answers to these and similar questions, the authors suggest, is to provide sincere, valued and well-managed reward and recognition (R&R) programs that attract and retain talented individuals, develop and share their knowledge, and motivate them to continue specific behaviors and actions. Inskeep and Hall make a strong argument that well-defined and supported talent and knowledge management programs are strategic imperatives for success in today's global business environment.

The authors of the next chapter, Patrick Schutz and Donald Carpenter, focus their attention on performance management and its sometimes elusive and confusing relationship with talent and knowledge management. Perhaps the main reason for such feelings of confusion and elusiveness, the authors emphasize, is that management practitioners in each of the three disciplines tend to become somewhat nearsighted within their own specialized environments and time constraints. Nevertheless, the authors continue, a relationship does exist. As discussed in their earlier chapter dealing with the broad function of HR planning, all three are related via the duty and responsibility of designing and implementing policies, procedures, and practices that are intended to enhance the inimitable competitive advantage gained by the organization through strategically directing the activities of its human resources.

The final part of this book deals with organizational learning and development. In the first chapter of this final section, Dennis Briscoe argues that the effective management of organizational talent is directly linked to organizational learning, which is paramount in today's hyper-competitive global economy. The chapter addresses the nature of that linkage, first defining talent and talent management and organizational learning in the global environment and then describing how these concepts are so intricately connected, relying closely on each other.

Drawing on knowledge management, social capital, and talent management literature, the next chapter by Rhonda Jones suggests that effective knowledge management rests primarily with an organization's ability to enable the exchange, enhancement, and application of social capital, which results from the deliberate and active management of employee talent. The author contends that talent management leads to the enhancement of social capital, which is key to knowledge management, and which in turn is essential to organizational competitiveness. In other words, in order for a firm to remain competitive, it must constantly manage the acquisition, flow, and application of knowledge; in order to manage knowledge, organizations should maintain and enhance their social capital; and in order to establish social capital, firms must first manage employee talent.

In the concluding chapter of the book, 'Certifying knowledge and skills is critical for talent management,' Jim Graber and William Rothwell discuss the necessity for a blueprint for systematizing and improving knowledge and skills of an organization's workforce. According to the authors, organizations use many approaches to capture, multiply, and transfer knowledge, such as formal training, mentoring, expert networks, best practice databases, and professional gatherings. Although these practices are very valuable, their ability to transfer knowledge consistently to other employees is not entirely clear. Employee certification, on the other hand, is a rigorous and proactive approach to knowledge and skills management. It systematically addresses knowledge/skill acquisition and transfer. The chapter introduces a comprehensive approach to employee certification (named CT[5]), and provides two contrasting case studies that highlight the manner in which certification can be tailored to organizational needs.

REFERENCES

Barney, J. (1991). Firm resources and sustained competitive advantage. *Journal of Management*, **17**(1): 99–120.

Barney, J. (1995). Looking inside for competitive advantage. *Academy of Management Executive*, **9**(4): 49–61.

Bhagat, R.S., Kedia, B.L., Harveston, P.D., and Triandis, H. (2002). Cultural variations in the cross-border transfer of organizational knowledge: An integrative framework. *Academy of Management Review*, **27**(2): 204–221.

Bloom, B.S. (1956). *Taxonomy of Educational Objectives, Handbook I: Cognitive Domain.* New York: David McKay.

Boudreau, J.W. and Ramstad, P.M. (2005). Talentship and the new paradigm for human resource management: From professional practice to strategic talent decision science. *Human Resource Planning*, **28**(2): 17–26.

Cohen, W.M. and Levinthal, D.H. (1990). Absorptive capacity: A new perspective in learning and innovation. *Administrative Science Quarterly*, **35**(1): 128–152.

Csikszentmihalyi, M. (1996). *Creativity: Flow and the Psychology of Discovery and Invention.* New York: HarperCollins Publishers.

Currie, G. and Kerrin, M. (2003). Human resource management and knowledge management: Enhancing knowledge sharing in a pharmaceutical company. *International Journal of Human Resource Management*, **14**(6): 1027–1045.

Fournies, F.F. (1999). *Coaching for Improved Work Performance* (3rd edition). New York: McGraw-Hill.

Goleman, D. (1995). *Emotional Intelligence: Why it Can Matter More Than IQ.* New York: Bantam Books.

Goleman, D. (1998). *Emotional Intelligence at Work.* New York: Bantam Books.

Grant, R.M. (1996). Towards a knowledge-based theory of the firm. *Strategic Management Journal*, **17**(Winter special issue): 109–22.

Guest, D.E. (1987). Human resource management and industrial relations. *Journal of Management Studies*, **24**(5): 503–521.

Gupta, A.K. and Govindarajan, V. (2000). Knowledge flows within multinational corporations. *Strategic Management Journal*, **21(4)**: 473–496.

Haesli, A. and Boxall, P. (2005). When knowledge management meets HR strategy: An exploration of personalization-retention and codification-recruitment configurations. *International Journal of Human Resource Management*, **16**(11): 1955–1975.

Hansen, M.T., Nohria, N., and Tierney, T. (1999). What's your strategy for managing knowledge? *Harvard Business Review*, March–April: 106–116.

Harrow, A.J. (1972). *A Taxonomy of the Psychomotor Domain: A Guide for Developing Behavioral Objectives.* New York: David McKay.

Illegems, V. and Verbeke, A. (2004). Telework: What does it mean for management? *Long Range Planning*, **37**(4): 319–334.

Krathwohl, D.R., Bloom, B.S., and Masia, B.B. (1964). *Taxonomy of Educational Objectives, Handbook II: Affective Domain.* New York: David McKay.

Lam, S.S.K. and Schaubroeck, J. (1998). Integrating HR planning and organizational strategy. *Human Resource Management Journal*, **8**(3): 5–19.

Lewis, R.E. and Heckman, R.J. (2006). Talent management: A critical review. *Human Resource Management Review*, **16**(2): 139–154.

Michaels, E., Handfield-Jones, H., and Axelrod, B. (2001). *The War for Talent.* Boston, MA: Harvard Business School Press.

Nonaka, I. and Takeuchi, H. (1995). *The Knowledge-Creating Company.* New York: Oxford University Press.

Paik, Y. and Choi, D. (2005). The shortcomings of a standardized global management system: The case study of Accenture. *Academy of Management Executive*, **19**(2): 81–84.

Polanyi, M. (1966). *The Tacit Dimension.* London: Routledge and Kegan Paul.

Prahalad, C.K. and Hamel, G. (1990). The core competence of the corporation. *Harvard Business Review* (May–June): 79–91.

Sadler-Smith, E. and Shefy, E. (2004). The intuitive executive: Understanding and applying 'gut feel' in decision-making. *Academy of Management Executive*, **18**(4): 76–91.

Storey, J. and Quintas, P. (2001). Knowledge Management and HRM. In Storey, J. (ed.) *Human Resource Management: A Critical Text.* London: Thomson Learning, pp. 339–363.

Tulgan, B. (2002). *Winning the Talent Wars: How to Build a Lean, Flexible, High-Performance Workplace.* New York: W.W. Norton & Company.

Vance, C.M. (1990). Intra-organizational knowledge-sharing groups: Applications and benefits for training and development. *Training and Management Development Methods*, **4**(2): 13–21.

Vance, C.M., Boje, D.M., Mendenhall, M.E., and Kropp, H.R. (1991). A taxonomy of learning benefits from external knowledge-sharing meetings. *Human Resource Development Quarterly*, **2**(1): 25–35.

Vance, C.M., Groves, K.S., Paik, Y., and Kindler, H. (2007). Understanding and measuring linear/nonlinear thinking style for enhanced management education and professional practice. *Academy of Management Learning and Education*, **6**(2): 167–185.

Wright, P.M. and Haggerty, J.J. (2005). Missing variables in theories of strategic human resource management: Time, cause, and individuals. *Management Revue*, **16**(2): 164–173.

PART 1

HR planning and staffing

2. Critical considerations of talent management and knowledge management for effective HR planning

Patrick F. Schutz and Donald A. Carpenter

INTRODUCTION

Effective strategic management involves processes of both strategy formulation and implementation. A primary purpose of human resource (HR) planning is to join in the strategic management effort to assist the organization in formulating and achieving its strategic objectives (Greer, 2001). Certainly, the quality of an organization's strategic management effort will depend upon the nature of the human talent, at all levels, that the organization is able to attract and mobilize through careful HR planning in formulating and implementing strategy. Thus, talent management (TM) is integral to HR planning, and the ongoing management of an organization's human talent provides essential support to an organization's effective strategic management process.

Knowledge management (KM) processes also play a central role in the effectiveness of HR planning in serving strategic management. An organization's human talent generates, obtains, and transfers critical knowledge used in strategy formulation. Knowledge transfer is also critical for developing understanding and ability to carry out strategy, and is essential for feedback and control in strategy implementation. In this chapter we will examine in more detail the central positions that both talent management and knowledge management play in effective HR planning. We also will examine important conditions and practices that should exist to enhance the impact of TM and KM on HR planning, and ultimately the strategic management process.

TALENT MANAGEMENT AS AN ESSENTIAL CONTEXT FOR HR PLANNING

As central to effective HR planning, talent management implements 'integrated strategies or systems designed to increase workplace productivity by developing improved processes for attracting, developing, retaining and utilizing people with the required skills and aptitude to meet current and future business needs' (Lockwood, 2005: 1). Essentially, in an organization where talent management is valued as a predominant cultural belief, everyone *should* be concerned with developing an internal workforce that is highly skilled and capable as well as energetic and inspired. Theoretically, the entire firm should be committed to rewarding appropriately the accomplishments of the individuals in its workforce and attending to their developmental and personal/professional needs. Similarly, the entire firm should also be engaged in a continuous *search* for talented individuals in all positions and departments who complement the cultural underpinnings and add value to the potential for meeting organizational objectives. The responsibility for TM accountability does not simply reside within the confines of the normal functions of human resource management. Since TM encompasses all aspects of a firm, the creation of a TM culture should start at the highest echelon(s) of management. Like all major change initiatives, it is necessary for the CEO to be involved in the design, creation, and support of the TM cultural underpinning (much like total quality management [TQM] must be supported by the highest levels of authority in the firm).

Mucha (2004; quoted in Lockwood, 2005: 1) cogently asserts that some of the primary attributes of TM are not merely important to organizations, but may be essential: 'The ability to execute business strategy is rooted in the ability to attract, retain, and develop key talent. Successful talent management creates the most enduring competitive advantage. No company can afford to be unprepared for both the best and worst of times.' A review of the current literature reveals that there is some agreement on the fundamental characteristics of TM. Activities related to recruitment, succession planning, human capital management, human resource planning, and performance management seem to represent the core activities of TM (McTernan, 2003; Hartley, 2004; Lockwood, 2005; McCauley & Wakefield, 2006; Stockley, 2007). Morton (2007: 2) suggests that TM 'is about behavior—the thoughts and actions that consistently, over time, become organizational culture. Talent management is more that something "to do", it is something "to be", a way of working and achieving both near and long-term success.'

To some, the term 'talent' in the phrase 'talent management' refers to two specific populations and services are different for denizens of each of the contexts. One context includes top managers and professionals who are the driving forces that lead the organization forward: a small percentage (16%) of the total organizational workforce. The other context includes the set of TM practices that are geared toward the workforce in general (Hansen, 2007)

According to a 2006 Towers Perrin survey, HR executives in 250 North American, mid-size and large organizations identified groups that they consider to be talent:

Senior leadership	86%
Mid-level employees with leadership potential	82%
Key contributors/technical experts	76%
Entry-level	48% (Hansen, 2007: 6)

It appears, however, that from an international/global perspective the majority of information about TM defines the practice as ubiquitous—transcending all departmental, divisional, and hierarchical boundaries. But, it is difficult to argue against the premise that ultra-valuable employees, by virtue of their unique and perhaps scarce talents, receive significant attention from talent managers. In response to the ubiquitous nature of TM, McCauley and Wakefield (2006: 5) assert that:

Globally, fewer and fewer managers and professionals are ready to fill these leadership roles, and companies worldwide find themselves competing for a smaller pool of talent . . . With HR focusing on hiring, training, and succession planning, talent management is traditionally an HR responsibility. Today's top companies, however, know that a single department's potential effectiveness is limited; the key to a successful program lies with the cooperation of all departments, with all managers across the breadth of their operations.

Wood (2006: 2) suggests that at least the *recruitment* function of TM is not necessarily restricted to senior professionals and executives. As an example of a way in which the recruitment function is changing to meet the needs of the rapid retirement of employees who were part of the post-WWII baby boom, the chemical industries:

are starting to react to the shortage of young recruits, with efforts including forming closer links with universities for R&D projects that could lead to jobs for the researchers involved. Some are also setting up R&D centers in the developing world, particularly China and India, getting the benefit of lower staff costs, and access to a larger supply of chemistry and engineering graduates.

No doubt this type of talent recruitment strategy is being employed by companies around the globe who may have had no post-WWII baby boom, but nonetheless feel the impact of the distinct shortage of young talent who possess math and science credentials.

Talent gap analysis, staffing, education of employees, and the cooperation of all departments and managers is essential to TM. Development of a *talent mindset* is also critical, in addition to the advancement of employee leadership knowledge, skills, and abilities (KSAs), determining leadership needs, coaching and making certain that feedback is always available to employees (McCauley & Wakefield, 2006).

Employee retention is a significant property of TM, in both the *public* and private sectors. Referring to the term 'talent,' McTernan (2003: 1) suggests that although the term may have been derived from the creative industries, even public services have a need to recognize that when the talent (employees) 'move in the public services knowledge, experience and relationships go with them.'

In a recent issue of *Reliable Plant magazine*, John Ha (2006: 2) presents a list of seven attributes of TM. They are cited here in their entirety because of their succinct wording and the provocative, albeit basic, questions following each:

1. *Corporate identity*:
    Who are you as an organization? Do you have the desired culture? Do all of your employees understand your vision, mission and core values or beliefs? What keeps your employees coming to work each day? What drives their behavior in the workplace with your customers and with one another?
2. *Recruitment and selection*:
    How do you identify and select the 'right' people for your organization? Is it based on gut feel? Is it based on their education and skill level?
3. *Performance management and coaching*:
    Are you properly managing performance and providing the kind of coaching employees need to improve?
4. *Employee development and training*:
    Are you developing your employees? Are you helping them identify a plan to improve their skill set and maximize their potential?
5. *Compensation, rewards and benefits*:
    Are you properly rewarding your employees? Are you helping them identify a plan to improve their skill set and maximize their potential?
6. *Success planning and leadership development*:
    Do you have a plan in the event that 'Joe gets hit by a bus?' How are you creating tomorrow's leaders?
7. *Compliance, policy and procedures*:
    Do you have your ducks in a row? Are you meeting your legal obligations? How are you handling employee relations?

Although Ha's jargon is somewhat colloquial and the questions simplistic, it is that very simplicity that lends credence to the list. TM is not necessarily complicated, but its reach throughout the organization is extensive.

However, it seems that TM is not necessarily as popular or prevalent as a reading of the current literature might lead one to think. Several studies indicate that even with all the recent attention given to TM and its rational argument, and despite the rhetoric and justifications, some organizations are reluctant to implement its full complement of strategies and practices. *Corporate Training & Development Advisor* newsletter (2006: 5) cites statements made by SuccessFactors' director of marketing communications, Stacey Epstein, regarding its study of 1100 US companies in April and May of 2007: Among other things, the study found that '58% [of the responding companies] had no succession planning strategy in place, 56% offered no rewards for performance for most employees, 35% had no official corporate goals or objectives, and 22% did not conduct performance reviews.' Epstein stated that the survey was mailed out to directors and vice-presidents in companies ranging from 25–25 000 employees. Perhaps also significant to a discussion of TM is that the SuccessFactors survey indicated that '54% of the respondents were not aligning [departmental] goals with corporate strategy, 48% were not cascading goals through the organization, and 47% were not giving employees visibility into management and corporate goals' (ibid.).

McKinsey & Company queried senior executives of global companies and asked them to rank order several obstacles that hamper or block programs from becoming value-added in terms of their respective businesses. Summarized by *T&D* (2007: 16), eight critical barriers reached the top of the list. Following are those critical barriers to successful implementation of TM and the percentage of respondents who ranked them:

54%   Senior mangers don't spend enough time on talent management.
52%   Line managers are not sufficiently committed to people development.
51%   Thought that silos discourage collaboration and resource sharing.
50%   Line managers are unwilling to differentiate high versus low performers.
47%   Senior leaders do not align talent management and business strategies.
45%   Line managers ignore chronic under-performance.
39%   Planning or allocation do not match right people to roles.
38%   CEO or senior team don't have shared view of pivotal roles.

Another barrier to the acceptance and implementation of a full-bodied TM mindset is mentioned by Hansen (2007: 2) when she cites the aforementioned 2006 Towers Perrin survey that indicates that:

only half of the respondent companies, however, believe that HR has the skills across a wide range of managerial support activities needed to effectively deliver on the talent management role. More than two-thirds say their HR department does not have the skills necessary to measure employee engagement on an ongoing basis or to evaluate the return on workforce-related investments.

Measuring TM initiatives and processes, and integrating TM processes with HR software systems appear to offer some help to mitigate the ambiguity surrounding TM. Likierman (2007) suggests that HR's credibility can be strengthened, and the TM program bolstered by linking the TM objectives with the overall objectives of the organization. He advises that measurement of the program should focus on achievements of TM programs rather than the processes used to accomplish the goals. Frauenheim (2006) reports that there is a shift toward companies buying software application programs that are intended to be bundled together to increase the potential for synergetic coordination between them. He cites (2006: 2) Jason Corsello, analyst of a market research firm:

> The main factor behind the buying shift, is that organizations recognize they can make better use of their workforce data when they integrate applications such as performance and compensation management. 'The suite approach is finally starting to take off. The true value is starting to resonate.'

Frauenheim cites Troy Kanter of HR software firm Kenexa, who illustrates the synergetic value of combining HR software stand-alone products with other products such as those used in performance appraisal and selection: 'By connecting applications, organizations can assemble profiles of successful workers from performance management software and then use those profiles in a recruiting application to guide their hiring' (ibid.). Although organizations seem to be buying multiple software programs for their various HR functions (i.e., recruiting, selection, compensation, safety, performance appraisal, etc.) it may be that those companies are still a long way from truly integrating them.

The International Association for Human Resource Information Management and the consulting firm Knowledge Fusion conducted a study in 2006 that indicated that nearly 78% of the respondents saw the priorities of TM changing, while only slightly over 22% thought those priorities would remain about the same; none of the respondents thought that the TM priorities would decrease in importance. Do those companies integrate their talent management business processes? Six percent indicated that their processes were fully integrated. This is significant considering that only a few years ago total integration of these processes was nearly non-existent. Fifty-three percent responded that their TM business processes were somewhat integrated and 31.6% indicated a little integration, while only a slight 9.3% of the respondents reported no integration.

The acceptance and implementation of TM as an essential mindset and practice supporting competitive advantage may require a paradigm shift on the part of the organization, and should be a top priority for comprehensive

HR planning. For instance, if an organization is currently departmentalized, perhaps by function (e.g., sales, production, HR, IT, etc.), there may very well be significant barriers to cross-communication and cross-fertilization of ideas and knowledge. Nothing new or earth-shaking about that. However, this situation presents an inherent barrier to TM and will significantly reduce the potential for reaping the benefits of a robust TM culture. The paradigm shift would entail creating a TM mindset that is championed from the very top level of the organizational structure (CEO, CFO, etc.). Certainly this is not an impossible task; rather, it is a challenge that many companies around the globe are struggling with. They want the extremely value-added, benefit-laden concept of TM to work for them but the real or imagined barriers to its implementation may seem insurmountable. We are not suggesting that departmentalization needs to be eliminated for TM to take hold. Rather, departmentalized organizations need to work a bit harder at implementing and maintaining an effective TM culture than organizations with a more flattened, flexible structure. A case in point: if TQM can become a predominant force in an organizational culture, TM can also become predominant. Like TQM, TM must have change agents, champions, and provide immediate as well as intermittent rewards for the participants.

KNOWLEDGE MANAGEMENT AS A CENTRAL PROCESS OF HR PLANNING

Knowledge is a key asset in any organization. Knowledge differentiates one organization from the next, and might well be the most important asset in an organization. However, knowledge is arguably the least well-managed asset in most organizations. Knowledge management, according to Turban et al. (2006: 353), 'refers to the process of creating or capturing knowledge, storing and protecting it, updating and maintaining it, and using it whenever necessary.' Knowledge is awareness, familiarity or understanding gained through study or experience. This definition provides a wide range of possibilities, from consciousness about an idea to a more automatic, reflexive skill in handling a complex concept or task. Knowledge management, through effective processes of knowledge generation, sharing, and transfer throughout the organization, plays an essential role for HR planning in supporting strategy formulation and implementation. We will now examine this role in more detail, with particular emphasis upon more formal knowledge management systems supported by our advancing technologies.

Knowledge can be either tacit or explicit. The former is defined as 'personal, context-specific, and hard to formalize and communicate. It consists of experiences, beliefs and skills. Tacit knowledge is entirely subjective and is often acquired through physically practicing a skill or activity' (Pearlson & Saunders, 2004: 287). Explicit knowledge is more easily captured and reported. It is often confused with 'information,' as it often appears on the same types of reports. Therefore, it is important to differentiate between knowledge and information. Computer literacy textbooks typically explain that information is comprised of organized (i.e., processed) facts. An *information processing system (IPS)* stores, organizes, sorts, and otherwise manipulates facts into a variety of formats that are presented to users on schedule or on demand. An IPS can be limited or quite rich, but it deals with *information*. Any knowledge that is brought to or drawn from the information is affected by the user.

A *knowledge management system (KMS)*, by comparison, is much more sophisticated in terms of what it stores as well as how it manipulates and how it presents knowledge. The classical information processing algorithms and techniques must be augmented by more complex methods. The means of capturing knowledge must be more complicated. Above all, the motivation behind the use of a KMS and the justification for the implementation of a KMS must be considered at a deeper level.

As previously stated, knowledge is a most important asset in most organizations. Knowing how to perform a task in the most effective manner for a given situation differentiates a master worker from an apprentice. If such knowledge is lost, an organization operates less effectively and less efficiently until it relearns that knowledge. In most cases, it is some degree of knowledge that provides competitive advantage, allows customer relationships to function more smoothly, keeps supply chains working, wins the day in negotiations, and counsels troubled employees. Despite the importance of knowledge to an organization, most organizations do not have formal knowledge management systems. This is not to say that managers don't appreciate knowledge and what it means to their organizations. Indeed, forward-thinking managers would like be able to manage knowledge. They simply don't know how, or, if they do know how, they don't have the resources to do it effectively.

INTERACTION OF KM AND TM IN ONGOING HR PLANNING

First and foremost, knowledge is held by human talent, especially in the absence of a computer-based, formalized knowledge management system. Knowledge is the basis for the talents managed by talent management. And recruiting, developing, and retaining workers with appropriate knowledge sets that can be applied to achieving company objectives represent areas of focus for ongoing HR planning. There can be significant costs associated with designing and implementing a formal KMS as part of an organization's efforts in knowledge management. It takes a lot of time and effort to establish a KMS. Besides the costs of computer hardware, software, network and supplies costs, and floor space, there also is the cost of training not only the knowledge workers and technical staff, but also all those who will be using the KMS. Of course, there are also opportunity costs. To obtain a genuine commitment to a strategy using a formal KMS, a paradigm shift must occur in most organizations. Simply stated—but not simply accomplished—corporate culture must change to accommodate a KMS.

In a free enterprise system, much of the motivation to perform is based on the incentive tied to work desired and performed. And the performance of a large percentage of workers is based on the knowledge they hold. Consequently, employees can feel threatened when their knowledge is codified and transferred to the collective KMS. The incentive for them to expand their knowledge is reduced, and the incentive for them to become social loafers increases. In a relatively small work group, workers often do share knowledge for the benefit of the group. However, in a large corporation, they don't even know the names or locations or jobs of the employees who can tap into the company-held knowledge that was previously their personal domain. For a summary of this and other cultural problems with implementing KM, see McNurlin and Sprague (2006: 543–545).

In order to effectively implement a KMS in a large organization, management needs to adopt a strategy of changing the corporate culture, based to a large extent on the input of talent managers and HR professionals. The strategy needs to address more innovative incentives for sharing information rather than traditional incentives, which are based on possessing information. It also needs to address the transition to the new nature of tasks that workers perform as their jobs are adjusted to the knowledge culture.

Another challenge must be considered before committing to the implementation of a KMS: the nature of knowledge gathering. Most people possess expertise that they apply on a routine basis without thinking much about the processes used. When questioned as to how they arrived at a decision or performed a task, the answer most often is, 'I don't know.' Getting a worker to describe in detail the knowledge that he or she possesses can be frustrating for both the worker and the KMS professional. As knowledge is captured to be placed into a knowledge management system, it must be categorized according to its nature and potential usage. In an information management system, data and information are stored in files according to their type; for example, classical data are stored in files that are divided into fields and records, large narratives are stored in text files, pictures and drawings are stored in image files, audio is stored in sound files, and so on. In a

KMS, those file types are used as well; for example, knowledge can be derived from an architectural drawing stored in an AutoCAD file format. However, the nature of knowledge requires storage and algorithms that go beyond the classical and reflect the manner in which humans process knowledge.

Since the dawn of the computer era, researchers have expanded the range and scope of the discipline of *artificial intelligence* in order for computers to mimic the methods that humans use to store and process knowledge. Several distinct categories have emerged and algorithms for processing those have been implemented in software, much of which is commercially available.

Many human applications of knowledge are *rule-based*. If a condition exists, one performs in a certain manner. If one is cold, one might put on a sweater. If the supply of paper clips in the supply room runs low, the supply administrator initiates an order for more paper clips. If a mason needs to put a half brick at the end of a row in a fireplace, and if there is an unused half-brick close at hand, he or she uses that half-brick—otherwise (i.e., else) he or she breaks a brick into halves.

Such 'if-then-else' logic is readily implemented into classical programming methods using mainstream computer languages. Such software, called *expert systems*, work well in limited domains of knowledge and are the simplest examples of artificial intelligence in action. One noteworthy example is MYCIN, a medical diagnostic system that leads one, question by question, though the process to pinpoint an ailment from a set of symptoms. MYCIN was emptied of its medical knowledge and was distributed as an *expert system shell* known as E-MYCIN (Empty MYCIN). A user could replace the medical rules with, say, electronics or automotive rules and create a computer diagnostic or automobile diagnostic system.

Rule-based systems rely on discrete conditions. Not all of the knowledge held by humans is appropriately discrete. For instance, if a worker says it is cold in his or her office, is that the same level of cold felt by another worker? Or would other workers refer to the temperature as chilly, frigid, or perhaps less warm than desired? What is the boundary between cold and chilly? Such scales have meanings based on the individual. Additional capabilities are needed to allow a KMS to deal with such qualitative subtleties. Fortunately, appropriately named *fuzzy logic* has been devised to mimic the manner in which the human brain deals with such situations.

Two other interrelated approaches that the human brain uses for managing information can be described as *chunking* and *pattern recognition*. As one drives along the interstate highway at meal time, even in an unfamiliar area, and notices the roadside sign that displays a number of internationally known logos of fast food restaurants, one immediately knows the majority of what to expect at the next exit. Associated with a particular logo in the driver's brain is stereotyped knowledge about menu selection, price range, cleanliness levels, quality, decor, parking, drive-through windows, and even workers' uniforms. Large chunks of information are stored together in the driver's brain. On the job, workers similarly apply such large chunks of information. A salesperson, for instance, can relate dozens of facts about a customer based on the trigger of the customer's name.

As an exhibition of his or her talent, a chess expert can engage in competition against several opponents simultaneously, walking around the room and stopping briefly at each chess board to make his or her move. That is possible as chess experts' brains deal with patterns of chess boards. Likewise, experts in other domains recognize and process patterns of information as knowledge. For example, a football quarterback steps to the line of scrimmage, quickly analyzes how the defensive players have aligned, and changes the play his team is to run. Such chunking and pattern recognitions can be found in all lines of work. An effective KMS needs to include algorithms to handle such sets of knowledge. While the storage of chunks and patterns can be accommodated in classical file structures, traditional computer languages are not as efficient as languages such as LISP (list processor) or Prolog to accomplish the algorithms.

All the above techniques and more can be blended into another category of knowledge processing known as *case-based reasoning*. Consider the power that an organization could derive if the capability existed to compare the characteristics of a decision currently at hand to instances where similar decisions had been made months or years ago, decisions that had been forgotten by the decision-maker or that had been made by other decision-makers no longer with the company. Consider the even greater power that can accrue if the KMS has ability to compare instances wherein, on the surface, there appears to be no similarity among those instances. Consider the greater power to bring knowledge into the decision that is external to the company. For instance, if a company was faced with the need to expand production facilities to make more widgets, wouldn't it be great if its KMS could inform managers that there was a ready supply of trained but unemployed widget workers in a location with vacant factory space close to good transportation facilities and to suppliers of raw materials that comprise widgets?

Such capability would not only incorporate case-based reasoning, but would also include use of *software agents*, which search for specific combinations or patterns of data. Such software agents typically employ algorithms similar to those used by a *search engine* on the World Wide Web. The difference between the two is that a search engine reacts to the search line provided by a human and comes to a conclusion fairly rapidly, while a software agent runs in a continuous manner. Software agents use a set of parameters that can be more complex than the search line given to a search engine and not only actively look through a designated range of storage locations but also lie in wait for new entries to be made into those storage locations.

Search engine and software agent technology, along with the other methods mentioned above, can also be used in what has become known as *data mining.* In its most limited form, data mining involves users issuing queries to a database to obtain information or knowledge as they encounter the need. In a more advanced version of data mining, intelligent software agents—equipped with rule-based, fuzzy, chunking, pattern-recognition, case-based, and other logic—continually search the corporate knowledge warehouse looking for any relationships that can be found and reporting on the relationships whenever they are found. This is known as *knowledge creation.*

Consider an illustration of a quiet, non-self-promoting employee who, unbeknownst to supervisors, has contributed to the success of a corporation on numerous occasions by applying his or her wisdom behind the scenes to dozens of co-workers who receive credit for the outcome. Such an employee seldom gets recognized or rewarded for those contributions. Yet a data mining capability of a fully installed, full-featured KMS could create knowledge of that employee's worth to the organization and pass that knowledge to appropriate supervisors. One place where a record of such informal contributions exists is in e-mail exchanges between that worker and his or her co-workers. An intelligent data mining application could examine such e-mail and find instances of cooperation or expressions of gratitude between co-workers, then connect those by project names or data sets used to successful (or failed, for that matter) projects, even though the project information is stored in other locations and in other formats. Thus, to reward and reinforce this important ongoing knowledge management activity related to knowledge generation and transfer, this approach is able to give credit where credit is due. And more fundamentally, thoughtful consideration for the development and use of such knowledge management tools affecting individual and organizational decision-making and performance should be an important priority in HR planning.

CONCLUSION

According to our premise, TM provides an essential philosophical and cultural context for managerial decision-making and behavior, and is particularly related to various HR functional areas such as staffing, training, performance management, compensation, and employee relations. As a fundamental context for HR planning, TM provides the universe within which HR functional practices should be carried out. In a later chapter in this book we examine this important context of TM in which the particular practice of performance management can operate most effectively and efficiently. For effective organizational performance, all HR functional areas must reinforce and be congruent with an organizational culture of talent management. A major priority of HR planning is to ensure that this TM culture is developed and integrated within all of the HR functional areas, as well as supported and reinforced by all leaders and managers within the organization.

For example, what would happen if an organization needed to hire new and scarce talent for the mechanical engineering department, but the present compensation strategy did not allow the company to be a pay leader in the organization's industry? And, what if the present recruitment strategy were to attract the 'best and the brightest' wherever they can be found? These two HR functional strategies are incongruent and therefore operate at odds with each other. The recruiters would be severely hampered by the restrictive compensation strategy. By the same token, the compensation specialists might then experience significant pressure from the recruiters to change a compensation policy that perhaps they had no authority to change.

Incongruence within an organization (including HR systems) can create friction between departments and often promotes cognitive dissonance on the part of individual employees. Effective knowledge management may serve as an effective feedback mechanism for noting this friction and underlying incongruence, and relaying this information back to managers and decision-makers for appropriate action. Based on a common high commitment to the value of talent management throughout the organization, KM can also help avoid this incongruence through its integrating role in effective HR planning. Referring to the previous example, in a TM culture the recruitment folks, via KM processes, would gather relevant data and information about the local labor market and the compensation costs necessary to attract the scarce talent that is needed by the mechanical engineering department. That information would be transmitted to both the mechanical engineering department and the compensation department, and an informed and consistent decision could be made quickly and accurately.

A strong commitment to the value of talent management and the use of effective processes of knowledge management is essential for HR planning. This dual commitment will determine *what* competencies the individual employees and organization as a whole should possess and develop, and *how* these talents should be developed and imparted within the organization. In addition, KM plays a critical role in sensing and providing feedback on how effectively the various HR functional practices are implemented and integrated within the organization, providing opportunity for correction where needed. Thus, TM and KM provide essential support to HR planning in its basic responsibility of preparing for and providing human talent with appropriate knowledge assets to enable effective strategy formulation, and the informed human talent needed for implementing those strategic plans.

REFERENCES

Corporate Training & Development Advisor. (2006). Most companies are not integrating the talent management process, survey finds. Stamford, CT: Simba Information, **11**(14): 5.

Frauenheim, E. (2006). Talent management software is bundling up. *Workforce Management*, **85**(19): 35.

Greer, C.R. (2001). *Strategic Human Resource Management: A General Managerial Approach* (2nd edition). Upper Saddle River, NJ: Prentice Hall.

Ha, J. (2006). Talent management: What's it mean? *Reliable Plant Magazine*, **5**(2006): 2.

Hansen, F. (2007). What is talent? *Workforce Management*, **86**(1): 12.

Hartley, D.E. (2004). Tools for talent. *T&D*, **58**(4): 20.

Likierman, A. (2007). How to measure the success of talent management. *People Management*, **13**(4): 46–47.

Lockwood, N. (2005). Talent management overview. *Talent Management Series Part I.* Alexandria, VA: Society for Human Resource Management.

McCauley, C. and Wakefield, M. (2006). Talent management in the 21st century: Help your company find, develop, and keep its strongest workers. *Journal for Quality and Participation*, **29**(4): 4.

McNurlin, B.C. and Sprague, R.H. Jr. (2006). *Information Systems Management in Practice* (7th edition). Upper Saddle River, NJ: Pearson-Prentice-Hall, pp. 529–547.

McTernan, J. (2003). Staff shortages now cost so much it is time to re-examine the way we do business. *Community Care*, 1469: 19.

Morton, L. (2007). Talent management: A critical way to integrate and embed diversity. Retrieved 6 June, 2007 from http://www.workinfo.com/free/Downloads/259.htm

Pearlson, K.E. and Saunders, C.S. (2004). *Managing and Using Information Systems* (2nd edition). New York: John Wiley and Sons, pp. 274–302.

Stockley, D. (2007). Talent management concept. Retrieved 6 June, 2007 from http://derekstockley.com.au/newsletters-05/020-talent-management.html.

T&D (2007). Talent management barriers. **61**(2): 16.

Turban, E., King, D., Lee, J., and Viehland, D. (2006). *Electronic Commerce 2006: A Managerial Perspective.* Upper Saddle River, NJ: Pearson Education, Inc., pp. 353–357.

Wood, A. (2006). Nurturing talent. *Chemical Week.* **168**(34): 5.

3. Talent staffing systems for effective knowledge management

Mark L. Lengnick-Hall and Leticia S. Andrade

While it may sound like a new idea, management and staffing systems designed to utilize knowledge in organizations can be traced back to antiquity. Neilson (2001: 35) describes how knowledge management and human resource management (HRM) were (probably) combined to build the pyramids in Egypt:

> Referring to his papyrus blueprints and sand table model, the chief architect begins: 'we are going to build a pyramid that is 756 feet square in plane and 481 feet high. The angle of inclination of the triangular faces will be 51.5 degrees. The base will cover about 13 acres and I estimate this pyramid will consist of 2,300,000 dressed stones averaging 2.5 tons each.'

> After much trial and error trying to pull 2.5-ton blocks of sandstone over the desert sands, you learn that putting logs underneath the stone blocks and using ramps saves on the back muscles. This knowledge is passed on to other work crews. As crew members are transferred to other jobs or recruited to fight in the Pharaoh's army, this 'know-how' becomes a generally accepted practice in the pyramid and military construction business. After several decades of hard work, you and your compatriots finish construction ahead of schedule and below cost estimates.

Few people would disagree that knowledge is becoming an increasingly important factor in firm success (Grant, 1996; Liebeskind, 1996; Teece, 1998; McFadyen & Cannella, 2004). As illustrated in the example above, it takes the support of HRM practices, such as staffing and training and development, to transform knowledge into 'know-how' and utilize it to achieve organizational objectives. Globalization and growing connectedness through such means as the internet and telecommunications technology have quickened the pace for competition and placed a premium on knowing what the next trend is and rapidly mobilizing resources to develop a product or provide a service that takes advantage of opportunities—before rivals enter the fray. And, while every firm and every industry is not competing in a hypercompetitive market (D'Aveni, 1994), even firms in more stable industries find that the need to reduce costs and increase efficiency emphasizes the importance of knowledge and learning as key ingredients to their success. While traditional approaches to HRM served organizations well in the 20th century, new and innovative approaches are needed for the 21st century and the knowledge economy (Lengnick-Hall & Lengnick-Hall, 2003). A key component of this new approach to HRM is its emphasis on developing staffing systems that provide the necessary talent for effective knowledge management.

In a knowledge economy, organizations need a stock (supply) and flow (movement) of talent to survive and compete. As defined in the dictionary, talent is 'the natural endowments of a person, a special often creative or artistic aptitude, and general intelligence or mental power' (Merriam-Webster Online, 2007). From a human resource management perspective, our definition of talent includes the natural endowments of all employees in the organization who carry or embody knowledge, skills, abilities, and other characteristics (KSAOs). It is not sufficient simply to hire people to perform specific jobs; organizations need the knowledge that individuals can bring to the workplace and apply to solving problems and creating innovations (Leonard-Barton, 1995; Anand, Gardner, & Morris, 2007). Boudreau and Ramstad (2007: 2) take a broader perspective on talent. They describe it as 'the resource that includes the potential and realized capacities of individuals and groups and how they are organized, including within the organization and those who might join the organization.' Viewing the organization as a repository of knowledge, it is important to recognize that the knowledge of the firm ultimately lies in its people (Nonaka, 1994; Grant, 1996). That is, it is the people who embody the know-how of the firm. Organizations need individuals to have knowledge when they come to work, to acquire knowledge over time, and to share their knowledge with others in the organization. Moreover, the knowledge of the firm rests in the organization of its human resources (Kogut & Zander, 1992). Therefore, organizations need to manage both people and knowledge for talent to be effectively utilized to achieve competitive benefits.

The purpose of this chapter is to integrate talent staffing systems with knowledge management. Rather than throw the baby out with the bath water, we show that a combination of traditional HRM policies, programs, and practices, along with some new perspectives and approaches, can be used to help organizations develop staffing systems that effectively manage people and knowledge. The chapter is organized as follows. First, we define key concepts from the knowledge management literature. Since much confusion can arise over abstract terminology, we believe it is necessary to establish a common frame of reference before proceeding. Second, we describe organizational staffing systems as a means for managing employee stocks and flows. Rather than focusing narrowly on recruitment and selection, we take a broader perspective on managing the movements of employees into, within, and out of the organization. Third, we integrate the management of employee stocks and flows (talent staffing systems) with knowledge stocks and flows (knowledge management systems). The objectives of a knowledge management system have implications for how talent staffing systems can best be designed to achieve desired outcomes. Finally, we offer some suggestions for research and practical implications.

KEY CONCEPTS FROM THE KNOWLEDGE MANAGEMENT LITERATURE

Knowledge is a multidimensional construct and has been examined from several different perspectives (Spender, 1996). Many authors distinguish between information and knowledge (see, for example, Newell et al., 2002). Leonard and Sensiper (1998: 112) define knowledge as 'information that is relevant, actionable, and at least partially based on experience.' Knowledge is information that is linked to potential actions because an individual is able to use it, whereas data are any signals that can be sent by an originator to a recipient, and information is simply data that are intelligible to the recipient (Davenport & Prusak, 2000; Lengnick-Hall & Lengnick-Hall, 2003). In the pyramid example, the outside temperature of 120 degrees would be considered data. The fact that people get exhausted at that temperature is information—data in context. And, recognizing that it is more productive to haul heavy stones early in the morning or later in the day when it is cooler is knowledge—information linked to actions.

Knowledge is frequently categorized as taking two forms: *explicit* and *tacit*. Explicit knowledge can be formalized, codified, and communicated, and is often gained through formal education, training programs, and experience on the job (DeNisi, Hitt, & Jackson, 2003). In the pyramid example, explicit knowledge can be found in the blueprints and sand table model created by the architect to communicate his design to the builders. Thus, explicit knowledge can be communicated through such means as written documents, formal presentations, books, manuals, formulas, specifications, lectures, diagrams, and so on. On the other hand, tacit knowledge is that which people know but cannot explain (Polanyi, 1966). It is not teachable, not articulated, and not observable in use, but instead is rich, complex, and undocumented (Davenport & Prusak, 2000). It is grounded in experience and difficult to express through mere verbal instruction—individuals know it but cannot articulate and explain it (DeNisi et al., 2003). In the pyramid example, tacit knowledge might be found in the stone moving crew's observations or by their becoming involved in situations. For example, one crew member discovers that by tapping on the stone and listening to the sound that it makes, he can identify where best to make a smooth cut. Others in the crew observe and listen along beside him and gain the same knowledge over time. The tacit knowledge acquired would be unique to the group.

Both explicit and tacit knowledge can be directed to accomplish organizational objectives through a combination of knowledge management and human resource management. The workers in the pyramid example were encouraged to share what they learned about moving stone blocks with other crews. For example, one crew might learn from an accident that water spilled on the ground in front of the stones helped them slide the stones more easily. Other crews in the same proximity observing this phenomenon would then incorporate it into their own behaviors. This knowledge would then be transferred to other crews throughout the construction site. More formally, *knowledge transfer* is the process through which an individual, team, department, or division is affected by the experience of another (Argote et al., 2000) and it represents one of the most important means by which organizations can gain competitive advantage through knowledge. In the pyramid example, knowledge transfer both sped up the construction process, and probably saved lives as well.

Knowledge can be thought of as a raw material in need of further processing—through conversions—that make it available and useful for changing behaviors, improving performance, and creating innovations. Nonaka and Takeuchi (1995) describe four modes of *knowledge conversion* between explicit and tacit knowledge: (1) *socialization*—from tacit to tacit, (2) *externalization*—from tacit to explicit, (3) *combination*—from explicit to explicit, and (4) *internalization*—from explicit to tacit. Socialization uses shared experiences whereby individuals acquire tacit knowledge from others through observation, imitation, and practice. Externalization uses metaphors, analogies, concepts, hypotheses, or models to articulate tacit knowledge into explicit concepts. Combination uses media such as documents, meetings, telephone conversations, or computerized networks to combine different bodies of explicit knowledge. Internalization uses oral stories, documents, manuals, and diagrams to help individuals convert explicit knowledge into shared mental models or technical know-how. These four modes of conversion form the basis for an organization to gain competitive advantage through knowledge assets.

In addition to the explicit/tacit knowledge distinction, knowledge can also be categorized as *general* versus *specific* (Becker, 1964). This is particularly useful for designing talent staffing systems for knowledge management since its focus is on the individual level of analysis. General knowledge, or public knowledge, resides in the public domain and it is applicable across firms in a variety of industries (Matusik & Hill, 1998). For example, knowledge of basic math, reading, and writing resides in the public domain, and someone who possesses that knowledge can apply it across virtually all businesses. On the other hand, specific knowledge is narrower in focus with application in only some situations (Lepak & Snell, 2003). *Occupation-specific knowledge* is that which is relatively codified throughout a broader professional or institutionalized group. The HRM body of knowledge is codified throughout the group of human resource professionals and even certified through the Society for Human Resource Management. *Industry-specific knowledge* is that which, though in the public domain, is applicable only to a particular industry. These bodies of knowledge must be obtained in order for practitioners to be certified or to gain legitimacy in the field. For instance, computer industry certifications signify possession of this form of knowledge. *Firm-specific knowledge* is that which can only be applied in a particular organization, such as knowledge of an organization's filing system or internal administrative procedures. Employees bring all four forms of knowledge to the organization in varying amounts (ibid.). Through knowledge management and HRM, the talents of employees can be directed to accomplish desired organizational objectives, such as solving problems and creating innovations.

Knowledge management is an encompassing term that usually covers three broad capabilities: *knowledge acquisition and creation, knowledge capture and storage*, and *knowledge diffusion and transfer* (Sparrow, 2006). Knowledge acquisition and creation refers to the generation of new knowledge fundamental to the long-term viability of the enterprise. Knowledge capture and storage refers to the creation (and maintenance in usable form so that it remains valuable) of an inventory of knowledge so the organization knows what it possesses and where it resides. Knowledge diffusion and transfer refers to the subsequent mobilization and flow of knowledge within the organization that creates knowledge-based value. Together, these three processes form the basis of gaining a competitive advantage through knowledge. However, knowledge must be applied to solving problems and creating new ideas if it is to have any effect on a firm's competitive position (Lengnick-Hall & Lengnick-Hall, 2003). Furthermore, for an organization to learn, it must create *absorptive capacity*, or the ability to identify, assimilate, and use additional knowledge (Cohen & Levinthal, 1990). Since, typically, individuals or groups cannot take in additional knowledge that is too different from their current knowledge base, organizations engage in practices that increase their absorptive capacities over time. A well-managed talent staffing system and knowledge management system can thus contribute to increasing an organization's absorptive capacity.

In summary, firms configure knowledge-based resources to create value through *knowledge stocks* and *flows* (Morris, Snell, & Lepak, 2005). Knowledge stocks include competencies, dynamic capabilities, routines, new ideas, and innovation and they can help organizations create competitive advantage through the effective use, manipulation, and transformation of various organizational resources required to perform a task. Knowledge flows include the movement of knowledge within and across firms that is essential for innovation and continuous adaptation. As Lepak and Snell (2003) note, it is the configuration of knowledge stocks that provides a basis for competitive advantage, whereas the renewal and recombination of those stocks allow a firm to sustain that advantage. Therefore, the integration of effective talent staffing systems and knowledge management is critical for creating knowledge stocks and flows necessary for gaining and sustaining competitive advantage.

MANAGING EMPLOYEE FLOWS THROUGH TALENT STAFFING SYSTEMS

Employees join organizations, get promoted, get demoted, transfer laterally to different jobs, retire, leave voluntarily, leave involuntarily, come back after being rehired, and even die on the job. They don't stay put; they move, sometimes for their own benefit, sometimes for the benefit of the organization, and sometimes for the benefit of both. These movements of employees into, within, and out of organizations—or *employee flows*—some planned and some unexpected, make staffing organizations a continual challenge. As employees flow into, within, and out of the organization, managers or organizations must figure out how to retain, or transfer valuable knowledge. For example, when an employee retires, how do organizations capture, or retain the specialized knowledge that they possess? When viewed from an employee flows perspective, staffing systems encompass decisions about employee movements. See Figure 3.1.

There are several employee flows that can occur in organizations. First, employees can be obtained externally (i.e., move from outside to inside) in three primary ways: (1) applicants can be recruited, selected, and hired from the outside, (2) former employees can be rehired (e.g., laid-off employees can be rehired), or (3) employees can be rented (e.g., contingent workers, such as part-time workers, independent contractors, and retirees). Second, once inside the organization, applicants (who are now employees) can move vertically, horizontally, or diagonally. Vertical movements include promotions (upward) and demotions (downward). Horizontal movement includes lateral transfers, such as those between equivalent jobs in the same

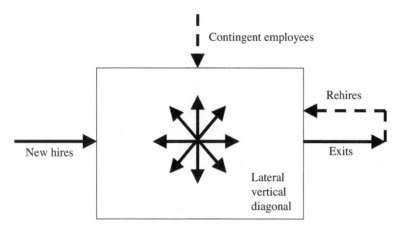

Figure 3.1   Employee flows

department (division, unit, etc.) or to equivalent jobs in different departments. Diagonal movement includes changing job families or occupations, such as moving from a human resource professional job to a line manager job in manufacturing. Third, employees can leave the organization either voluntarily (e.g., for a job at another company or to retire from work altogether), or involuntarily (e.g., terminated for job performance, laid off due to budget issues, or in some cases due to death).

Any employee movement triggers a potential cascade of staffing decisions (Thibodaux & Rouse, 2005). For example, if a manager leaves the organization voluntarily, there are several options for replacing him or her. The organization can hire someone from outside, hire someone from inside, or not fill the job at all. If the organization hires someone from outside, this has the least effect on overall employee flows—only one replacement is necessary. On the other hand, if the organization promotes a current employee to fill the position, there are now at least two employee moves: the current employee into the manager's job and then someone to fill the promoted employee's job. Again, depending upon whether the organization goes outside for the replacement, or hires someone from within, multiple staffing decisions can be the result.

Mathematically, these employee movements can be modeled using Markov analyses, which use historical movement rates of employees between jobs as probabilities to predict future movements for planning purposes (Heneman & Sandver, 1977; Thibodaux & Rouse, 2005). Additionally, these employee flows can be incorporated into utility analyses to determine the benefits versus costs for alternative staffing strategies (Boudreau & Ramstad, 2003).

The important point is that taking a bird's eye view of employee flows and developing staffing systems—with an emphasis on systems (i.e., interacting component parts)—allows organizations to manage employee movements proactively to achieve desired objectives. As previous research has shown, for example, some turnover (employee flows out of the organization) is functional and healthy for an organization's survival (e.g., Dalton, 1997), and sometimes it even makes sense to hire (employee flows into the organization) in poor economic times (i.e., countercyclical hiring) to gain competitive advantage over rivals when economic times improve (Greer, 1984). A staffing perspective of managing employee flows is thus more likely than a focus on individual staffing decisions to result in a steady source of human capital that is constantly renewed and adaptable to changes in the environment. From an employee flows perspective, individual staffing decisions, such as whom to promote or whom to transfer are viewed in the larger context of how they affect the overall stock and flow of talent in the organization.

Neither talent staffing systems nor knowledge management systems in isolation are adequate for effectively creating competitive advantage through knowledge assets in a firm. Each is a subsystem of the larger organizational system, and optimizing subsystems (i.e., doing each part well separately) does not result in maximum organizational system performance (von Bertalanffy, 1974). Consequently, what is needed is the integration of the two subsystems—working together—to accomplish desired organizational goals.

INTEGRATING TALENT STAFFING SYSTEMS AND KNOWLEDGE MANAGEMENT SYSTEMS

Talent staffing systems and knowledge management systems are inextricably intertwined. Let's return to our pyramid example. Imagine two scenarios for the staffing of stone moving crews. In the first scenario, crews are formed and reformed on a daily basis. The composition of crews change frequently, so little opportunity exists for creating cohesion within the group. Furthermore, since the crews in the first scenario are not allowed to communicate with other crews (perhaps for fear of an uprising), the capacity to transfer knowledge throughout the construction site is hindered or eliminated. In the second scenario, stone moving crews are kept intact over time. The composition of crew members remains fairly stable (with the exception of losses due to death and injury), and the groups are able to become cohesive. Furthermore, keeping the crews together creates an opportunity for team learning. When allowed to communicate with other groups (in contrast to the first scenario), crews can share what they learn, and best practices can be diffused throughout the construction site. The design of talent staffing systems can play a significant role in facilitating these aspects of knowledge management. This can be accomplished by designing organization structures and processes that promote knowledge acquisition, capture, and transfer, as well as developing timelines for employee transfers that capitalize on familiarity and group cohesion and recognize the benefits of broad social ties and diversity of experience. In the next sections, we examine ways in which talent staffing systems can be integrated with knowledge management systems to develop knowledge assets that can create competitive advantage for organizations.

Objectives of a Talent Staffing System for Effective Knowledge Management

While talent staffing systems for effective knowledge management must be tailored to particular organizational characteristics, there are some general goals and objectives shared across all organizations:

1. Hire individuals who have knowledge and expertise (explicit and tacit; often specialized) to contribute to solving problems and creating innovations. Hire for knowledge gaps, not job gaps. Hire for knowledge, not jobs.
2. Hire for social capital (who you know) in addition to human capital (what you know). Hire individuals that have both valuable social networks and the capacity to create new social capital.
3. Hire individuals who can teach and communicate what they know to others.
4. Adapt jobs, work, tasks, and locations to employees rather adapting employees to a particular job and/or location to attract, motivate, and retain knowledge workers.
5. Capture the knowledge of employees (either through technology or embedding it in social systems) before they leave—either voluntarily or involuntarily.
6. Retain employees who are motivated and have the capacity to learn continuously. Encourage turnover of those who can't or won't learn continuously.
7. Create a climate and culture that supports knowledge creation, capture, and diffusion.
8. Develop strategies for minimizing knowledge loss and knowledge spillover.

First, organizations need to hire individuals who have knowledge and expertise (explicit and tacit; oftentimes specialized) to contribute to solving problems and creating innovations. This is more important in knowledge-intensive firms (Horwitz, Heng, & Quazi, 2003; Anand et al., 2007) and for knowledge worker jobs (Newell et al., 2002) than in other firms and jobs, but even in less knowledge-intensive firms and in jobs requiring less knowledge, it is still a desirable goal to attain. For key knowledge workers, organizations need to place more emphasis on hiring for knowledge and less emphasis on hiring for particular jobs (Lepak & Snell, 2003). For example, professional law firms hiring attorneys may seek individuals with particular knowledge such as experience and specialization in labor law, family law, and so on. Thus, hiring for knowledge gaps is frequently more important than hiring for job gaps (Brelade & Harman, 2000).

Second, while hiring for human capital (or knowledge) that individuals bring to the organization is crucial, hiring for social capital may be equally important (Newell et al., 2002; Swart & Kinnie, 2003). Social capital refers to 'the goodwill that is engendered by the fabric of social relations and that can be mobilized to facilitate action' (Adler & Kwon, 2002: 17). From this perspective, the networks of friends, colleagues, and associates that an individual brings to an organization expand the opportunities for importing knowledge into the organization from external sources. In addition, the social capital that an individual develops while within an organization is equally important for expanding its knowledge assets.

Third, organizations need to hire individuals who can teach and communicate what they know to others. It is necessary, but not sufficient to hire individuals with needed knowledge and expertise. Organizations also need employees who can transfer their knowledge to individuals and groups.

Fourth, for key knowledge workers, adapting jobs, work, tasks, and locations to employees rather than adapting employees to a particular job and/or location is an important means to attract, motivate, and retain them (Horwitz et al., 2003; Ronen, Friedman, & Ben-Asher, 2007). Key knowledge workers are more likely to be scarce in the labor market and demand more flexible work arrangements, as well as more likely to make valued contributions to the organization when their needs are met.

Fifth, organizations need to capture the knowledge of employees (either through technology or embedding it in social systems) before they leave—either voluntarily or involuntarily. This applies to both full-time permanent employees and part-time contingent employees.

Sixth, some employees are more important because they have the ability to learn continuously and contribute over a longer time period. Special emphasis should be placed on efforts to retain them. On the other hand, some employees don't have the ability to learn continuously (or don't exert the effort), and consequently are less valuable over a longer time period. Turnover of these employees is both desirable and healthy for the organization.

Seventh, organizations need to create a climate and culture that nurtures and supports knowledge acquisition, capture, and diffusion. This is necessary both to attract talented workers with needed knowledge and to ensure that, once hired, the talented workers have the motivation and opportunity to apply their knowledge for the benefit of the organization. This is particularly important for preventing *knowledge hoarding*, or employees' reluctance to share knowledge for fear of becoming expendable.

Eighth, organizations need to develop strategies for minimizing knowledge loss and knowledge spillover. When employees who are deeply embedded in social networks within an organization leave, the effect of their departures can often be greater than the loss of a single employee (Fisher & White, 2000). Their departures may have negative effects on knowledge flows within the organization.

Additionally, when employees who have firm-specific, and especially proprietary, knowledge leave the organization, the potential for knowledge spillovers to competitors is a serious concern. This is also a worry when hiring contingent workers who may acquire firm-specific knowledge while working for the organization and then later share that knowledge with competitors. Together, these overarching objectives provide a basis for designing talent staffing systems that support effective knowledge management within organizations and prevent undesirable, and often unintended, knowledge leakage to other organizations. Specific staffing strategies that facilitate each of the components of knowledge management—acquisition, capture, and transfer—will be discussed next.

Talent Staffing System Components to Promote Knowledge Acquisition and Creation

The knowledge an organization possesses reflects the cumulative knowledge of the individuals that flow through it over time. Thus, attracting and hiring individuals with needed knowledge forms the foundation for knowledge management effectiveness. Without high-quality raw materials (i.e., knowledgeable employees), even the most sophisticated knowledge management system will yield few benefits.

Make, buy, or rent knowledge

There are three primary ways in which organizations can acquire knowledge through talent staffing systems: make it, buy it, or rent it (Davenport & Prusak, 2000). First, the 'make' decision is one in which the organization hires individuals with fundamental knowledge and the capacity to learn, and further develops them over time. It is akin to hiring talented athletes for a team sport without regard to the position they will play and then developing their talents to fill one or more roles. An organization might hire a knowledgeable individual and then use him or her in several capacities: as an individual contributor or as a member of one or more teams—cross-functional, multidisciplinary, and even inter-organizational (Jackson, Hitt, & DeNisi, 2003). Since it requires time to develop individuals with this strategy, an organization cannot fully reap the benefits of this approach in the short term.

Second, the 'buy' decision is one in which the organization hires individuals with particular needed knowledge that can be applied to solving problems and creating innovations immediately. The organization can reap the benefits of this approach in the short term, and, if it pays attention to retention issues, can reap the benefits in the long term as well. In some cases, through mergers and acquisitions, organizations buy entire groups of employees with needed knowledge at one time; or through strategic alliances, organizations can rent the needed knowledge of other organizations. When IBM purchased Lotus at 14 times its book value, it was not simply purchasing software. It was buying the knowledge that created collaborative software applications and had the absorptive capacity to envision the next generation of communications and information-sharing software (Davenport & Prusak, 2000). However, the mobility of individuals within acquired or merged firms can make this wholesale purchase of knowledge approach risky. There is no guarantee that key individuals in the acquired firms will stay on in their jobs. Furthermore, the acquisition process may disrupt the ecology of the knowledge-creating environment (ibid.) and thus dilute or destroy the hoped for attainment of knowledge.

Third, the 'rent' decision is one in which the organization hires (for a specific period of time on a contractual basis) individuals with particular needed knowledge that can be applied to solving problems and creating innovations immediately. And, while there is no expectation to retain these individuals in the long term, there is a hope that their knowledge can be captured before they leave. Davis-Blake and Hui (2003) identify three determinants for contracting for talent: (1) the firm-specificity of required knowledge, (2) the nature of interdependencies in the project, and (3) the desired type of flexibility. Contracting for talent is most feasible in the following situations:

1. *Low firm-specificity of required knowledge*   The knowledge is public and not private (firm-specific), and the risk of transferring private knowledge to contractors is minimal.

2. *Few interdependencies in the project* Key project tasks are not highly interdependent, the tasks are not heterogeneous with respect to the level of required interdependence, and contracting for talent is unlikely to create significant violations of the psychological contract.
3. *Need for functional, numerical or financial flexibility* The goal is functional flexibility (redesigning the work so that the organization does not maintain its staff employees for whom it has insufficient and irrelevant demand to warrant the development of an internal capacity to do that work). Or the goal is numerical flexibility (efforts to redesign work so that workforce size can be adjusted easily to match the volume of work) and adequate contractor responsiveness to organizational changes and concerns can be assured. Or the goal is financial flexibility (efforts by managers to reintroduce greater competition among individual workers, thus reducing the expense of performing specific organizational functions) and the costs of contracting are not extremely high and the firm is unlikely to incur high switching costs in the future.

Davis-Blake and Hui (2003) note that when contracting for talent, firms typically invest relatively few resources in capturing and retaining knowledge generated with and by contract talent and that using contract talent to increase an organization's absorptive capacity may be problematic anyway due to the firm-specific nature of much product or process knowledge. Nevertheless, opportunities for acquiring knowledge through renting employees should not be ignored. For example, explicit knowledge brought into the firm by contract employees is easily captured if documentation is required.

The human resource architecture for knowledge
Not all workers possess the same knowledge, nor is all knowledge equally important to organizational success. The decision to make, buy, or rent knowledge is contingent upon a number of factors, but one of the most important is organizational strategy. The strategic direction of the organization determines which jobs (Kaplan & Norton, 2004; Becker & Huselid, 2006) and which employees are most important or key to success. Lepak and Snell (1999) have described the organization's human resource architecture as consisting of four distinct groups of employees categorized by two dimensions: strategic value and uniqueness. Strategic value refers to how important the employees are to the successful realization of the organization's strategy. Uniqueness refers to how easy or difficult it is to obtain needed skills in the labor market.

One group of employees, termed *knowledge-based employees*, are those who are critical to the organization's strategic success and more difficult to obtain in the labor market because they must possess more specific types of knowledge. Consequently, employees in this group are typically hired as a 'make' decision (i.e., hire and develop) when there is adequate time to do so, or hired as a 'buy' decision (i.e., hire for immediate contribution) when time pressures are urgent and there is a specific knowledge gap to fill.

A second group of employees, termed *job-based employees*, are likewise critical to the successful realization of an organization's strategy, yet the knowledge they possess is more general in nature or at least specific only at the occupational level. This is knowledge that is more easily purchased in the open market. Employees in this group are typically hired through a 'buy' decision, since their knowledge base allows them to begin making contributions immediately once they start work. However, since the knowledge possessed by employees in this group is more general in nature (e.g., accounting knowledge), they can be rented as well, although there may be risks of knowledge spillover if rented employees share what they learned at one organization with another.

A third group of employees, termed *alliance partners*, have low strategic importance but high uniqueness. That is, their direct impact on strategic success is not as critical, but their knowledge base is unique and more difficult to obtain in the labor market. Furthermore, either making or buying this knowledge is not a sound organizational investment decision. Consequently, organizations typically rent these employees, obtaining their knowledge on an as-needed basis.

A fourth group of employees, termed *contract workers*, have both low strategic importance and low uniqueness. Consequently, these workers are typically obtained through outsourcing arrangements, whereby the organization does not hire them as employees and they perform tasks for which such fears as knowledge spillover are virtually non-existent.

Lepak and Snell's typology of employee groups is useful for determining make, buy, or rent decisions for obtaining knowledge. However, it provides little insight into more specific decisions on whom to hire from among applicants, or whom to hire from among contingent employees. Decisions on whom to hire will likely depend on the organization's overall strategy or objectives (Bechet & Walker, 1993). For that, we need the traditional HRM tools of job analysis and KSAO (knowledge, skill, ability, and other characteristics) specification.

The KSAOs of knowledge workers
Davenport and Prusak (2000) note that in few firms are jobs dichotomized between thinkers (knowledge work) and doers (labor). And, while Lepak and Snell's (1999) typology identifies one employee group as low in strategic value and low in uniqueness, there is no implication that that group does not

require knowledge to perform needed tasks. However, the degree to which some firms infuse knowledge management throughout different employee groups does vary. While some firms emphasize knowledge management within obvious knowledge-oriented jobs, they place less emphasis on it in other more operational jobs. One company that instills knowledge management into all roles throughout the organization is Chaparral Steel. At Chaparral, even line steelworkers visit customers to better understand their requirements, attend industry seminars, and perform production experiments (ibid.). A security guard was even purported to have been observed reading a steelmaking textbook. The greater the infusion of knowledge management throughout an organization, the more emphasis needs to be put on hiring employees who have KSAOs that focus on capabilities for making contributions of knowledge no matter where they reside in the organizational hierarchy or what jobs they perform. But, what are those needed KSAOs?

While several researchers have proposed lists of knowledge worker KSAOs (e.g., Brelade & Harman, 2000; Horwitz et al., 2003; Swart & Kinnie, 2003), none have used as thorough and systematic a process for identification as Pulakos, Dorsey, and Borman (2003). Pulakos et al. developed a taxonomy of job performance for knowledge-based competition that extended a previous model proposed by Campbell et al. (1993). In addition to technical competence in a relevant content specialty (e.g., accounting, engineering, etc.), Pulakos et al. identified three additional performance dimensions: (1) building and applying knowledge, (2) sharing knowledge, and (3) maintaining knowledge. Behavioral definitions of each of these dimensions are specified as follows:

1. *Building and applying knowledge* Gather information and sift through it to identify key issues and gain an accurate understanding of a situation or content area; analyze data, integrate data, and think 'outside the box' to create new knowledge, enhance a knowledge base, or develop solutions; develop new and innovative strategies, approaches, tools, and products that increase competitive advantage; anticipate changes in competitive and market demands and address these proactively; exploit technology to enhance productivity and performance.
2. *Sharing knowledge* Share knowledge and expertise freely in written or oral form to help others accomplish goals; collaborate effectively with others to arrive at solutions, innovate, or implement; develop effective networks with other experts to facilitate information and knowledge exchange; document, organize, and capture knowledge for reuse by others; package and present information in a meaningful manner (style, tone, level of detail) that is on-point, persuasive, and effectively addresses the receiver's needs and expectations.

3. *Maintaining knowledge*   Demonstrate enthusiasm and curiosity for learning and advancing knowledge; develop and maintain specialized knowledge, skills, and expertise that enable significant contributions to work outcomes; stay abreast of new methods or content areas.

Pulakos et al. then developed a list of predictor constructs for the three performance dimensions and had experienced selection experts judge their relevance for each of the proposed performance dimensions. This resulted in the following KSAOs by performance dimensions: (1) building and applying knowledge: reasoning ability, critical thinking, fluency of ideas, creativity, information gathering, information integration, problem solving, initiative, content-relevant experience, and domain-specific knowledge; (2) sharing knowledge: active listening, writing, speaking, interpersonal flexibility, and cooperativeness; and (3) maintaining knowledge: reading comprehension and willingness to learn. To assess these KSAOs for knowledge-based competition, the authors assert that measures of past experience relevant to the performance dimensions (such as biodata measures), and high-fidelity assessments (e.g., job- or computer-based simulations) may hold more promise than general cognitive ability and personality measures alone. Swart and Kinnie (2003) describe a quasi-situational interview used for selecting knowledge workers at a software company. As part of the interview, recruits needed to show how they would share their innovative ideas and cutting-edge know-how within a project team. In addition, a strong emphasis was placed on organization fit. By focusing on organization fit, the company was able to establish shared mental models and a continued commitment to sharing knowledge.

Recruiting knowledge workers
While it is difficult to generalize across all workers, those considered knowledge workers may require different means for effective attraction/recruiting. Horwitz et al. (2003) propose that to attract, retain, and motivate knowledge workers, organizations need to provide challenging work, create a work culture that permits relative autonomy, celebrate achievement, and develop a sense of purpose, direction, and excitement. Additionally, organizations must be willing to share gains, foster effective communication, demonstrate concern for people by respecting the dignity of the individual, provide enabling resources (such as new technology), and enable employees to acquire skills to increase their employability in both internal and external labor markets. Tampoe (1993) identified four key motivators for knowledge workers: personal growth (the opportunity for individuals to realize their potential), operational autonomy (a work environment in which knowledge workers can achieve the tasks assigned to them), task

achievement (a sense of accomplishment from producing work that is of high quality and relevance to the organization), and money rewards (an income that is a just reward for their contribution to corporate success and that symbolizes their contribution to that success).

What recruitment strategies and sources work best for knowledge workers? Pulakos et al. assert that knowledge workers are generally people who have ties and loyalties to their occupations, so recruiting them through channels such as professional associations and societies, conferences, and publications, as well as the internet, are likely to be the most effective ways to reach them. This both recognizes and reinforces the connection between social capital and knowledge management described earlier. Additionally, as much research has shown, employee referrals are one of the best sources of desirable applicants. This should be true for knowledge workers, too. Poaching—or attracting applicants from competitors—is another source of knowledge workers. As Pulakos et al. note, hiring experienced workers from competitors can allow for expansion into new areas and markets where these individuals have already established expertise.

Horwitz et al. used a structured questionnaire administered to respondents in a sample of knowledge-intensive firms in Singapore to assess the effectiveness of strategies used to attract, motivate, and retain knowledge workers. The most effective strategies were (1) offering a compensation package that may include a sign-on bonus and funded further studies, (2) a proactive recruitment program using head hunters, targeted advertisements, and on-campus recruitment, focusing on those who are seen to fit into the culture easily, and (3) internal filling of positions, based on a career plan that positions the employer as the choice employer.

Summary

In summary, an organization can acquire knowledge by making it, buying it, or renting it through its staffing system. Each decision involves trade-offs regarding the urgency of obtaining the knowledge, the ability to capture the knowledge for long-term use, and the ability to control knowledge spill-over to unwanted parties. The decision to make, buy, or rent knowledge is also contingent upon its strategic value and uniqueness. Consequently, some employees possess more valuable knowledge than others. Major job performance dimensions for knowledge workers include technical competency, building and applying knowledge, sharing knowledge, and maintaining knowledge. Specific KSAOs have been identified for each of these performance dimensions. While it is difficult to generalize about all knowledge workers, it seems that to attract them requires providing challenging and meaningful work, autonomy, monetary rewards, and the opportunity to continue acquiring knowledge and skills—both at work and outside of work. The most effective recruiting sources for knowledge workers may include employee referrals, professional associations and their publications, as well as poaching from competitors.

Talent Staffing System Components to Promote Knowledge Capture and Storage

Organizations need some means for capturing and storing knowledge so it can be more easily shared across people and groups, and so when individuals leave the organization, some of what they know remains behind. *Organizational memory* is the means by which organizations store knowledge for future use (Olivera, 2000). It is formed by dispersed knowledge (e.g., held by people and documents) and the integrating mechanisms that make it accessible. *Organizational memory systems* are sets of knowledge retention devices (e.g., people and documents) that collect, store, and provide access to the organization's experience.

Codification and personalization strategies
Hansen, Nohria, and Tierney (1999) identified two primary ways that organizations capture and store knowledge. Each strategy has different implications for talent staffing systems. With a *codification* strategy, an organization attempts to capture knowledge—in particular explicit knowledge—by having employees document what they do and what they know. Hansen et al. describe this as a 'people-to-documents' approach and the objective is to get employees to write, document, and make explicit what they know or have learned in a manner that allows other employees to learn from them. Rather than reinvent the wheel each time a similar problem or opportunity is confronted, a codification strategy enables an organization to reuse knowledge in productive ways. Hansen et al. describe how the Anderson Consulting company was able to use codified knowledge to service clients faster and better than their competitors. By taking off-the-shelf templates and other aids, Anderson consultants could, with some modifications, adapt previously used solutions to new customers. A codification strategy can be particularly effective when implemented with information system technology, whereby employees can contribute to, have access to, and use knowledge through various communication devices. However, this strategy does not require sophisticated technology to be implemented.

For organizations pursuing primarily a codification strategy, there are some important implications for talent staffing systems. First, organizations will want to hire employees who have, among other KSAOs, the ability to reuse knowledge and implement solutions. For example, individuals who are capable of identifying problems, articulating those problems in a way that will yield possible solutions through an internet search, and then using that information to solve a problem would be valuable. Second, it would be desirable to hire people who can articulate what they know and contribute, usually in written form, to a knowledge database. Equally important is hiring people who enjoy teaching others and sharing what they know rather than hoarding knowledge as a source of personal power.

With a *personalization strategy*, an organization attempts to capture knowledge—in particular, tacit knowledge—by having employees share what they know and have learned with others through person-to-person contact. Hansen et al. (1999) describe this as a person-to-person approach and the objective is to develop social networks that connect people with needed knowledge to one another. With this approach, tacit knowledge is conveyed from one person to another with the expectation that it will be applied to a particular situation. Since this type of knowledge cannot be easily captured in documents and other codified forms, it is embedded in people and their networks instead. Hansen et al. describe how the consulting company Bain invests less in codified systems of knowledge capture and more in developing and retaining employees who have specialized knowledge and capabilities that can be accessed by their colleagues. A personalization strategy relies less on information technology for capturing knowledge, but may use it for identifying who knows what (expert locators) and how to access people with needed knowledge.

For organizations pursuing a personalization strategy, there are some important implications for talent staffing systems. First, organizations will want to hire employees who have, among other KSAOs, critical and analytical skills and the ability to share knowledge with others through personal interaction. For example, individuals who are capable of problem solving and tolerating ambiguity and who are capable of mentoring others would be valuable. With this approach, every employee is a teacher and a student. Second, organizations will want to increase the awareness of who knows what and who is working on what within the company. This can be accomplished through the use of skill profiling systems and corporate yellow pages. Additionally, communities of practice, thematic help desks manned by knowledge area specialists, and knowledge fairs may be used to capture knowledge and make it more accessible (Cross, Parker, & Borgatti, 2002).

Capturing knowledge of retiring employees
Capturing the knowledge of retiring employees is sometimes ignored until it is too late. In the words of Joni Mitchell, 'you don't know what you've got till it's gone.' The loss of employees, especially in large numbers, can represent massive losses of organizational knowledge accumulated over a

long period of time. If the knowledge has not been codified or passed on through some other means to remaining employees, it could be disastrous for an organization's continued effective functioning. For example, at NASA, due to downsizing and cost-cutting, the engineers who designed the Saturn 5 rocket used to launch the lunar landing craft were encouraged to take early retirement. When they left, 20 years of experience and expertise about the design trade-offs that had been made in building Saturn rockets left with them. As one NASA engineer lamented: 'If we want to go to the moon again, we'll be starting from scratch because all of that knowledge has disappeared. It would take at least as long and cost at least as much to go back' (DeLong, 2004: 11–12).

The Tennessee Valley Authority (TVA) has developed a novel approach to the problem (Fisher, 2006) that has been described as triaging knowledge at risk (DeLong, 2004). Recognizing that it was about to lose many senior and knowledgeable employees due to retirement, and worried about what that would do to operations, the TVA in 1999 began by asking line managers three questions: (1) What knowledge is likely to be lost when particular employees leave? (2) What will be the business consequences of losing that knowledge? and (3) What can be done to prevent or minimize the damage? Then, it took the following steps. First, it identified who would be retiring when by simply asking employees in a questionnaire when they were planning to retire. Second, each employee was given a score of 1 to 5, with 1 denoting someone who didn't plan to leave for six years or longer, and 5 identifying someone who would be leaving within a year. Third, managers and supervisors rated each employee 1 to 5 (5 being critical) in terms of how essential their knowledge is to the operations. Fourth, the attrition score was multiplied by the critical-knowledge score to arrive at a metric indicating where immediate action needed to be taken. Fifth, the TVA used both codification and personalization strategies to capture the knowledge of these valuable retiring employees.

For example, knowledge of whom to call at General Electric (explicit knowledge) can be documented easily. However, passing on tacit knowledge requires person-to-person contacts. As a case in point, a steamfitter foreman at one plant had learned over many years that by tapping on a pipe with a wrench and listening for a particular sound, he could detect corrosion inside feed water pipes. In that case, the TVA assigned a younger engineer to shadow him before he retired. From a talent staffing strategy standpoint, the TVA is able to both capture the knowledge of retirees before they leave (through shadowing) and fast-track the next generation of employees so they are able to become competent more quickly.

In addition to capturing knowledge before retirees leave, organizations have other staffing strategies for obtaining knowledge from these employees.

One solution is to offer employees flexible phased retirements (DeLong, 2004). This could include a number of job design alternatives, including reduced responsibilities, reduced work hours, flex time, and job sharing. These strategies essentially slow down the employee flow out of the organization—hopefully long enough to capture the knowledge of these employees. Another solution is to rehire retired employees as consultants or temporary workers. Hiring retirees back, even on a temporary or part-time basis, allows organizations both to continue using their knowledge and to capture their knowledge before they are gone for good (ibid.). Monsanto has a Retirement Resource Corps (RRC) that enables the company to employ recent retirees on a per diem basis either to train the next generation of employees or to work on projects for which they have knowledge and expertise. An additional means of using retirees is as mentors. Both NASA and Sandia Labs hire retirees to mentor junior employees, thus freeing up more senior employees to focus on project tasks.

Summary
In summary, organizations need to develop means for capturing and storing knowledge so it can be shared with other employees both in the present and in the future. There are two primary ways in which organizations can capture and store knowledge—either through codification or personalization. Through codification, organizations separate the knowledge from the employees by storing it in documents and other tangible outlets. Through personalization, organizations store knowledge in the employees themselves. Each approach has different implications for talent staffing systems. While it is critical to capture and store the knowledge of current employees, it is also important to capture and store the knowledge of employees who are leaving. Since retirements are one form of employee flows out of the organization that can be planned for, specific means can be used to capture and store what employees know before they leave.

Talent Staffing System Components to Promote Knowledge Transfer and Diffusion

It is not enough for an organization simply to acquire and create—and capture and store—knowledge. That knowledge must also be diffused and transferred (1) individual to individual (usually expert to novice), (2) individual to group (either to broaden availability of specific knowledge or to preserve knowledge until a successor is named, (3) group to individual (transferring knowledge to a new member), and (4) group to group (preserving one group's knowledge over time, or broadening access to specific knowledge, such as best practices) (DeLong, 2004). Practices for transferring knowledge can be characterized as either direct or indirect (ibid.). *Direct knowledge transfer* involves personal interaction between the sender and receiver, and includes such practices as face-to-face meetings, after-action reviews, mentoring programs, communities of practice, and storytelling. *Indirect knowledge transfer* involves little or no personal interaction between sender and receiver, and includes such practices as interviews, documentation (such as written reports or lessons-learned databases), and training. Both direct and indirect knowledge transfer practices have implications for talent staffing systems. Next, we discuss those practices where talent staffing systems are most likely to have a more direct impact on knowledge transfer.

Mentoring

Mentoring occurs between two people in which the more experienced and knowledgeable mentor provides a host of career development (e.g., sponsorship, exposure, visibility, coaching, protection, and challenging assignments) and psychosocial (e.g., role modeling, acceptance, confirmation, counseling, and friendship) functions to a protégé (Murrell, Crosby, & Ely, 1999). From a knowledge transfer standpoint, mentoring relationships are effective for directly transferring critical implicit and tacit work-related knowledge (DeLong, 2004). From a talent staffing perspective, several questions must be addressed.

First, where should the organization place emphasis on mentoring relationships? This requires prioritizing the transfer of knowledge from the most essential personnel.

Second, who should serve as mentors? Current employees may view mentoring as an added burden that detracts from their work. To alleviate this problem, some organizations, such as NASA, have brought back retirees to serve as mentors.

Third, how do you match mentors with protégés? Research suggests that voluntary (or informal) mentoring relationships are more effective than formal ones, and that formal relationships are less effective for women than men (Ragins & Cotton, 2000). Also, from a knowledge transfer perspective, mentoring can serve as a means for developing a protégé's social capital. The protégé gains exposure and introductions to those in the mentor's social network.

Finally, a staffing alternative that is less involved, but similar to mentoring is shadowing. With shadowing, employees observe a more experienced employee in his or her daily tasks over a (usually short) period of time. While not as rich in depth as mentoring, this can be an effective staffing strategy for transferring knowledge from a more experienced employee to a new or inexperienced one, without entailing some of the costs of more long-term and formal mentoring relationships.

Using employees as trainers

Another, sometimes overlooked, staffing strategy that facilitates knowledge transfer is to use employees as trainers. When employees are selected to train their peers and colleagues, they have the opportunity to share their unique knowledge and expertise with others. Their credibility as trainers is enhanced since they are typically successful at what they do within the organization and their profession. Additionally, selecting employees to serve as trainers may be seen by them as a reward and recognition of their contributions to the organization. They may feel that their knowledge and expertise is valued by the organization. Consequently, using employees as trainers may not only be an effective means for knowledge transfer; it may also be an effective means for retaining critical knowledge workers.

Job rotation

Job rotations are lateral transfers of employees between jobs in an organization (Campion, Cheraskin, & Stevens, 1994). They are typically used as a staffing strategy for employees early in their careers more so than for those in late career. Job rotation may serve as one means for employees to increase their networks of contacts. Additionally, job rotation may facilitate the transfer of company culture. At Air Products and Chemicals, new hires with engineering and information technology degrees, as well as MBAs and PhDs, participate in three job rotations averaging ten months each (DeLong, 2004). The company arranges the first assignment, but then the employees must find their second and third assignments themselves. The company also encourages these employees to take assignments in areas that they might not otherwise consider, to enhance their knowledge bases.

Expatriates

An expatriate assignment is a staffing strategy involving a job transfer that takes the employee to a workplace that is outside the country in which he or she is a citizen (Mendenhall, 2005). From a knowledge transfer perspective, expatriates know how the parent company operates and can pass on this knowledge to the local employees. Expatriates represent one type of boundary-spanner that may be important for developing social capital (Kostova & Roth, 2003). Network ties with peer expatriates, local working partners, and local friends may serve as channels for social resources, such as informational, emotional, instrumental, and appraisal support (Sparrow, 2006). While much has been written about selecting employees for foreign assignments, most has been concerned with cross-cultural and family adjustments.

From a knowledge management perspective, staffing concerns should additionally focus on abilities of expatriates to transfer knowledge and develop social capital abroad (ibid.). Equally important as selecting and staffing expatriates for international assignments is the process of repatriation. Repatriation refers to the process of returning expatriates home from international assignments (Gregersen, 2005). While repatriation focuses on assisting expatriates and their families to the adjustment of moving back home, effective talent staffing systems must also consider how to integrate the employee back into the organization. Expatriates may face challenges as they re-enter an organization. For example, there may be changes in the organization's rules or procedures that occurred while the expatriate was abroad, requiring that that expatriate unlearn old ways of operating before new learning and knowledge transfer can occur. As mentioned earlier, expatriates acquire valuable knowledge while overseas, therefore organizations need to exploit this new knowledge and utilize the talents that were acquired abroad.

Teamwork
The use of various types of work teams is a commonly used staffing strategy, especially in knowledge-intensive firms. For example, knowledge teams are groups of employees who perform interdependent knowledge work and who are collectively responsible for a product or service (Mohrman, 2005). They are often composed of members with a number of different highly advanced disciplines, each with knowledge bases that only partially overlap. Other types of knowledge teams include (ibid.): (1) work teams that deliver a service or product, (2) integrating teams that coordinate across various parts of the organization, (3) management teams that integrate various parts of the organization and (4) process improvement teams that examine and make changes to the work processes of the organization.

In staffing teams for effective knowledge management, it is important to realize that employees may participate as members of several teams—on one as a team leader, on another as an expert adviser, on one project team that requires frequent meetings and close working relationships, and on another project team that requires working more alone with infrequent meetings of the larger team (Jackson et al., 2003). For example, NASA instituted a policy whereby technical experts have to make available up to 20% of their time to other projects instead of being dedicated only to one program (DeLong, 2004).

Some work environments may be very dynamic, causing new teams to be formed, old teams to be reconfigured, and some old teams to be disbanded. The fluid nature of team formation and dissolution serves both adaptation and knowledge transfer processes well, especially in rapidly changing environments, but it makes staffing more complex. A premium is placed on hiring individuals who have needed expertise, the ability to function on different types of teams, adaptability, and high tolerance for change. Since team structures may change over time, there probably is a need to focus on organizational fit—individuals who are compatible with an organization's values and goals may be better equipped to serve on teams with different configurations of employees.

Succession and replacement planning

Succession and replacement planning are both traditional human resource staffing methods that can be used to facilitate knowledge transfer. However, in the past, succession planning, in particular, was primarily used for senior-level positions in organizations. When viewed from a knowledge management perspective, succession planning may also be used for managerial, professional, and technical workers in addition to senior-level executives. Some key staffing questions for knowledge management include: (1) What is the organization's current skill and knowledge base, and how will it need to change, given its strategy? (2) How do organizations plan for replacing key knowledge workers? And (3) How do organizations make certain that successors have been adequately prepared to fill those critical positions? To answer these traditional human resource succession planning questions for knowledge management requires some reframing. For example, Northrop Grumman developed a discipline management program in which its main technical functions are broken down into 35 disciplines, such as software engineering, systems engineering, structural analysis, and subsystems (DeLong, 2004). Each discipline is assigned a manager who is responsible for all employee flows within the discipline across all projects in the business unit. These discipline managers are responsible for knowing all of the talent within their skill area so that better staffing decisions can be made. In essence, the discipline manager is responsible for ensuring that the company has adequate coverage in the assigned area at all times—and that these skills are managed effectively over time without major disruptions. Shell Chemical has a similar program, in which global skill resource managers are charged with ensuring that an adequate pipeline of talent is available to meet both current and future needs of the business.

Communities of practice

A community of practice is an informal cluster or network of people who work together sharing knowledge, solving problems, and exchanging insights, stories, and frustrations (Lesser & Prusak, 2000). Communities of practice are not constrained by geographic, business unit, or functional boundaries. They are formed around common tasks, common work interests, and common contexts (Lengnick-Hall & Lengnick-Hall, 2003). They can speed up the development of individuals' social capital as well as connect isolated professionals across an organization. Many communities of practice may exist in a single organization. Some communities of practice may extend beyond the organization's boundaries, transferring new knowledge into the organization. Best Buy uses communities of practice to transfer knowledge among employees involved in similar activities (DeLong, 2004). For example, car audio system installers are linked in mobile installation bays throughout the United States, allowing them to share tips and experiential knowledge with one another. Likewise, Best Buy has established communities of practice for each of its product areas, such as appliances, home theaters, and computers. Sales associates share their tips and insights about products and sales tactics with one another.

Communities of practice seem to provide a knowledge-related 'home base' for employees in much the same way those functional designations provide an operations-related 'home base.' Talent staffing systems would seem to benefit from using both of these anchors in recruitment and retention activities since both are important for helping employees see how they fit into the organization's work and its social fabric.

Summary

In summary, knowledge can be transferred between people either directly (from person to person) or indirectly (with little or no personal contact). Talent staffing systems can be used to facilitate the transfer of knowledge among employees. Mentoring is useful for transferring critical implicit and tacit knowledge between people, but current employees may resist efforts to participate due to their own workloads. Staffing some training programs with employees as trainers is another effective way to transfer knowledge and retain valued employees. The practice of job rotation has been around for a long time, but takes on added importance when viewed from a knowledge transfer perspective; job shadowing offers some of the benefits of job rotation without the long-term costs and commitments. Similarly, expatriate staffing assignments present the opportunity to transfer knowledge from the parent company to the local employees, as well as import knowledge into the organization via the expatriates' social networks. As team members in knowledge-intensive firms, employees may serve in many team roles. This requires hiring people for organization fit that are capable of versatile contributions when needed. Succession planning in knowledge-intensive firms requires focusing on developing a pipeline of organizational skills that are continuously renewed and available for deployment. And, finally, communities of practice can be established as informally staffed knowledge transfer systems within an organization. Talent staffing systems can play a major role in the success of transferring knowledge among employees in an organization.

ISSUES IN INTEGRATING KNOWLEDGE MANAGEMENT AND TALENT STAFFING SYSTEMS

The integration of knowledge management and talent staffing systems is still a relatively new area of practice and research. And, it has been made more difficult due to the turf battles over where responsibility for knowledge management should reside. Knowledge management has frequently been viewed as an information technology function in organizations, resulting in an emphasis on codified knowledge acquisition, storage, and transfer. On the other hand, the human resource function has been the primary organizational leader in both developing talent staffing systems and transferring much tacit knowledge among employees. Clearly, taking a more holistic approach to knowledge management and talent staffing systems should enable organizations to compete more effectively on the basis of their knowledge assets. However, many challenges must be overcome to realize this goal. See Table 3.1.

In the area of knowledge acquisition and creation, research is beginning to shed light on the decisions of making, buying, or renting knowledge. However, much less is known about what types of configurations, or mixes, of these approaches yield the best outcomes for organizations pursuing particular strategies or operating in particular environments. From a practical standpoint, organizations face the challenge of retaining valued knowledge workers once they are hired. Since these workers typically have high value externally, ways to embed them in an organization (see, for example, Mitchell, Holtom, & Lee, 2001) seem particularly important. And, while some organizations attempt to acquire knowledge wholesale through buying other companies or merging with them, there is no guarantee that the employees (and their knowledge) will remain after the purchase or merger.

In the area of knowledge capture and storage, recent research is beginning to shed light on the two primary methods of codification and personalization (e.g., Haesli & Boxall, 2005). How talent staffing systems can facilitate the capture and storage of knowledge must be viewed from both a current employee's and a leaving employee's perspective. Capturing the knowledge of employees while they are with an organization (be it a long or short time) is critical for increasing an organization's absorptive capacity and potential to gain competitive advantage through knowledge. From a practical standpoint, organizations need to be concerned that employees may leave before their knowledge has been captured (particularly consequential for long-term knowledgeable employees); contingent employees may only do the jobs they are hired for, but not transfer their knowledge to

Table 3.1 Issues in integrating knowledge management and talent staffing systems

Knowledge Management Capabilities and Goals	Talent Staffing System Strategies	Issues
Knowledge acquisition & creation: acquire and create knowledge that provides a basis for competitive advantage; increase absorptive capacity	Make, buy, or rent individual knowledge through external hires Buy the knowledge of groups of employees through acquisitions and mergers Rent the knowledge of groups of employees through strategic alliances	Knowledgeable employees are valuable externally and difficult to retain Key employees in acquired firms may not remain after the acquisition
Knowledge capture & storage: capture and store knowledge that can be accessed for solving problems and creating innovations	Personalization Codification	Employees may leave before their knowledge has been captured Contingent employees may only do the job, but not share their knowledge Contractual barriers may make it difficult to capture knowledge through strategic alliances
Knowledge diffusion & transfer: diffuse and transfer knowledge between individuals, from individuals to groups (and vice versa), and across teams throughout the organization	Mentoring Employees as trainers Job rotation Expatriates Teamwork Succession and replacement planning Communities of practice	Knowledge hoarding Knowledge spillover and loss Team fit

the organization (an opportunity lost); and while strategic alliances may offer ways to capture the knowledge other organizations have acquired, contractual barriers may limit these opportunities.

Finally, in the area of knowledge diffusion and transfer, much has been published and research interest appears to be high. We know more about how to diffuse and transfer knowledge through various means, but we still don't know how to deal with pragmatic problems that may affect competitive advantage and strategic effectiveness. For example, hoarding knowledge is a big problem in many organizations. Individuals face the dilemma of either keeping what they know to themselves (to protect their personal value) or sharing what they know with others (making themselves vulnerable to job loss). Identifying reward structures and organizational climates conducive to knowledge transfer remains a thorny issue.

Additionally, knowledge spillover and loss confronts organizations as a difficult challenge. Since employees really are volunteers and can leave at any time, how do you prevent them from taking proprietary knowledge and knowledge that affects competitive advantage with them? Legal and contractual requirements offer only limited protection. Lastly, in transferring knowledge, many organizations are moving to more team-based structures. This presents both problems and opportunities: problems in locating individuals with the knowledge, flexibility, and adaptability to take on many roles, and opportunities to limit knowledge loss and increase the organization's absorptive capacity.

The ancient Egyptians may have solved many of the problems of integrating talent staffing systems with knowledge management. Some of what they learned has been passed on through the codified knowledge they left behind on the pyramid walls. However, we will never know what tacit knowledge they learned and transferred while accomplishing their amazing engineering feats. And, despite our incredible technological advances, we have a long way to go to match their organizational accomplishments.

Instead, we must reinvent the wheel (and learn what they probably knew) for a more globally connected world environment that we face today and in the future.

REFERENCES

Adler, P.S. and Kwon, S.W. (2002). Social capital: Prospects for a new concept. *Academy of Management Review*, 27: 17–40.

Anand, N., Gardner, H.K., and Morris, T. (2007). Knowledge-based innovation: Emergence and embedding of new practice areas in management consulting firms. *Academy of Management Journal*, 50(2): 406–428.

Argote, L., Ingram, P., Levine, J.M., and Moreland, R.L. (2000). Knowledge transfer in organizations: Learning from the experience of others. *Organizational Behavior and Human Decision Processes*, **82**(1): 1–8.

Bechet, T.P. and Walker, J. (1993). Aligning staffing with business strategy. *Human Resource Planning*, **16**(2): 1–16.

Becker, B.E. and Huselid, M.A. (2006). Strategic human resources management: Where do we go from here? *Journal of Management*, **32**(6): 898–925.

Becker, G.S. (1964). *Human Capital*. New York: Columbia University Press.

Boudreau, J.W. and Ramstad, P.M. (2003). Strategic I/O Psychology and the Role of Utility Analysis Models. In Borman, W., Ilgen, D., and Klimoski, R. (eds), *Handbook of Psychology*. New York: Wiley, pp. 193–221.

Boudreau, J.W. and Ramstad, P.M. (2007). *Beyond HR: The New Science of Human Capital*. Boston, MA: Harvard Business School Press.

Brelade, S. and Harman, C. (2000). Using human resources to put knowledge to work. *Knowledge Management Review*, **3**(1): 26–29.

Campbell, J.P., McCloy, R.A., Oppler, S.H., and Sager, C.E. (1993). A Theory of Performance. In Schmitt N. and Borman W.C. & Associates (eds) *Personnel Selection in Organizations*. San Francisco: Jossey-Bass, pp. 35–70.

Campion, M.A., Cheraskin, L., and Stevens, M.J. (1994). Career-related antecedents and outcomes of job rotation. *Academy of Management Journal*, **37**(6): 1518–1542.

Cohen, W.M. and Levinthal, D.A. (1990). Absorptive capacity: A new perspective on learning and innovation. *Administrative Science Quarterly*, **35**(1): 128–152.

Cross, R., Parker, A., and Borgatti, S.P. (2002). *A Bird's Eye View: Using Social Network Analysis to Improve Knowledge Sharing and Creation*. Retrieved 15 July, 2007 from http://www-935.ibm.com/services/au/igs/pdf/g510-1669-00-cpov-a-birds-eye-view.pdf.

Dalton, D.R. (1997). Employee transfer and employee turnover: A theoretical and practical disconnect? *Journal of Organizational Behavior*, **18**(5): 411–413.

D'Aveni, R.A. (1994). *Hypercompetition: Managing the Dynamics of Strategic Maneuvering*. New York: Free Press.

Davenport, T.H. and Prusak, L. (2000). *Working Knowledge*. Boston, MA: Harvard Business School Press.

Davis-Blake, A. and Hui, P.P. (2003). Contracting Talent for Knowledge-based Competition. In Jackson, S.E., DeNisi, A.S., and Hitt, M.A. (eds) *Managing Knowledge for Sustained Competitive Advantage: Designing Strategies for Effective Human Resource Management*. San Francisco: Jossey-Bass, pp. 178–208.

DeLong, D.W. (2004). *Lost knowledge: Confronting the Threat of an Aging Workforce*. Oxford UK: Oxford University Press.

DeNisi, A.S., Hitt, M.A., and Jackson, S.E. (2003). The Knowledge-based Approach to Sustainable Competitive Advantage. In Jackson, S.E., DeNisi, A.S., and Hitt, M.A. (eds), *Managing Knowledge for Sustained Competitive Advantage: Designing Strategies for Effective Human Resource Management*. San Francisco: Jossey-Bass, pp. 3–36.

Fisher, A. (24 July, 2006). Retain your brains. *Fortune*, **154**(2): 49–50.

Fisher, S.R. and White, M.A. (2000). Downsizing in a learning organization: Are there hidden costs? *Academy of Management Review*, **25**(1): 244–251.

Grant, R.M. (1996). Toward a knowledge-based theory of the firm. *Strategic Management Journal*, **17**(Winter): 109–122.

Greer, R.C. (1984). Countercyclical hiring as a staffing strategy for managerial and professional personnel: Some consideration and issues. *Academy of Management Review*, 9(2): 324–330.

Gregersen, H.B. (2005). Repatriation. In Cartwright, S. (ed.), *The Blackwell Encyclopedia of Management* (2nd edition). Malden, MA: Blackwell Publishing, pp. 1–319.

Haesli, A. and Boxall, P. (2005). When knowledge management meets HR strategy: An exploration of personalization-retention and codification-recruitment strategies. *International Journal of Human Resource Management*, 16(11): 1955–1975.

Hansen, M.T., Nohria, N., and Tierney, T. (1999). What's your strategy for managing knowledge? *Harvard Business Review*, 77(2): 106–116.

Heneman, H.G., III and Sandver, M.G. (1977). Markov analysis in human resource administration: Applications and limitations. *Academy of Management Review*, 2(4): 535–542.

Horwitz, F.M., Heng, C.T., and Quazi, H.A. (2003). Finders, keepers? Attracting, motivating and retaining knowledge workers. *Human Resource Management Journal*, 13(4): 23–44.

Jackson, S.E., DeNisi, A.S., and Hitt, M.A. (eds) (2003). *Managing Knowledge for Sustained Competitive Advantage: Designing Strategies for Effective Human Resource Management*. San Francisco: Jossey-Bass.

Kaplan, R.S. and Norton, D.P. (2004). *Strategy Maps: Converting Intangible Assets into Tangible Outcomes*. Boston, MA: Harvard Business School Press.

Kogut, B. and Zander, U. (1992). Knowledge of the firm, combinative capabilities, and the replication of technology. *Organization Science*, 3(3): 383–397.

Kostova, T. and Roth, K. (2003). Social capital in multinational corporations and a micro-macromodel of its formation. *Academy of Management Review*, 28(2): 297–317.

Lengnick-Hall, M.P. and Lengnick-Hall, C.A. (2003). *Human Resource Management in the Knowledge Economy: New Challenges, New Roles, New Capabilities*. San Francisco: Berrett-Koehler.

Leonard, D. and Sensiper, S. (1998). The role of tacit knowledge in group innovation. *California Management Review*, 40(3): 112–132.

Leonard-Barton, D. (1995). *Wellsprings of Knowledge-building and Sustaining the Sources of Innovation*. Boston, MA: Harvard Business School Press.

Lepak, D.P. and Snell, S.A. (1999). The human resource architecture: Toward a theory of human capital allocation and development. *Academy of Management Review*, 24(1): 31–48.

Lepak, D.P. and Snell, S.A. (2003). Managing the Human Resource Architecture for Knowledge-based Competition. In Jackson, S.E., DeNisi, A.S., and Hitt, M.A. (eds), *Managing Knowledge for Sustained Competitive Advantage: Designing Strategies for Effective Human Resource Management*. San Francisco: Jossey-Bass, pp. 127–154.

Lesser, E.L. and Prusak, L. (2000). Communities of Practice, Social Capital, and Organizational Knowledge. In Lesser, E.L., Fontaine, M.A., and Slusher, J.A. (eds), *Knowledge and Communities*. Boston: Butterworth Heinemann, pp. 123–131.

Liebeskind, J.P. (1996). Knowledge, strategy, and the theory of the firm. *Strategic Management Journal*, 17(Winter): 93–107.

Matusik, S.F. and Hill, C.W.L. (1998). The utilization of contingent work, knowledge creation, and competitive advantage. *Academy of Management Review*, 23(4): 680–697.

McFadyen, M.A. and Cannella, A.A., Jr. (2004). Social capital and knowledge creation: Diminishing returns of the number and strength of exchange relationships. *Academy of Management Journal*, **47**: 735–746.

Mendenhall, M.E. (2005). Expatriate Assignment. In Cartwright, S. (ed.), *The Blackwell Encyclopedia of Management* (2nd edition). Malden, MA: Blackwell Publishing, pp. 126–127.

Merriam Webster (2007). Talent. Retrieved 20 July, 2007 from http://www.merriam-webster.com/dictionary/talent.

Mitchell, T.R., Holtom, B.C., and Lee, T.W. (2001). How to keep your best employees: Developing an effective retention policy. *Academy of Management Executive*, **15**(4): 96–108.

Mohrman, S.A. (2005). Knowledge Work. In Cartwright, S. (ed.), *The Blackwell Encyclopedia of Management* (2nd edition). Malden, MA: Blackwell Publishing, p. 218.

Morris, S., Snell, S.A., and Lepak, D.P. (2005). An Architectural Approach to Managing Knowledge Stocks and Flows: Implications for Reinventing the HR Function. In Burke, R. and Cooper, C. (eds), *Reinventing HR*. London: Routledge Press, pp. 31–54.

Murrell, A.J., Crosby, F.J., and Ely, R.J. (1999). *Mentoring Dilemmas: Developmental Relationships in Multicultural Organizations*. Mahwah, NJ: Lawrence Erlbaum Associates.

Neilson, R.E. (2001). Knowledge management: A timeless concept? *The Military Engineer*, **93**(611): 35–36.

Newell, S., Robertson, M., Scarborough, H., and Swan, J. (2002). *Managing Knowledge Work*. Houndmills, UK: Palgrave.

Nonaka, I. (1994). A dynamic theory of organizational knowledge creation. *Organization Science*, **5**(1): 14–37.

Nonaka, I. and Takeuchi, H. (1995). *The Knowledge-creating Company: How Japanese Companies Create the Dynamics of innovation*. Oxford: Oxford University Press.

Olivera, F. (2000). Memory systems in organizations: An empirical investigation of mechanisms for knowledge collection, storage and access. *Journal of Management Studies*, **37**(16): 811–832.

Polanyi, M. (1966). *The Tacit Dimension*. New York: Anchor Books.

Pulakos, E.D., Dorsey, D.W., and Borman, W.C. (2003). Hiring for Knowledge-based Competition. In Jackson, S.E., DeNisi, A.S., and Hitt, M.A. (eds), *Managing Knowledge for Sustained Competitive Advantage: Designing Strategies for Effective Human Resource Management*. San Francisco: Jossey-Bass, pp. 155–177.

Ragins, B.L. and Cotton, J.L. (2000). Marginal mentoring: The effects of type of mentor, quality of relationship, and program design on work and career attitudes. *Academy of Management Journal*, **43**(6): 1177–1194.

Ronen, S., Friedman, S., and Ben-Asher, H. (2007). Flexible Working Arrangements: Societal Forces and Implementation. In Gilliland, S.W., Steiner, D.D., and Skarlicki, D.P. (eds), *Managing Social and Ethical Issues in Organizations*. Greenwich: Information Age Publishing, pp. 3–51.

Sparrow, P. (2006). Global Knowledge Management and HRM. In Stahl, G.K. and Bjorkman, I. (eds), *Handbook of Research in International Human Resource Management*. Cheltenham, UK and Northampton, MA, USA: Edward Elgar, pp. 113–138.

Spender, J.C. (1996). Making knowledge the basis of a dynamic theory of the firm. *Strategic Management Journal*, **17**: 45–62.

Swart, J. and Kinnie, N. (2003). Sharing knowledge in knowledge-intensive firms. *Human Resource Management Journal*, **13**(2): 60–75.

Tampoe, M. (1993). Motivating knowledge workers: The challenge for the 1990s, *Long Range Planning*, **26**(3): 49–55.

Teece, D.J. (1998). Capturing value from knowledge assets: The new economy, markets for know-how, and intangible assets. *California Management Review*, **40**(3): 55–79.

Thibodaux, N. and Rouse, R. (2005). Retaining key knowledge in the utility industry. *Knowledge Management Review*, **8**(4): 16–19.

von Bertalanffy, L. (1974). *Perspectives on General System Theory*. New York: Edgar Tashdjian & George Braziller.

4. Attracting and retaining Generation Y knowledge worker talent

Siri Terjesen and Regina-Viola Frey

INTRODUCTION

In most parts of the developed world, the working age population will decrease over the next 50 years. For example, declines of 12, 8, 6, and 5% are expected in Japan, Canada, Australia/France, and the United States respectively. See Figure 4.1.

These statistics are driven by low birth rates, the retirement of Baby Boomers and increased life expectancies. Coupled with statistics indicating that the number of knowledge-based jobs requiring university education and expert skill sets will grow as developed economies continue to shift from manufacturing to service industries, the latest highly educated population to enter the labor force, Generation Y (born 1977–94) are in great demand. In developed economies, Generation Y employees currently comprise roughly 20% of the workforce but will reach 40% in just five years.

Generation Y

Generation Y people are the latest cohort to join the workforce and are also referred to as 'Millennials' and the 'Dot.com generation.' Generation Y follow the 'Builders' (born before 1946), the Baby Boomers (born 1946–64) and Generation X (born 1965–79), and precede Generation Z (born 1995–2009). Generation Y are primarily the children of Baby Boomers. Prior studies indicate that Generation Y workers, when compared with their Generation X and Baby Boomer counterparts, are more adaptable, confident, able to multi-task and technologically savvy (NAS Recruitment, 2006). Generation Y employees plan to move around and want to work faster and harder than their colleagues and want to be 'climbing the corporate ladder by their sixth month on the job' (ibid.: 6). Other studies describe Generation Y employees as more entrepreneurial, optimistic, socially responsible, innovative, and self-interested than earlier generations

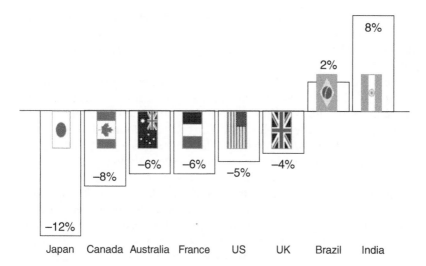

Source: US Census Bureau: International Database.

Figure 4.1 *Working age (15–64) population: % change expected 2005 to 2025*

in the labor force (Drake International, 2006). A survey (ibid.) of over 3000 Generation Y employees reports the following about the cohort:

- Ambitious: 81% of Generation Y employees expect to be promoted in two years or they will move.
- Seek development: 90% of Generation Y employees would stay longer with an employer, given the right training and development.
- Value empowering leadership styles: 97% of Generation Y employees value a leadership style that involves empowerment, consultation, and partnering and will leave if they don't get it.
- Prefer large firms: 37.5% of Generation Y employees prefer a large (50+ staff) firm, compared with just 27.3% of Baby Boomers.
- High turnover: 63% of Generation Y employees stay less than two years with an employer.

As the last statistic indicates, firms employing Generation Y may face retention challenges. Around the world, turnover rates vary, with estimates including 16% in the United Kingdom (PersonnelZone, 2006) and 22% in the United States (Jackson, 2006). Employee turnover is expensive. Costs vary from $13 000 (ibid.) to 25% of annual salary (Kepner-Tregoe, 1999).

Turnover rates are highest among women (Moncrief et al., 2000) and newcomers (Wanous, Stumpf, & Bedrosian, 1979). For example, individuals aged 20–24 are three times more likely to change jobs than individuals aged 45–54.

Professor Christian Scholz (2003) has coined the term 'Darwiportunism' to describe the Darwinian 'survival of the fittest' struggle among firms competing for employees and the 'opportunistic' behavior of Generation Y employees who seek personal development, fun, social recognition, and rewards. Darwiportunism represents a great challenge to talent management efforts to attract, retain, motivate, and develop talented employees. The massive shortage of skilled workers in the future suggests that Generation Y employees can be more selective about the organizations where they will work and how they will structure their careers. Darwiportunism highlights the importance of knowledge management in talent management: first, in terms of determining the most effective sources and methods for recruiting talent; second, the external dissemination of company knowledge provides a desirable but realistic view of the organization.

This chapter is concerned with the attraction and retention positions and programs for Generation Y employees. These two components of HR planning are essential to an organization's talent management and knowledge management processes. Attraction is important to establish the pool from which individuals can be hired, while retention efforts are devoted to keeping these individuals engaged in their careers. Following an overview of the extant literature on attraction and retention as well as pertinent gender differences, we present results from two research studies that dovetail findings on Generation Y talent management. The first study examines Generation Y college graduates' assessment of the attractiveness of organizational attributes and their perceived presence in three typical graduate employers: a management consultancy, a media corporation, and an investment bank. One of the most important findings of the research presented is that gender differences with respect to career aspirations are very pronounced within Generation Y, despite the widespread popular view that there will have been a degree of convergence between young professional men and women. The second study explores 12 corporate HR recruiters' assessments of policies and programs geared to the retention of Generation Y workers. The studies are complementary and provide insight into two sides of talent management. We discuss implications for practitioners interested in attracting and retaining Generation Y knowledge worker talent. We conclude with statements from Generation Y members about what they are looking for in their careers.

ATTRACTING GENERATION Y: RESULTS FROM A STUDY OF GRADUATES OF UK UNIVERSITIES

Overview of Literature and Research

Later in this section, we report results from the Terjesen, Freeman, and Vinnicombe (2007) study (Study I) of Generation Y organizational attribute preferences. This study was motivated by earlier findings of significant sex differences in new graduate applicant attraction outcomes (Connerley, Carlson, & Mecham, 2003) and calls for further research on the process and dynamics of recruitment decision-making (Breaugh, 1992; Breaugh & Starke, 2000) and factors related to applicant attraction (Rynes, 1991; Powell & Goulet, 1996; Connerley et al., 2003), including analysis by sex (Thomas & Wise, 1999). A meta-analysis of 242 US studies of sex differences and similarities in job attribute preferences by Konrad et al. (2000) revealed generational differences in job attribute preferences by gender and sex, suggesting the need for research on the next generation to join the labor force.

Attracting applicants is central to the talent management process as firms establish a pool of applicants who are both attractive to the organization and attracted to the organization (Wanous, 1992). In the graduate recruitment market, firms invest large amounts of time and money to attract applications from soon-to-be-minted university graduates for management trainee, professional, and technical positions (Rynes & Boudreau, 1986; Breaugh, 1992). Organizational attributes are a key factor in applicant attraction (Rynes, 1991) and an applicant's positive first impression of an organization increases the likelihood of post-interview attraction (Turban, Forret, & Hendrickson, 1998) and offer acceptance (Powell & Goulet, 1996). Thus, the external dissemination of knowledge about a firm is important in providing a realistic but desirable picture of the corporation.

Market for Generation Y knowledge workers and increase in female labor force

Much of the expected growth in the labor force in developed countries will come from women joining the labor market. For example, in the United Kingdom, an 80% increase in the number of women in the labor market (Labour Force Survey, 2003) is driven by both women returning to the workforce after leaves of absence as well as the increase in female graduates. In the United Kingdom, there are approximately 25 000 more female graduates than male and the female students' academic performance (measured by first and upper second class degrees) exceeds that of their male counterparts (HESA, 2003). Traditionally, female graduates have been more likely to enter the public sector. Of the 3.9 million male and female graduates in the UK labor market, 63% of men are employed in the private sector, compared with just 49% of women (Labour Force Survey, 2003). Young female graduates are joining the private sector: 65% of female employees with university degrees aged 21–25 work in the private sector, but lag the same-age group of males, of whom 83% work in the private sector (ibid.). The ratio of men and women in higher managerial and professional positions varies by age group, with ratios ranging from 1.7 (16–24-year-olds) to 2.1 (35–44-year-olds) to 3.5 (55–69-year-olds) (Labour Force Survey, 2005), indicating more sex equality among the Generation Y members of the UK workforce than other generations.

Self-schema

Individuals' perceptions of themselves (self-schema) generally reflect sex differences (Bem, 1981; Ruble & Martin, 1998). Previous research identifies sex differences in job attributes (see Konrad et al., 2000), however little work examines organizational attributes, especially among individuals who are about to enter the labor market. Self-schema is an individual's psychological construction of self, based on a number of aspects, most commonly gender. There are two classifications of gender self-schema: male gender self-schema (associated with masculinity and career roles) and female self-schema (associated with femininity and family roles) (Bem, 1981). Male gender self-schema is generally based on roles, norms, values, and beliefs that are considered appropriate for men. In contrast, female gender self-schema is largely based on roles, norms, values, and beliefs held about women. Individuals usually seek gender self-schema that reflect their sex (ibid.), although there are individual differences in the extent of incorporation of gender stereotypes and roles in self-schema.

Most research on gender self-schema and work preferences focuses on individuals at later stages of their careers. However, Konrad et al.'s (2000) meta-analysis of US studies of job attribute preferences reports significant sex differences consistent with gender roles and stereotypes, particularly the gender stereotype that interpersonal relationships are more important to women. Based on Williams and Best (1990), Konrad et al. (2000) summarize the masculine roles (and corresponding job attributes) as follows: income provider (earnings, benefits, security, openings), dominance (leadership, responsibility, power), aggression (power), achievement (opportunities for promotion, challenge, task significance, accomplishment), autonomy (freedom/autonomy), exhibition (prestige, recognition) and endurance (challenge, not physical work environment). Feminine roles (and corresponding job attributes) include homemaker (good hours, easy commute, location, not opportunities for travel), affiliation (opportunities to make friends, working with people, not solitude), nurturance (opportunities to help others), succorance (good co-workers, good supervisor), deference (not leadership), and abasement (not power).

Early research on male and female managers argues that the traditional role for men is income provision, hence men should be more likely to place a higher importance on salary (Lacy, Bokemeier, & Shepard, 1980). Recent research reports that men are more likely to indicate preferences for organizational attributes that are consistent with male gender self-schema and masculine stereotypes. Attributes such as pay and status represent objective career success (Nicholson, 2000). In their careers, women's satisfaction is linked to the development of interpersonal relationships (Powell & Mainiero, 1992). When compared with their female counterparts, Eddleston, Veiga and Powell (2006) find that male managers are more likely to prefer status-based career satisfiers and less likely to prefer socio-emotional career satisfiers. Furthermore, self-schema better explain female managers' preferences: female managers' gender self-schema mediate the relationship between sex and socio-emotional career satisfiers, however male managers' self-schema do not mediate the relationship to status-based career satisfiers (Eddleston et al., 2006). We suspect that male and female organizational attribute preferences will be strongly linked to gender self-schema.

As described above, gender self-schema reflects an individual's construction of self. Within the recruiting context, it is interesting to explore how this self-perception is linked to potential organization employers. A second theory, person-organization fit, is useful when considering the link to organizations.

Person-organization fit
The Attraction-Selection-Attrition (ASA) model (Schneider, 1987) describes how individuals seek organizations that they perceive to have characteristics similar to their own. These ideas were extended to person-organization fit theory, which describes the extent of congruence of patterns between individuals' values and those of an organization (Chatman, 1989). The person-organization fit literature is concerned with how individuals select organizations to join and generally focuses on the later stages of the recruitment process. For example, individuals who perceive a closer fit to the organization to which they have been recruited are more likely to adjust quickly and feel most satisfied (Chatman, 1991). Perceived fit is an important early step in the 'matching model' of individuals and organizations in the recruiting process (Wanous, 1992).

An extensive body of person-organization fit literature explores how individuals are attracted to organizations with attributes aligned to their personal characteristics (e.g., Tom, 1971; Chatman, 1989; 1991; Cable &

Judge, 1994; 1996). A recent meta-analysis of 71 studies reveals that characteristics of organizations predict applicant attraction outcomes (Chapman et al., 2005). Thus, individuals who perceive a strong fit with an organization will be attracted to apply. Coupled with the theory of reasoned action (Ajzen & Fishbein, 1980; Ajzen, 1991), person-organization fit suggests that graduates' attitudes influence their intentions to apply. We are interested in the salience of these ideas in the context of a specific employer, a management consultancy.

Study I

The first study examined final year university students' preferences at the beginning of the recruitment process when many make the initial decision to apply to firms. We explored which organizational attributes attract Generation Y male and female graduates to apply for a job and the perceived presence of these attributes in three popular UK graduate employers: a management consultancy, an investment bank, and a media corporation.

Methodology
The subjects were Generation Y full-time undergraduates at the top 22 UK universities who were looking for a job, but not yet in possession of an offer. Subjects were also disqualified if they reported that they had been in contact with recruiters from one of the organizations that they were evaluating, as recruiter behavior can influence applicants' perceptions.

This study involved two phases. In Phase One, 32 repertory grid interviews[1] identified the attributes that undergraduates use to differentiate between ten potential employers. In Phase Two, a shortlist of 20 attributes was used in a survey collected from 862 students. The respondents were 35% female science students, 25% female arts students, 30% male science students, and 10% male arts students. The internet-based survey asked respondents to rate the attributes according to personal importance. The students also provided their perceptions of three major graduate employers (a management consultancy, an investment bank, a media corporation) against the 20 attributes and the likelihood that they would apply for a job.

Respondents filled in demographic data including sex, university, and degree course. The following questions were asked with respect to each of the 20 organizational attributes listed in Table 4.1:

- Organizational attributes by importance: 'Imagine that a graduate employer existed that was ideal for you personally. Please indicate the extent to which you would agree with the following statements: "My ideal employer would" ". . . invest heavily in the training and

Table 4.1 Mean ratings of organizational attributes by importance

Organizational Attribute	Mean Rating	Significance
Invest heavily in the training and development of their employees	6.15	
Really care about their employees as individuals	6.13	f ***
Clear opportunities for long-term career progression	6.11	
Variety in daily work	6.05	f ***
Dynamic, forward-looking approach to their business	5.83	
Friendly, informal culture	5.62	f **
Opportunity, in the early years, to move around the organization and work in different areas/role	5.57	
Freedom to work on your own initiative	5.43	
Scope for creativity in your work	5.41	
Employ people with whom you feel you will have things in common	5.24	f *
A pure meritocracy (rewards and promotions based on performance)	5.13	
Offer the opportunity for international travel	4.98	
Use your degree skills	4.97	f **
Widely regarded as a highly prestigious employer	4.94	
Very high starting salary	4.92	m ***
Relatively stress-free working environment	4.91	f **
Opportunity to work (and live) abroad	4.70	
Internationally diverse mix of colleagues	4.51	f ***
Require you to work standard working hours only	3.89	f ***
A small organization	3.38	

Note: Significant differences: f = females rate higher; m = males rate higher. * $p < 0.05$; ** $p < 0.01$; *** $p < 0.001$.

development of their employees" from 1–7, where 1 = strongly disagree and 7 = strongly agree.'
- Perception of three organizations: 'Based on your current perceptions of [management consultancy, media corporation, or investment bank], please tell us to what extent you agree or disagree with the following: "The [management consultancy, media corporation, or investment bank] offers . . ." "a very high starting salary" from 1–7 where 1 = strongly disagree and 7 = strongly agree.'
- Likelihood to apply: 'How likely are you to apply to [management consultancy, media corporation, or investment bank] from 1–7 where 1 = very unlikely and 7 = very likely.'

Results

Organizational attributes Our research in Study I identified nine significant differences in organizational attributes. Men rate only one attribute as significantly higher than women do in importance: 'a very high starting salary.' In contrast, the women indicate significantly higher preference for eight attributes. These attributes are, in order of significance: 'really care about their employees as individuals,' 'variety in daily work,' 'internationally diverse mix of colleagues,' 'require you to work standard working hours only,' 'friendly, informal culture,' 'use your degree skills,' 'relatively stress-free working environment,' and 'employ people with whom you feel you will have things in common.' All findings are reported in Table 4.1.

Perception of three organizations There are significant differences between the graduate mean ratings of the three organizations on nearly all of the attributes. See Table 4.2. This confirms that students can differentiate among employers at a relatively early stage of the job search process. For example, the students perceive the media corporation to offer more scope for creativity at work (5.44) and a relatively stress-free working environment (3.74) than the management consultancy (creativity = 4.56; stress-free = 3.06) or the investment bank (creativity = 3.94; stress-free = 2.51) (all $p < 0.01$).

Organizational attractiveness and likelihood to apply We then examined if there is a positive relationship between the attractiveness of organizational attributes and likelihood to apply. Previous studies identify a positive relationship between organizational attributes and initial attraction (Turban et al., 1998) and job acceptance (Powell & Goulet, 1996). We extended this work by examining the applicants' self-reported likelihood to apply using a correlation analysis, finding a positive and significant relationship (all $p < 0.001$). The correlations for the management consultancy, media corporation, and the investment bank were 0.440, 0.332 and 0.436 respectively.

To test our ideas, we focused on one organization. We selected management consultancy as the industry that is one of the most popular employers of UK graduates. For example, a recent survey of 3800 students at 32 UK universities reports four management consultancies among the top 15 preferred graduate employers (Universum, 2004).

We used multiple regression analyses to examine the relationship between likelihood to submit an application to the management consultancy (dependent variable) and perceptions of organizational attractiveness

Table 4.2   Mean ratings and differences in perceptions of management consultancy, media corporation, and investment bank (t-tests)

Organizational Attribute	Management Consultancy Mean Rating	Media Corporation Mean Rating	Investment Bank Mean Rating	Management Consultancy vs. Media Corporation	Management Consultancy vs. Investment Bank	Media Corporation vs. Investment Bank
Invest heavily in the training and development of their employees	5.83	4.73	5.46	**	**	**
Really care about their employees as individuals	4.41	4.50	4.08	*	**	**
Clear opportunities for long-term career progression	5.61	4.91	5.48	**	**	**
Variety in daily work	4.91	5.28	4.32	**	**	**
Dynamic, forward-looking approach to their business	5.84	4.73	5.51	**	**	**
Friendly, informal culture	4.20	4.59	3.51	**	**	**
Opportunity, in the early years, to move around the organization and work in different areas/roles	5.13	4.82	4.79	**	**	–
Freedom to work on your own initiatives	4.68	4.84	4.30	**	**	**
Scope for creativity in your work	4.56	5.44	3.94	**	**	**
Employ people with whom you feel you will have things in common	4.21	4.68	3.95	**	**	**

Table 4.2 (continued)

Organizational Attribute	Management Consultancy Mean Rating	Media Corporation Mean Rating	Investment Bank Mean Rating	Management Consultancy vs. Media Corporation	Management Consultancy vs. Investment Bank	Media Corporation vs. Investment Bank
A pure meritocracy	5.04	4.11	5.16	**	**	**
Offer the opportunity for international travel	5.39	5.15	5.44	**	–	**
Use your degree skills	4.16	3.95	4.03	**	*	–
Widely regarded as a highly prestigious employer	6.12	5.69	6.07	**	–	**
Very high starting salary	5.78	3.83	5.95	**	**	**
Relatively stress-free working environment	3.06	3.74	2.51	**	**	**
Opportunity to work (and live) abroad	5.22	4.90	5.29	**	*	**
Internationally diverse mix of colleagues	5.39	5.32	5.42	–	–	*
Require you to work standard working hours only	2.81	3.14	2.70	**	*	**
A small organization	1.80	1.61	1.91	**	**	**

Note: * $p < 0.05$; ** $p < 0.01$.

Table 4.3　Relationship between attractiveness and likelihood to apply to management consultancy: summary of multiple regression results

Organizational Attribute	Total Stand. Coeff.	Women Stand. Coeff.	Men Stand. Coeff.
Employ people with whom you feel you will have things in common	0.199	0.173	0.178
Friendly, informal culture	0.110	0.136	0.261
Offer the opportunity for international travel	0.127		
Internationally diverse mix of colleagues	−0.104		0.128
Use your degree skills	0.096		0.130
Really care about their employees as individuals	0.112	0.108	0.148
Very high starting salary	0.098		
Dynamic, forward-looking approach to their business	0.073	0.108	
Require you to work standard working hours only	−0.079		
Scope for creativity in your work	0.088		
Widely regarded as a highly prestigious employer			0.089
Opportunity, in the early years, to move around the organization and work in different areas/roles			−0.123
R^2	0.274	0.240	0.333

Note:　All attributes reported are statistically significant at $p < 0.001$.

(independent variables). The analysis was conducted for both the total sample and the male and female respondents separately.

Table 4.3 reports those attributes that are significant in predicting likelihood to apply to the management consultancy, together with associated betas indicating the size and direction of effect. All organizational attributes reported were statistically significant ($p < 0.001$), however the R^2 is low. This may be due to the reduction of the 84 common constructs identified in Phase One to a shortlist of 20 for the Phase Two survey. The attributes explained more of the 'likelihood to apply' for male students ($R^2 = 0.333$) than for female students ($R^2 = 0.240$).

Table 4.3 also reveals that the most important predictor of likelihood to apply to the management consultancy, for the sample as a whole, is 'employ people with whom you feel you will have things in common.' In descending order of importance, the other key attributes for the population of male and female students are 'offer the opportunity for international travel,' 'really care about their employees as individuals,' 'friendly, informal culture,' a 'very high starting salary,' 'use your degree skills,' 'scope for creativity in your work,' and a 'dynamic, forward-looking approach to their business.' Two attributes are negatively related to applicants' preference: 'an internationally diverse mix of colleagues' and 'require you to work standard working hours only.' Interestingly, in the case of the former, the students indicate a preference for employers that will offer them the 'opportunity for international travel' (0.127), for example to go out and see the world, but not to an 'internationally diverse mix of colleagues', for example being surrounded by foreigners (−0.104).

The results provide further evidence of differences between male and female respondents in relation to their assessments of the attractiveness and likelihood to apply to the management consultancy. Second, the results suggest that females who rate the management consultancy highly on the following attributes, in descending order of importance, are most likely to apply: 'employ people with whom you feel you will have things in common,' 'friendly, informal culture,' 'really care about their employees as individuals,' and 'dynamic, forward-looking approach to their business.' Seven attributes are significant for the men, providing further evidence of differences between the sexes in their assessments of the management consulting firm's attractiveness and of the effect of graduates' assessments on their likelihood to apply. For men, the positive attributes, in descending order of importance, are 'offer the opportunity for international travel,' 'employ people with whom you feel you will have things in common,' 'very high starting salary,' 'really care about their employees as individuals,' 'use your degree skills,' and 'widely regarded as a highly prestigious employer.' Interestingly for men, the 'opportunity, in the early years, to move around the organization and work in different areas/roles' is negatively related to organizational attractiveness.

RETAINING GENERATION Y: RESULTS FROM A STUDY OF HR PRACTITIONERS IN GERMAN FIRMS

Study II

In this section, we report results from the Frey (2006) study of HR practitioners' perceptions of policies and programs to retain Generation Y

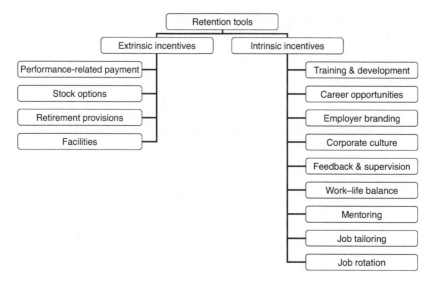

Figure 4.2   Extrinsic and intrinsic incentives

employees. While organizational attrition can come from quits, lay-offs and retirements, retention management practices usually focus on voluntary quits. For the purpose of our study of retention management practices in German firms, we focus on policies and programs directed to retain younger employees with the highest performance and potential. There are two classifications of retention tools: extrinsic and intrinsic incentives. See Figure 4.2. Extrinsic incentives include performance-related payment, stock options, retirement provisions and facilities. Intrinsic incentives include training and development, career opportunities, employer branding, corporate culture, feedback and supervision, work–life balance, mentoring, job tailoring, and job rotation.

Methodology
We employed a two-stage modified Delphi technique to survey 12 human resource managers of medium- and large-sized German multinational enterprises. The Delphi technique is a method for obtaining estimations and opinions from a panel of independent experts over two or more rounds. After each stage, an independent administrator provides an anonymous summary of the experts' estimations. When experts' assessments have changed little between rounds, the process is terminated and final assessments are based on the average. In Stage One, we asked the experts for their insights on how best to retain highly qualified Generation Y employees. In

Stage Two, we asked HR managers to rate the 13 retention tools from Figure 4.2 on a 1–5 scale and then to select the five most powerful tools for retaining highly educated employees.

Results

Expert insight Our experts expressed a variety of attitudes toward retention of Generation Y knowledge workers. Some experts viewed the loss of talented Generation Y knowledge workers as a critical concern for the company that required strategic action, while others stated that their companies did not perceive a need to develop such a strategy. We summarize the discussion with quotes from our interviews about programs to retain Generation Y knowledge workers:

- Offer training and development and pleasant corporate culture: 'If you have to close down a site and people hear this through the grapevine, the best leave the sinking ship first. Thus, only a pay-to-stay bonus keeps them on board for the last half year. But to keep them in the long run, they have to be offered good training and development and a pleasant corporate culture.'
- Strong brand image as preferred employer: 'We already compete with other companies for the highly talented graduates. Our problem is that we are no shiny car producer or cool FMCG [fast-moving consumer goods] company since we produce large industrial constructions. Graduates can choose and they often decide to join the more consumer-oriented firms. Thus, we have to actively recruit talent and build a strong image as preferable employer.'
- Work–life balance: 'As most of the employers offer competitive salaries, we have to differentiate ourselves with creative solutions to improve the work–life balance of our employees. Home offices and part-time solutions are necessary.'
- Offer interesting challenges: 'We suppose that the average time an employee stays with the same company will decline. Thus, lifelong employment will become absolutely obsolete. We try to see it realistically. We cannot grant an employee paternal protection from unemployment or other accidents. But we can promise to do everything we can to keep him up to date. We can offer interesting challenges.'

Retention tools In Stage Two, the experts were asked to assess the power of some of the retention tools identified in Stage One, from 1 (completely ineffective) to 5 (highly effective). The results are displayed in Table 4.4.

Table 4.4   Retention tools

Rank	Retention Tool	Mean
1	Career opportunities	4.42
2	Feedback	3.93
3	Corporate culture	3.92
4	Training & development	3.86
5	Job rotation Performance-related payment	3.71
6	Employer branding	3.64
7	Mentoring	3.50
8	Stock options	3.15
9	Retirement provisions	3.14
10	Job tailoring Work–life balance	2.93
11	Facilities	2.69

DISCUSSION

Studies I and II explore the attraction and retention of Generation Y knowledge workers respectively. Taken together, our findings add to our understanding of talent management and knowledge management processes. We begin by reflecting on the 20 most sought job attributes (see Table 4.1). Konrad et al.'s (2000) meta-analysis identified 39 commonly identified job attributes from 242 previous studies. While many attributes are also identified in our sample, we note the absence of students' mention of benefits (e.g., medical, life insurance), job security, physical work environment, solitude, easy commute, geographical location, and feedback. This provides some anecdotal evidence that, compared with previous generations, Generation Y look for different qualities in their employers.

We extend earlier research by analyzing likelihood to apply to three organizations by male and female undergraduates, and explore the relationship to organizational attractiveness. Our findings corroborate the importance of certain organizational attributes for applicant attraction (Rynes, 1991; Wanous, 1992) and with regard to sex and gender. This study finds sex differences exist in both the importance of organizational attributes and the perceived extent of their presence in three organizations that recruit heavily from the graduate market.

In line with other work on gender self-schema, our results suggest that men place greater importance on a high starting salary. We had expected the male students to identify with this masculine gender role. However, we

had also expected male students to identify more with the masculine stereotype for the following three attributes: 'clear opportunities for long-term
career progression,' 'opportunity, in the early years, to move around the
organization and work in different roles,' and 'widely regarded as a highly
prestigious employer.' In fact, none of these attributes revealed differences
that were significantly more significant for men. This suggests that
Generation Y men and women are more similar than different with regards
to these traditionally masculine stereotypes.

We found that women indicate a greater preference for 'feminine' organizational attributes. Based on the Konrad et al. (2000) meta-analysis, we
suspected that female students would identify more strongly with the feminine stereotypes of 'friendly, informal culture' and 'employ people with
whom you feel you will have things in common' and the feminine gender
role 'require you to work standard working hours only.' Indeed, all were
true and significant. Interestingly, the non-gender-typed intrinsic attributes
'variety in daily work' and 'use your degree skills' were also more true and
significant for the women in our sample. We did not have any expectations
about three other attributes: 'care about their employees as individuals,'
'relatively stress-free working environment,' and 'internationally diverse
mix of colleagues,' however all were found to be significantly more important for women. Taken together, our findings suggest organizational attributes explain more of Generation Y female preferences than those of their
male counterparts. It may be that women, even at the career entry stage,
adapt behaviors that are more associated with traditionally masculine
gender roles and stereotypes.

Our second study examined HR practitioners' perceptions of retention
tools. We distinguished three groups of retention tools with differing relevance for retaining highly qualified employees. We defined 'must-have'
retention tools like performance-related payment, career opportunities and
rich training and development, as well as 'possible to have' tools such as job
rotation, retirement provisions, and coaching. However, the third group,
'underestimated' tools, might grow more important in the near future.

CONCLUSIONS AND IMPLICATIONS

The study of graduating university students' perceptions of organizational
attributes and reported likelihood of application offers several key contributions for academics and practitioners. First, we add to the emerging
body of early applicant impressions of organizations (Gatewood, Gowan,
& Lautenschlager, 1993; Cable & Graham, 2000) by identifying the organizational attributes used by UK undergraduates to differentiate among

potential employers at the job application stage. Building on gender self-schema, we distinguish sex differences with regard to attributes on two levels: importance of ascribed benefits and the attributes favored more highly by women can be related to female gender self-schema's emphasis on relationship-based organizational characteristics and career satisfiers. The study finds that male and female respondents hold different perceptions of three potential employers. Finally, as expected, desirability of perceived organizational attributes is linked to likelihood to apply.

Taken together, the repertory grid interviews with Generation Y students produce a list of desired organizational attributes that vary from earlier work in the field (e.g., Posner, 1981). These findings are not surprising given that most Generation Y students (born 1977–94) were not even born when Posner's (1981) and other studies of labor force perceptions were published. Our sample's five most preferred attributes are 'invest heavily in the training and development of their employees,' 'care about their employees as individuals,' 'clear opportunities for long-term career progression,' 'variety in daily work,' and 'dynamic, forward-looking approach to their business.'

HR planning and recruiting professionals should become familiar with the organizational attributes desired by Generation Y graduates. Recruiters may be pleased with these results in that it is an arguably more realistic goal to change perceptions about one's organization than to change the more fundamental views of the importance of certain attributes. Thus, the external dissemination of knowledge about the corporation is of critical concern to talent managers. Following work on realistic presentation (Wanous & Colella, 1989; Wanous, 1992), recruiters should only advertise those attributes that are true for the organization. Firms that emphasize unrealistic attributes will quickly be recognized by the new graduate recruits who will depart for other organizations that they perceive to have these attributes. New recruits who do not sense a strong fit with the organization are more likely to leave (Chatman, 1991) and the churning of graduate employees constitutes a great cost to the firm in terms of lost time, morale, and possibly customer trust and goodwill. Furthermore, it takes time for new employees to become productive, impacting firm performance (Watson Wyatt, 2006).

Private UK employers seek applicants from the over 125 000 degree graduates each year. One of the main implications of the study to practice is that a segmented approach is needed if the male and female Generation Y undergraduate population is to be assessed effectively. There is little evidence of sex segmentation activity in the existing recruitment marketplace. Regardless of the popular view that the values of young men and women are increasingly converging and possibly contrary to the professed view of young women themselves, female undergraduates value, to a greater extent than male, organizational characteristics that reflect gender self-schemas.

This presents both a considerable challenge and a great opportunity to organizations wishing to increase their representation of women. Employers may wish to consider gender roles and stereotyping and sex in a broader sense.

A second key trend is that today's workers are likely to forego 'organizational careers' in favor of 'boundaryless' or 'protean' careers that are based on self-direction and the pursuit of psychological success in one's work (Hall & Moss, 1998). Generation Y careers may be characterized by work across a range of organizations, leveraging external networks, or based on internal standards for personal or family reasons. In all cases, a boundaryless career perspective acknowledges the subjective construction of individuals' careers, in spite of structural constraints. Recent research indicates that individuals' subjective career success is based on realms such as work–life balance and fulfillment (Heslin, 2005).

Generation Y employees are already having and increasingly will have a significant impact upon the competitive advantage of organizations. A clear understanding of the needs, preferences, and general characteristics of this new and growing labor sector, as well as particular differences presented by male and female employees, is essential for today's and future successful talent management efforts. In addition, information generation and knowledge sharing about the most effective measures for attracting, managing, and retaining Generation Y employees should be a major priority of HR-related knowledge management efforts in organizations.

We conclude with excerpts from essays from Generation Y students. These are potent samples of the new employee voices that managers and HR professionals should carefully and thoughtfully attend to in planning for and leading successful organizations in the future.

Eva Marie Knoll, born 1982, Germany; graduate of University of Hamburg
Long term, I am interested in a career in media management for broadcast and electronic media. In the short term, I plan to work in management consulting.

I am career-oriented but do strongly believe that a balance between professional and personal fulfillment is not a contradiction but much more a question of how to exploit and pursue choices that best comply with an individual set of values at a certain point in time.

Just recently I decided in favor of an employment since I could negotiate to work from another country, to which I plan to move due to personal reasons, and only occasionally have to return to the home office in Germany. In this case virtual meetings and internationally accessible offices reduce the necessity for trade-offs between personal and professional goals.

Regarding *interpersonal relationships*, the longer the working hours, the more important it is to be able to identify with colleagues (as well as the brand or the product) and work in a friendly and rather informal atmosphere that nevertheless allows competitiveness and professionalism. However, I dislike over-regulated and stiff codes of conduct, since I believe that an overly restrictive and complex environment distracts attention and energy from the actual process of value creation.

Edison Zhang, born 1987, USA; graduate of Duke University
I think that the first job that I get as a college graduate, although very important, is most likely not a career-type job. Instead, it serves more as a buffer time for me to explore different areas of the company business and figure out what the next step in my career path will be. It would likely be unrelated to the degree I am pursuing in college (engineering), but instead in an industry like investment banking or consulting that is directly related to the pursuit of my goal. Since I want to have the breadth and depth of skills and knowledge necessary to run my own business, I look for a job where I can learn the most in the shortest amount of time . . .

When it comes down to choosing which company to work for, the people and culture of the company are the most important factors. Because I am intentionally entering a profession where there is a steep learning curve, I expect there to be long hours and stress. However, I would only expect the stress to come from the work, not from the people I work with. I am attracted to a culture where my co-workers would help and guide me through stressful situations as mentors, and one where I would be rewarded for my contributions to the company. It is important for me that my co-workers are diverse, honest, and highly motivated, examples of the future leaders that will carry on the success of the company. Finally, in the end, I just want to be happy working alongside my co-workers and doing my job.

Elaine 'He' Bai, born 1984, Zhengzhou, China; graduate of Beijing Foreign Studies University
I do someday hope to be an entrepreneur and to help other entrepreneurs realize their dreams with my experience and networking fund. Especially nowadays, in China, there are so many opportunities, and so many social problems can be solved by the booming of SMEs and the spirit of entrepreneurship! I don't want to miss such a good timing, I want to be part of it, not only in China, also part of the world, if I can.

Luis Pellerano, born 1988, Santo Domingo, Dominican Republic; sophomore at Pontificia Universidad Catolica Madre y Maestra
I study law and work as a paralegal for Pellerano & Herrera, a law firm founded by my grandfather and his cousin over 50 years ago. A third-generation lawyer in Latin America is expected to do only one thing: go in,

move up, and take over. I fully recognize that going into the firm would be the safest choice. Nevertheless, I consider myself a risk-taker and wish to undergo the struggles of starting up my own business . . . I have made several proposals to my uncle (who runs the financial and administrative area of the firm) with the objective of branching out the firm . . . Living in the third world definitely has its drawbacks, but from an entrepreneurial standpoint, it's a ripe place for innovating and improving the status quo.

Katherine 'Kat' Teodosic, born 1985, Detroit, Michigan; graduate of Albion College

My future goals and career aspirations involve many different paths. Someday I want to run my own business, whether it is a boutique, gallery, or even a restaurant. I think it is necessary to get as much experience as possible in the workplace that one aspires to have a career in. I am hoping to intern at a large, successful PR firm in the Detroit area and this will give me hands-on experience in advertising, PR, and marketing.

Lisa Patel, born 1988, Lowell, Massachusetts; sophomore, University of California, Berkeley

My interests range from strategy consulting and brand management to international relations and South Asian studies, therefore my future career may not have a specific title or role. However, I know my career will be internationally based so I am more able to create a positive change not only in my immediate society, but around the world.

In the near future, I will help establish a non-profit entrepreneurial venture that benefits the Cal community. My long-term goal includes establishing a strategy consulting firm that incorporates many philanthropic consulting services on an international level. There, I hope to promote a collective, entrepreneurial, and challenging atmosphere where everyone has a shared vision for the firm.

NOTE

1. See Kelly (1955) and Easterby-Smith (1980) for detailed reviews of the repertory grid methodology.

REFERENCES

Ajzen, I. (1991). The theory of planned behavior. *Organizational Behavior and Human Decision Processes*, **50**(2): 179–211.

Ajzen, I. and Fishbein, M. (1980). *Understanding Attitudes and Predicting Social Behavior*. Englewood Cliffs, NJ: Prentice-Hall.

Bem, S.L. (1981). Gender schema theory: A cognitive account of sextyping. *Psychological Review*, **88**(4): 354–264.

Breaugh, J.A. (1992). *Recruitment: Science and Practice*. Boston, MA: PWS-Kent.

Breaugh, J.A. and Starke, M. (2000). Research on employee recruitment: So many studies, so many remaining questions. *Journal of Management*, **26**(3): 405–434.

Cable, D.M. and Graham, M.E. (2000). The determinants of job seekers' reputation perceptions. *Journal of Organizational Behavior*, **21**(8): 929–947.

Cable, D.M. and Judge, T.A. (1994). Pay preferences and job search decision: A person-organization fit perspective. *Personnel Psychology*, **47**(2): 317–348.

Cable, D.M. and Judge, T.A. (1996). Person-organization fit, job choice decisions, and organizational entry. *Organizational Behavior and Human Decision Processes*, **67**(3): 394–11.

Chapman, D.S., Uggerslev, K.L., Carroll, S.A., Piasentin, K.A., and Jones, D.A. (2005). Applicant attraction to organizations and job choice: A meta-analytic review of the correlates of recruiting outcomes. *Journal of Applied Psychology*, **90**(5): 928–944.

Chatman, J.A. (1989). Improving interactional organizational research: A model of person-organization fit. *Academy of Management Review*, **14**(3): 333–349.

Chatman, J.A. (1991). Matching people and organizations: Selection and socialization in accounting firms. *Administrative Science Quarterly*, **36**(3): 459–484.

Connerley, M.L., Carlson, K.D., and Mecham, R.L., III (2003). Evidence of differences in applicant pool quality. *Personnel Review*, **32**(1): 22–39.

Drake International (2006). Generation Y: Attracting, engaging and leading a new generation at work. White Paper.

Easterby-Smith, M. (1980). The design, analysis and interpretation of repertory grids. *International Journal of Man-Machine Studies*, **13**(1): 3–24.

Eddleston, K.A., Veiga, J.F., and Powell, G.N. (2006). Explaining sex differences in managerial career satisfier preferences: The role of gender self-schema. *Journal of Applied Psychology*, **91**(2): 437–445.

Frey, R.V. (2006). Retention strategien für High Potentials – eine qualitative Studie. Frankfurt: Johann Wolfgang Goethe University, December.

Gatewood, R.D., Gowan, M.A., and Lautenschlager, G.J. (1993). Corporate image, recruitment image and initial job choice. *Academy of Management Journal*, **36**(2): 414–427.

Hall, D.T. and Moss, J.E. (1998). The new protean career contract: Helping organizations and employees adapt. *Organizational Dynamics*, **26**(3), Winter: 22–37.

HESA (Higher Education Statistics Agency) (2003). *First Destinations of Students Leaving Higher Education Institutions 2001/02*. UK: HESA.

Heslin, P.A. (2005). Conceptualizing and evaluating career success. *Journal of Organizational Behavior*, **26**(2), 113–136.

Jackson, L.A. (2006). It's cheaper to keep 'em. *Black Enterprise*, **36**(7): 72.

Kelly, G.A. (1955). *The Psychology of Personal Constructs*. New York: Norton.

Kepner-Tregoe (1999). Avoiding the Brain Drain: What Companies are Doing to Lock in Their Talent. White paper. Available at: http://www.kepner-tregoe.com/PDFs/Avoiding_Brain_exec_KL457a.pdf. Accessed 9 January 2008.

Konrad, A.M., Ritchie, J.E. Jnr, Lieb, P., and Corrigall, E. (2000). Sex differences and similarities in job attribute preferences: a meta-analysis. *Psychological Bulletin*, **126**(4): 593–641.

Labour Force Survey (2003). *Summary of Labour Market Structure—aged 16+ (SA)—Spring*. UK: Office of National Statistics.

Labour Force Survey (2005). *Summary of Labour Market Structure—aged 16+ (SA)—Autumn*. UK: Office of National Statistics.

Lacy, W.G., Bokemeier, J., and Shepard, J.M. (1980). Job attribute preferences and work commitment of men and women in the United States, *Personnel Psychology*, **36**: 315–329.

Moncrief, W.C., Babakus, E., Cravens, D.W., and Johnston, M.W. (2000). Examining gender differences in field sales organizations. *Journal of Business Research*, **49**(3), 245–257.

NAS Recruitment (2006). Generation Y: The Millennials: Ready or Not, Here They Come. White paper. Available at: http://www.nasrecruitment.com/TalentTips/NASinsights/GenerationY.pdf. Accessed 9 January 2008.

Nicholson, N. (2000). Motivation-selection-connection: An Evolutionary Model of Career Development. In Peiperl, M., Arthur, M., Goffee, R., and Morris, T. (eds), *Career Frontiers: New Concepts of Working Life*. Oxford: Oxford University Press, pp. 54–75.

PersonnelZone Direct (2006). Archive. May. Available at: http:www.personnelzone.com. Accessed 9 January 2008.

Posner, B.Z. (1981). Comparing recruiter, student, and faculty perceptions of applicant and job characteristics. *Personnel Psychology*, **34**(2): 329–339.

Powell, G.N. and Goulet, L.R. (1996). Recruiters' and applicants' reactions to campus interviews and employment decisions. *Academy of Management Journal*, **39**(6): 1619–1640.

Powell, G.N. and Mainiero, L.M. (1992). Cross-currents in the river of time: Conceptualizing the complexities of women's careers. *Journal of Management*, **18**(2): 215–237.

Ruble, D.N. and Martin, C.L. (1998). Gender development. In Eisenberg, N. (ed.) *Handbook of Child Psychology* (Vol. 3). New York: Wiley, pp. 993–1016.

Rynes, S.L. (1991). Recruitment, job choice, and post-hire consequences: A call for new research directions. In Dunnette, M.D. and Hough, L.M. (eds), *Handbook of Industrial and Organizational Psychology* (2nd edition, Vol. 2). Palo Alta, CA: Consulting Psychologists Press, pp. 399–444.

Rynes, S.L. and Boudreau, J.W. (1986). College recruiting in large organizations: Practice, evaluation, and research implications. *Personnel Psychology*, **39**(Winter): 729–757.

Schneider, B. (1987). The people make the place. *Personnel Psychology*, **40**(3): 437–453.

Scholtz, C. (2003). Spieler ohne Stammplatzgarantie. Darwiportunismus in der neuen Arbeitswelt. Weinheim: Wiley-VCH, pp. 122–130.

Terjesen, S., Freeman, C., and Vinnicombe, S. (2007). Attracting Generation Y applicants: Organisational attributes, likelihood to apply and sex differences. *Career Development International*, **12**(6): 504–522.

Thomas, K.M. and Wise, P.G. (1999). Organizational attractiveness and individual differences: Are diverse applicants attracted by different factors?. *Journal of Business and Psychology*, **13**(3): 375–390.

Tom, V. (1971). The role of personality and organizational images in the recruiting process. *Organizational Behavior and Human Performance*, **6**(5): 573–592.

Turban, D.B., Forret, M.L., and Hendrickson, C.L. (1998). Applicant attraction to firms: Influences of organizational reputation, job and organizational attributes, and recruiter behaviors. *Journal of Vocational Behavior*, **52**(1): 24–44.

Universum (2004). *Universum Graduate Study: 2004 UK Edition*. Accessible at: http://www.universumeurope.com/ukgs.aspx. Accessed 9 January 2008.

US Census Bureau (2007). International database. Accessible at: www.census. gov/ipc/www/idb/. Accessed 9 January 2008.

Wanous, J.P. (1992). *Organizational Entry: Recruitment, Selection and Socialization of Newcomers*. Reading, MA: Addison-Wesley.

Wanous, J.P. and Colella, A. (1989). Organizational entry research: Current status and future directions. In Ferris, G.R. and Rowland, K.M. (eds), *Research in Personnel and Human Resources Management* (Vol. 7). Greenwich, CT: JAI Press, pp. 59–120.

Wanous, J.P., Stumpf, S.A., and Bedrosian, H. (1979). Job survival of new employees. *Personnel Psychology*, **32**(4): 651–662.

Watson Wyatt (2006). Maximizing the Returns on Investments in Human Capital: Lessons from Seven Years of Global Studies. Available at: http://www. watsonwyatt.com/us/pubs/insider/showarticle.asp?ArticleID=15205. Accessed 9 January 2008.

Williams, J.E. and Best, D.L. (1990). *Sex and Psyche: Gender and Self Viewed Cross-culturally*. Thousand Oaks, CA: Sage.

PART 2

Training and coaching

5. The role of social networks in managing organizational talent, knowledge and employee learning

Rob F. Poell and Ferd J. Van der Krogt

The concepts of talent management and knowledge management have a lot in common. Both are very popular concepts in organizations, although the notion of knowledge management has been around for longer than the idea of talent management. Both relate to ways in which organizations manage and develop their human resources with a view to optimal performance. Both concepts implicitly address the issue of learning in work and organizational contexts. A key challenge in talent management is making an organization attractive for employees and ensuring that they give their best. Providing them with excellent opportunities for learning, development, and growth is one way of ensuring competitive advantage. A core issue in knowledge management is using employee learning for the benefit of a broader organization. Organizations can thus manage both their knowledge and talent by systematically encouraging employee learning.

The discipline of human resource development, which evolved from the practical field of training and development, increasingly emphasizes the workplace as a (potentially) rich source of learning (Billett, 2001; Streumer, 2006). Social networks are put forward in this emerging debate as crucial carriers of workplace learning (Storberg, 2002; Kessels & Poell, 2004). On the one hand, participation in social networks can enhance the opportunities for talented employees to develop their competencies on the job, by augmenting the learning potential inherent in their work (Ellström, 2001; Tjepkema, 2003). On the other hand, social networks are important carriers of employee knowledge, embedded in their cultural and structural characteristics (Poell & Van der Krogt, 2002).

In literature as well as practice, all three notions of talent management, knowledge management, and social networks tend to be viewed from an organizational perspective as tools of management. This view, however, leads to unrealistic expectations of what these concepts can do for organizations. Many experts fail to recognize that organizations are also political arenas, where employees can pursue different interests than, for example, managers and/or HR professionals. In this chapter, we conceptualize the role of social networks from the perspective of individual employees as they participate in workplace learning activities, further develop their talents, and make their knowledge and expertise more productive. We present a framework to analyze such organizational processes, based on the notion of an individual employee's learning path, and the way in which social networks affect these.

This chapter presents a perspective on organizations as social networks of actors, which can help explain how employees (the talent pool of the organization) create individual learning paths and what constraints and opportunities they encounter in doing so. We use the theoretical framework of the learning-network theory (Van der Krogt, 1998; 2007), which emphasizes the structure of social networks as well as the actors operating from these networks (cf. Lin, 2002) to give rise to various organizational processes relevant to talent development and knowledge management. The chapter illustrates how individual employees' opportunities to engage in development are strongly dependent on the social networks from which they operate in the organization. Two such networks are particularly interesting, which we call, respectively, the work network (generated from the primary work process of the organization) and the learning network (generated from HRD interventions, i.e., the creation and execution of learning programs). These two networks provide learning-relevant experiences on which individual learning paths are based and they influence how individuals make meaning of these experiences. Thus, they also affect the opportunities for talent and knowledge management.

First, the chapter will introduce the central notion of an individual learning path. Second, it will elaborate upon the perspective on an organization as a social network of actors, building particularly on Mintzberg's theory of organizations (1989; see also Mintzberg, Ahlstrand, & Lampel, 1998). Third, the chapter will demonstrate how learning-relevant experiences gained by employees are affected by the structure of the work network. This social network is related to and perpetuates the primary work process in the organization. Fourth, it will focus on the way in which learning programs are organized to illustrate how the structure of the learning network that gives rise to HRD processes influences employees' learning-relevant experiences. Finally, the chapter will return to the question of how employees create individual learning paths, followed by the implications for talent management and knowledge management.

THE NOTION OF AN INDIVIDUAL EMPLOYEE'S LEARNING PATH

In order to manage their knowledge and talent pools, organizations offer employees work and learning experiences that contribute to individual professional development (Billett, 2001; Ellström, 2001). These experiences occur in three types of organizational process (Van der Krogt, 2007), namely, (1) the primary work process of the organization; (2) the human resource management (HRM) process; and (3) the human resource development (HRD) process. First, individual employees gain experiences relevant to learning in the primary work process of the organization by preparing, executing, and improving their everyday work. For example, a more experienced colleague shows them how to solve a particular problem on the job. Second, in the HRM process individual employees further their careers, which provides them with experiences as they acquire, maintain, and change job positions in organizations. For instance, they are subjected to job appraisals by their supervisor. Third, and probably easiest to recognize, in the HRD process employees engage in learning-relevant experiences specifically intended to contribute to their professional development. Obvious examples are participating in education programs and being coached by a supervisor (Van der Krogt, 2007).

The experiences gained in these three types of process by individual employees form the basis for their professional development. Each employee, however, will have to bring some form of coherence into the diverse experiences in order to make sense of them. We refer to this activity as the creation of a learning path by the employee. The concept of a learning path refers to a set of learning-relevant activities that are both coherent as a whole and meaningful to the employee. The activities are based on learning-relevant experiences gained in the organizational processes. Coherence and meaning are created by the employee through engaging in new learning-relevant experiences and/or 'discovered' by the employee through reflection on past experiences in the organizational processes (ibid.). Each employee thus creates his or her own learning path on the basis of experiences gained in various organizational processes.

Individual employees can create learning paths in various ways (Poell, 2005). One option is drawing up and executing a personal development plan (cf. Fenwick, 2004). Another possibility is conducting an individual learning project, that is, undertaking activities for a specific period of time with a view to learning about a particular theme relevant to the employee (cf. Clardy, 2000; Tough, 2003; Roberson & Merriam, 2005). A somewhat less structured approach is when an employee creates informal opportunities to gain learning-relevant experiences, for example by joining or forming a community of practice (Wenger, 1998). And, finally, to the extent that employees themselves engage in taking transfer-enhancing measures around formal training courses (Broad & Newstrom, 1992; Koslowski & Salas, 1997) that would resemble the creation of a learning path as well.

The creation of meaningful learning paths that contribute to individual employees' professional development depends on their position in the organization (Van der Krogt, 2007). More specifically, the various social networks from which employees operate have a large impact on the experiences that they can gain. In particular, the positions of actors in these networks and in the communication and consultation structures determine to a large extent how much impact an employee can exert on the organizational processes and, therefore, on the learning-relevant experiences he or she can gain from these. It is these social networks (cf. Lin's notion of social structure, 2002) that give rise to the organizational processes and the experiences relevant to the learning paths and professional development.

In the remainder of this chapter we will examine how individual actions and learning-relevant experiences that form the basis of a learning path are influenced by specific organizational processes and the networks of actors creating those processes. In this view, social networks are understood differently than traditional sociological conceptions of social networks. The view presented here suggests that social networks—their structure and actors—emerge from organizational processes. We suggest that the type of organizational process will have a large impact on the actors and the social structure of the network; these actors and structures then greatly influence employee learning and professional development. Consequently, the types of organizational processes in organizations determine in part what and how an employee learns. In the context of learning, social networks are not considered static snapshots of nodes and ties. Instead, social networks are self-perpetuating constellations of actors with specific meaning for those actors as they engage in organizational processes.

VIEWING THE ORGANIZATION AS A NETWORK OF ACTORS

The learning-network theory presented here (Van der Krogt, 1998; 2007) regards organizations as networks of actors; it is these social networks that influence organizational processes. In this view, organizational processes are shaped by interactions between various actors (e.g., employees, managers, HR professionals, clients, trade unions, professional associations, and so forth) who hold positions in different types of social network. All these actors are potential sources of knowledge and talent to the organization. From their various network positions, actors create three organizational processes that are crucial to the professional development of employees: the primary work, HRM, and HRD processes. The structure of each network comprises the positions (authority, responsibility, dependency) of the actors as well as the communication and consultation structures. The network structure determines each actor's opportunities for interaction, positional power (formal authority), and access to means and to other actors necessary for exerting influence. On the basis of their positions in the network structure, actors thus create processes that, over time, result in process structures.

This perspective on organizations and organizing is based on Mintzberg (1989; see also Mintzberg et al., 1998), who assumes that the organization of the primary work process depends on the structure of the actor network, that is, on the positions of actors and their power relations (cf. Garavan et al., 2007; Sambrook, 2007). Two important social structural characteristics of Mintzberg's organization types are: (1) the distribution of authority among actor positions—centralization vs. decentralization—reflected in the power and resources of each actor; and (2) the communication and consultation structures. Four specific types of actor constellation in Mintzberg's work are particularly interesting to our purpose, namely (1) the entrepreneurial organization; (2) the bureaucratic organization; (3) the organic unit organization; and (4) the professional organization. These four types clearly show the different positions of employees in the actor-network structure (cf. Lin's notion of social structure, 2002) that gives rise to the primary work process. They are illustrated below.

The entrepreneurial organization is characterized by a relatively loosely coupled actor network, meaning that employees in the primary work process have the individual autonomy to work directly with their own clients highly independent from one another (e.g., real estate brokers working in a partnership company). In the bureaucratic organization, the power relationships between actors are highly hierarchical and regulated. Employees in the primary work process (e.g., assembly line workers in a factory) are highly dependent on the technostructure (Mintzberg, 1989) of the organization, which designs the work procedures, and on the management, which enforces these procedures. The organic unit organization is characterized by egalitarian power relationships between actors and the primary process is organized in self-managing teams each working with their own set of clients (e.g., IT specialists developing company intranets for different industries). Employees operate strongly interdependently. In the professional organization, professionals in the primary process follow the methods and codes developed by the professional field outside their own organization (e.g.,

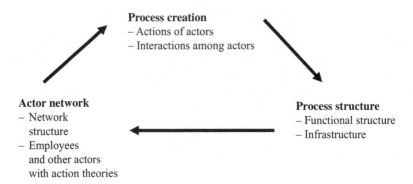

Process creation
– Actions of actors
– Interactions among actors

Actor network
– Network
  structure
– Employees
  and other actors
  with action theories

Process structure
– Functional structure
– Infrastructure

Figure 5.1   Process cycle: relationships between the network of actors, the
creation of processes, and the structure of processes

medical doctors in an academic hospital). Employees are highly dependent on their external colleagues and professional associations, who enforce the way in which the professionals work.

Organizations in Mintzberg's view can be viewed as network structures and actors creating, shaping, changing, and perpetuating the organizational processes described above (see Figure 5.1). The network structure in this view refers to the relationships of power and influence among the actors, that is, their authority and their formal position in the communication structure. Actors engage in the creation of processes on the basis of their action theories (i.e., their values and norms as well as their knowledge and skills; cf. Argyris & Schön, 1996). They create processes and tackle problems encountered while doing so. Actors apply their action theories and learn from doing so, as they interact with others who may hold different action theories.

The network structure, however, needs to be distinguished from the work process structure. Over time, actors in an organization carry out and improve work processes, which come to be embedded in the work process structure and the work network. Whereas the network structure comprises the responsibilities and communication channels needed to carry out work and improve work processes, the work process structure comprises the functional structure (i.e., the tasks and work procedures) and the infrastructural facilities (i.e., tools for carrying out work). Quality control is an important part of the work process structure, responsible for the systematic evaluation and improvement of the work process, meaning the division of tasks and jobs as well as the work procedures.

Besides the network and work process structures, Mintzberg's theory also addresses the values and norms as well as the knowledge and skills of the various actors in and around the organization (sometimes referred to as the action theories of actors; cf. Argyris & Schön, 1996). Actors do not always act according to the given structures in the organization; they also follow their own expertise and beliefs in shaping organizational processes. Actors learn as they develop their action theories, applying these in organizing work processes and thus gaining learning-relevant experiences.

Mintzberg's work focuses on the primary work process in organizations, paying little attention to HRM and HRD processes. The learning-network theory (Van der Krogt, 1998; 2007) attempts to fill that gap, assuming that each organization will develop various networks for organizing the primary work process, the HRM process, and the HRD process. A further assumption is that these actor networks will differ according to the type of process that it produces. Incidentally, Mintzberg's perspective on organizational structures seems to allude to such differentiation where he speaks about selective decentralization; power relations among actors differ according to the domain or process at hand. Likewise, Hanson (1979) showed how relationships between managers and professionals can differ according to the domains (work content or work conditions) under scrutiny.

The learning-network theory presented here uses both action theories (comprising knowledge, skills, norms, values; cf. Argyris & Schön, 1996) of actors and Mintzberg's network structures to explain how learning is organized. Highlighting both action theories and network structures provides the analytical tools to understand how employees learn while they are embedded in the organization. Developing one's action theories (i.e., learning) is an important mechanism to encourage the shaping and improvement of organizational processes. Action theories enable employees to interpret situations and act appropriately. New and old experiences are integrated into the existing action theory and get their meaning within that particular framework. The action theory itself can also be redefined, however, as learning involves a process of mutual adaptation between the existing action theory and (new and old) experiences.

Summarizing this section, we view an organization as a set of networks, each consisting of a network structure and actors with action theories (see Figure 5.1). From these networks, actors (forming the talent pool of the organization) create three types of process (work, HRM, and HRD), each thus leading to a process structure. The process structures, in turn, influence the activities carried out by the networks of actors, as the latter perceive and interpret process structures on the basis of their action theories. Actors act according to their perceptions and action theories from their positions in the network structures. By applying their action theories in organizing processes, actors develop these action theories (including their knowledge base); that is, they learn.

LEARNING-RELEVANT EXPERIENCES GAINED FROM THE WORK NETWORK

As illustrated above, the organization's human talent embodied in its employees gain experiences from the primary work process that are relevant to their learning and professional development and, therefore, to the organization's knowledge management. Which experiences they can gain depends on the type of work network and on the way in which work has come to be structured. This scenario will be illustrated in this section, which suggests that actor positions in the network structure generate different learning-relevant experiences. First, the way in which actors organize work will be modeled as a cycle. Then, four ideal types of work process will be introduced. Finally, this section will describe three dimensions on which work-network structures can differ.

How Actors Organize Work: A Cycle

The primary work process in an organization is brought about by actors in and around that organization. For example, in service organizations it is shaped by a client in interaction with one or several employees and other actors. Students in a secondary school, for instance, engage in their educational career together with teachers, mentors, counselors, their parents, and their fellow students. Patients in health care institutions work with doctors, nurses, specialists, and family members, in order to regain health.

To provide services employees use various facilities, such as technical equipment and protocols for treatments and quality control. Thus, over time, a work process structure comes into being, which can be characterized by a functional structure and a certain infrastructure (see Figure 5.2).

The actors in the work network can use the existing work structure to engage in new work activities. They do so based on their perception of the work structure. Their action theory about work also plays an important role, as it influences their perception and interpretation of the work structure as well as their actions in the work process. Their actions are also affected by their position in the work network (cf. Lin, 2002).

The positions of the actors in the work network delineate the boundaries within which they can operate. Their action theories, however, determine to what extent they can actually use that room, as their expertise and beliefs may limit the extent of their actions. Problems encountered in the work process influence how actors operate in learning-relevant work processes. Employees will try to reduce such problems by adapting their learning paths accordingly (e.g., by paying more attention to relevant topics).

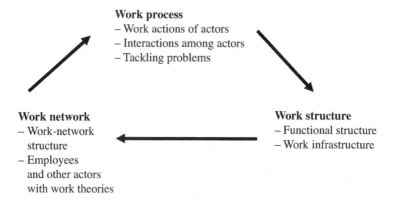

Work process
– Work actions of actors
– Interactions among actors
– Tackling problems

Work network
– Work-network
  structure
– Employees
  and other actors
  with work theories

Work structure
– Functional structure
– Work infrastructure

*Figure 5.2   Relationships between the work network, work process, and
work structure*

Managers will do so by acting strategically in the development of learning arrangements (e.g., by asking educators to design better fitting programs). Educators themselves obviously have learning and development as their job rather than as tools for them to use; they will, however, attempt to align themselves with the dominant actors to secure their relatively weak position (e.g., in bureaucratic organizations they will choose the side of management, while in organic unit organizations they will be more likely to affiliate themselves with the various autonomous teams).

Four Ideal Types of Work Process

As described above, employees create work processes together with other actors based on their positions in the work network. According to the learning-network theory, different work processes are expected to occur in different work networks. Table 5.1 typifies the different work processes according to their network structure and their work structure, which will be illustrated below. Depending on the type of work process, employees can gain different types of learning-relevant work experiences.

Individual work based in loosely coupled networks
This network structure can very well be characterized as an association of free professionals. The classical professions are often organized like this, for instance, lawyers working in their own firm, doctors who have their own practice, or solitary researchers in a university. Their autonomy at work is maximal, as the network is only a loose connection among the individual employees. Work and its improvement are individual processes tied to the

Table 5.1   Relationships expected between work-network structures and work structures

Structure of the Work Network		Work Structure
Loosely coupled network Individual autonomy Entrepreneurial organization	◄──►	Individual work By entrepreneurial employees Broad jobs
Vertical network Hierarchical, formalized relations Bureaucratic organization	◄──►	Programmatic work By centrally coordinated units Strong task division
Horizontal network Organic relations Unit organization	◄──►	Integrated work By teams Integrated jobs
External network Professional autonomy Professional organization	◄──►	Specialized work By professionals Disciplinary task differentiation

person. Individual employees decide on their own course of action, do their jobs individually, and make necessary adjustments by themselves. The interaction with clients is crucial, from the diagnosis of the problem, the setting of quality demands, the determining of a solution, to its evaluation. Direct feedback from the client gives the employee opportunities to adjust actions along the way as well.

Programmatic work based in vertical networks
This organization is characterized by a strong division of tasks, both in developing and planning work as well as in its actual execution. This structure can be observed, for example, in classical banks and training institutes offering popular off-the-shelf courses. Work is directed by managers and preparatory staff members from the technostructure of the organization. The client does not contact the individual employee directly but goes through the organization first. The strength of this network lies in its monitoring of quality standards, guaranteeing clients a predictable level of service. Dedicated quality officers or quality circles are often established to monitor the work process. Elaborate procedures and regulations are usually in place, as are systematic evaluation of work and refining protocols, all with a view to quality control.

Integrated work based in organic networks
This organization works with fixed teams each responsible for a particular type of product or service provided to a particular group of clients (e.g.,

students in a specific year group at school, patients with a specific disease pattern in residential care). In the extreme ideal-typical shape of this network structure, the employees cooperate very intensely with one another and their clients. Quality control is owned by teams of employees, who collect information, interpret it themselves, and have the authority to change their own way of operating as well.

Thematic work based in professional networks
The main characteristic of this organization is the use of specialized, complex methods with predictable outcomes (e.g., medical doctors operating in an academic hospital). Through a process known as pigeonholing, the professionals aim to match their clients to well-known methods yielding a large chance of success. Managers and clients have little impact on service provision. Quality control depends strongly on the (new) insights and methods developed within the professional field transferred to its professionals. The professional field develops new treatments or methods, which the individual professionals have to appropriate and apply in their day-to-day routine. Representatives from the professional field monitor to what extent the methods used in practice are still adequate and applied as intended. If necessary, the professional field will take measures, such as conducting further research to improve methods or offering their members more intensive professional development programs. The (formal as well as informal) professional networks are crucial within this network structure.

Three Dimensions in Work-Network Structures

Table 5.1 summarizes the different work processes according to their network structure and their work structure. As Figure 5.3 indicates, the positions and relations among the actors in the ensuing four ideal types of work-network structure can be presented along three dimensions: the vertical, horizontal, and external dimensions. The three dimensions can be regarded as axes delineating the space in which work-network structures can be situated.

Employees can gain a diversity of learning-relevant experiences from participating in the work process and solving problems thus encountered. Which experiences they gain depends strongly on the position of employees in the three dimensions of the work network (see Figure 5.3), according to the theory presented here. The learning-network theory suggests that if employees operate in a mainly vertical network they are likely to learn how to apply procedures better, whereas more horizontal networks will probably see them solving joint problems with their direct colleagues.

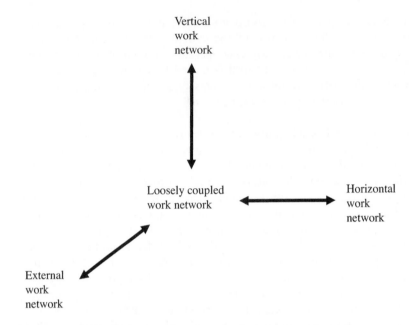

Figure 5.3 *Four ideal-typical work-network structures along three dimensions*

Professional networks offer many external learning opportunities, sharing experiences with colleagues from other organizations and experts. In loosely coupled networks, gaining learning-relevant experiences is mainly a function of the individual employee's efforts to improve his or her work.

LEARNING-RELEVANT EXPERIENCES GAINED IN THE LEARNING NETWORK

The previous section dealt with the learning-relevant experiences to be gained by employees from the primary work process in the organization. This section builds on that foundation and will focus on the human talent's experiences in one crucial HRD process, namely, organizing learning programs. In other words, the learning-network theory presented here suggests that both work processes (summarized in Mintzberg's four types) and HRD processes combine to influence what and how people learn, the development that is a crucial component of an organization's knowledge management. Precisely which experiences employees gain from HRD processes, however, depends strongly on the type of learning network and on the way in which learning has become structured over time. These points will be further illustrated below. First, the way in which actors organize learning networks will be modeled as a cycle. Then, the creation of learning programs by actors will be explained. Finally, this section will illustrate four ideal-typical learning programs that actors can create based in four ideal-typical learning networks.

Actors Organize Learning Networks: A Cycle

Over time, a specific learning network comes into being in every organization (Van der Krogt, 1998; 2007). The learning network is a constellation of actors who, from their positions and action theories, undertake learning-relevant activities. The latter become embedded in the learning structure, which in turn influences the learning-relevant activities of the actors. How the learning network is thus organized bears many similarities to the way in which work networks come about (cf. Figures 5.1 and 5.2).

In the learning network, various positions can be distinguished, just like in the work network (e.g., learning employees, consultants, training managers, content experts, supervisors, external training providers), with each position holding particular authority. Each actor has particular action theories about the purposes served by learning and about which learning-relevant activities should be undertaken. For example, employees may be of the opinion that they learn best by asking an experienced colleague, while their supervisor may want to send them to a formal training course. The learning network also has a climate, representing its values and norms about organizing learning-relevant activities in the organization.

Actors Create Learning Programs

One very important process organized by actors from the learning network is learning-program creation (see Figure 5.4). Usually a consultant initiates a learning program, charged to do so by a manager in response to a perceived problem. The consultant forms a program group consisting of several managers, content experts, and employees involved in the problem directly or indirectly. These actors may also come from outside the organization. The learning-program group analyzes the perceived problem and develops ideas about the learning theme (e.g., the goals of the learning program, a global description of the topic at hand), about the learning activities (e.g., courses, self-study, workplace training, experiments, mentoring, analyzing difficult work situations), and about the contexts in which employees can learn together (dyads, learning sets, e-learning, self-directed approaches).

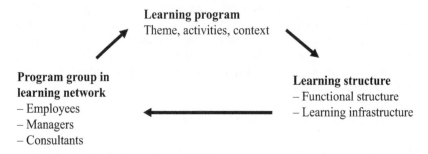

Figure 5.4   Learning-program creation

The program group is part of the learning network and holds its own position (e.g., 'Customer Focus Implementation Support Group,' 'Treatment Effectiveness Professional Development Group'). The individual members of the program group hold their own position in the learning network as well, which is usually one of the reasons why they were invited to join the program group in the first place. The program group needs to find its position in the learning network and build relationships with other actors, for instance external training institutes and content experts. The internal structure of the program group is also important, for example the responsibilities and relationships among the members. Just as crucial as the structural aspects, however, are the beliefs, knowledge, and skills of the actors in and around the program group, as it tries to reach a (more or less) shared problem definition and approach.

The program group takes into account the tasks and responsibilities of the actors involved as well as the usual procedures in place for developing learning programs. Another relevant consideration is the current learning infrastructure, which offers them didactic measures, existing programs, e-learning facilities, tests, and so forth. They may try to change the existing learning structure so as to be able to function well during the learning program.

Four Ideal Types of Learning Network

The structure of learning networks can be described in terms of three dimensions similar to those delineating the four work-network structures (cf. Figure 5.3), which together form a three-dimensional space. The space shows how differently learning networks may be structured, as they can differ on each particular dimension. The variety of learning networks is illustrated below (see Figure 5.5) by a description of the four ideal types at the end of each dimension. This subsection will also hypothesize which ideal types of learning program are likely to be created in each learning network.

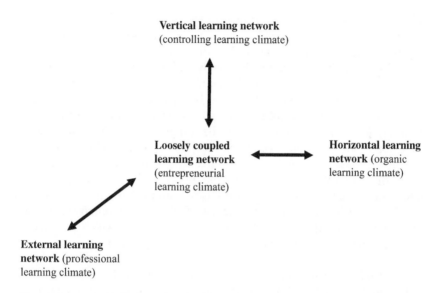

Figure 5.5 Four ideal-typical learning-network structures and their climates

The individual learning program based in a loosely coupled learning network
The relations among the actors in the loosely coupled learning network are characterized by individual responsibility supplemented by exchange and negotiation. The learning climate emphasizes entrepreneurship and creating learning programs is the responsibility of individual learners, who will agree on certain 'contracts' with one another. Employees set off on their own learning paths and use the opportunities offered by the organization as they go; opportunities that may be negotiated. They will organize learning programs together with their colleagues, as long as everyone's input is equal or some form of exchange is in place. For example, one employee may agree to provide a colleague with expert input if the latter is willing to counsel the former employee towards solving another difficult problem.

It is likely for individual-based learning programs to come into being in organizations with loosely coupled work and learning networks, character- ized by an entrepreneurial learning climate. Employees in these organiza- tions are expected to be self-directed and to feel responsible for their own work and further development. Usually a coordinator in the organization takes the initiative to form a program group willing to learn about a particular theme. The coordinator tries to get a number of employees interested in the topic through informal contacts and snowball strategies.

The employees each have their own interests in the topic, however they expect to learn most from each other. They are also sensitive to the learning infrastructure and facilities at their disposal.

At this stage the participants have only limited ideas about other possible program-group members. The learning theme is still very broad. Participants need to develop the topic by themselves using each other's experiences. Only limited collective decisions are made about learning contexts and learning activities, as the needs and preferences of the individual participants are taken into account as much as possible. It is likely that subgroups will emerge consisting of employees who expect to learn more from their other subgroup members than from others in the larger group, or who join a subgroup for pragmatic reasons. Evaluation will not be very systematic. The coordinator will justify the use of facilities to management and the individual participants will monitor the extent to which they learn enough to warrant further participation in the program group.

The centralized learning program based in a vertical learning network

The core of the vertical learning-network structure is based in the technostructure of the organization, often in dedicated HRD departments. This type is likely to be found in bureaucratic organizations with an extensive division of tasks. An important characteristic of this learning network is that *planning* forms the basis of training course design and delivery. Dedicated HRD professionals hold an important position in this network, as they plan and coordinate the learning programs and are often involved in delivery as well. Other experts and managers (as sponsors) are also involved in preparation, delivery, and evaluation. The learning programs are regulated and competence-based. The learning climate emphasizes control. Careful planning based on policy intentions and task analyses is deemed very important in this network. Program designers and experts engage in these activities extensively before delivery, which also takes into account the needs and possibilities of the learning employees.

Organizations offering this type of learning program will probably have a centrally coordinated learning network and a tightly regulated learning climate. The vertical dimension is strongly dominant here. The program in its ideal-typical extreme is designed, delivered, and evaluated according to fixed plans, as described in the traditional handbooks. It is often a line manager or HRD department that takes the initiative, as they perceive problems in the primary (work) process or in the labor market and expect a learning program to contribute to the solution. A consultant will then be assigned to design a learning program for a group of employees. The consultant will analyze the problem with the actor that provided the assignment and subsequently devise a plan for approval. Intended participants, their supervisors, and content experts may be consulted for elaboration of the plan, which will also be informed by the consultant's learning expertise and methods as far as budget and responsibilities allow. Examples of such methods include investigating the learning styles of the participants, assessing their prior knowledge, taking transfer-enhancing measures, incorporating workplace training exercises, arranging for coaching and mentoring by supervisors and direct colleagues, and conducting customization efforts targeted at the individual learning paths and needs of the participants.

The organic learning program based in a horizontal learning network
Work and learning are integrated in teams in this network. Problem finding, problem analysis, and problem reduction are important mechanisms to encourage learning in teams. A process consultant usually helps teams solve complex work problems. The different expertise and experience of the team members are employed to come up with new creative ideas or solutions. If supervisors are involved, they are engaged on an egalitarian basis with the learners or they may take on the role of consultant. Learning activities are undertaken while progress is being made and new insights are allowed to develop along the way. The team itself takes the initiative to bring in other experts or advisers. The learning climate is organic.

This program is expected to occur in organizations with team-based work arrangements and an organic learning network, where employees solve complex problems with clients in teams. The programs are usually also initiated in those teams, when they cannot solve their problems with the normal procedures. In this scenario, the team decides to put more systematic effort into solving the problem and may invite a process consultant to help them do so. Reflection is the dominant learning activity in this type of program, leading to the definition of a number of themes for subgroups to work on. What is characteristic here is the joint analysis and mutual learning process among the team members. This team-based learning about a jointly defined problem is what differentiates it from individual-based programs. The horizontal dimension of the learning network is much stronger here.

The collegial learning program based in an external learning network
This network comes into being when professionals from different organizations associate with each other, which is a precondition for the creation of professions. Professionals need to acquire and keep up to date with the necessary knowledge, skills, and beliefs that make up their profession. The professional association plays a central role in this network, as it tries to control the research institutes, the development labs, the method-development centers, the continuing professional education, the quality control, and the

career policies within the professional field. Professionals working in professional organizations (e.g., universities, hospitals, law firms, consultancy agencies) are thus heavily influenced by their profession and operate in a collegial learning climate.

Scientific research usually triggers the development of new techniques and methods (e.g., a new commercial MRI scanner based on years of lab studies). Professional development institutes, on this basis, provide the professionals (e.g., medical doctors who use MRI scans) with training courses, which the latter apply in their own work repertoire. The professionals are thus inspired by innovative insights and new methods developed in the professional field outside their own organization. Participants together with their external colleagues get acquainted with the professional body of knowledge, insights, norms, and codes valid within their discipline. Their everyday work is adapted to new scientific techniques by their participation in continuous professional development activities offered by dedicated institutes. Highly characteristic of this external learning-network structure is that professionals from several organizations create learning paths together. The other three learning-network types are usually restricted to actors from one and the same organization.

It is likely that this type of program occurs in traditional professional organizations, with highly specialized experts and a strong orientation on the profession and external colleagues. The idea to start an external, collegial learning program may be based on the professional field proposing new work methods. It may also be due to a specific problem that emerged in an organization, which several professionals are interested in analyzing and resolving together with external colleagues. The driving forces here are new methods and specialized topics. The relations within the program group are determined largely by the content expertise and positions of the actors in the profession. Studying literature and cases are favorite learning activities. Just as in individual learning programs, developing individual knowledge, skills, and values for work is very important. In collegial learning programs, however, a clearly delineated learning theme and the role of the profession are crucial, which is why the external dimension is emphasized.

This section has shown that the learning-network theory expects certain relationships to occur between the learning network of an organization and the learning programs created by the actors making up the organization's talent pool. Table 5.2 contains an overview of these expected relationships.

The Importance of Actors' Action Theories

The above descriptions of four ideal-typical learning networks and learning programs are based on the network structure and the learning climate.

*Table 5.2   Relationships expected between learning-network structures and
learning programs*

Structure of the Learning Network		Learning Program
Loosely coupled structure Entrepreneurial learning climate	←→	Loosely coupled program Individual-based
Vertical structure Controlling learning climate	←→	Centrally regulated program Competence-based
Horizontal structure Organic learning climate	←→	Organic program Problem-based
External structure Professional learning climate	←→	Collegial program Method-based

They intend to show how much learning networks can differ. Up to this
point in the argument we have not, however, taken into account the action
theories of the actors (i.e., their values, norms, knowledge, and skills;
cf. Argyris & Schön, 1996). So far, we have more or less assumed that actors
engage in learning programs in accordance with the network structure and
the learning climate. Of course, it is possible that their action theories show
similarities with the current climate and structures (as Figure 5.1 suggested). Fortunately, actors also have opportunities to place their own
emphases on their organizing actions, deviating from the current network.

Moreover, actors will not always act in accordance with their action theories, as the latter offer *opportunities* for interpretation and action rather
than prescribing or controlling actors' interpretations and actions. The
main reason why actions deviate from action theories, however, is that
different actors probably use different action theories. Managers, consultants, employees, and external actors each have their own action theories
and the desire to place their own emphases on the current learning network.
The interactions between the various actors will ultimately determine to
what extent their action theories become embedded in the network structure and climate of the organization.

HOW DO EMPLOYEES CREATE THEIR INDIVIDUAL
LEARNING PATHS?

The previous two sections have demonstrated the various learning-relevant
experiences that actors can gain from organizing processes created in two
types of network, namely, the work network that gives rise to the primary
(work) process in the organization, and the learning network that organizes

the crucial HRD process of learning-program creation. The chapter will now return to the question of how the human talent of the organization organizes their individual learning paths out of the many learning-relevant experiences in these processes. In other words, how do individual employees manage to make sense of the multitude of learning-relevant experiences in order to further their own professional development?

A learning path was defined as a set of learning activities that are both coherent as a whole and meaningful to the employee. Employees can organize their learning paths in many different ways. At the core, however, learning-path creation is about an employee recognizing and creating learning activities and experiences on the basis of a particular learning idea. Employees use the existing opportunities available through work and learning programs to gain experiences that can bring about meaningful learning to them. They can also create new opportunities for learning-relevant experiences to be integrated in their learning path.

Central to the notion of a learning path are the work experiences of employees. They will probably also take part in ad hoc learning activities, such as workshops, training courses, or coaching sessions. Important mechanisms for learning from work are, first, reducing the problems encountered in the work process and, second, improving the quality of services or products. Additionally, employees can learn by participating in the creation of learning programs, as Figure 5.3 indicated. The latter is more systematic than the former and has the advantage that employees not only learn from what they encounter during work but also influence learning programs so as to match their subsequent experiences with the learning path they have chosen.

A learning path emerges as individual employees make sense of the many learning opportunities on offer. This, in turn, can guide further learning activities that they undertake (e.g., studying a book or participating in a coaching session). Employees can create and bring order to their learning path along various 'lines.' These lines are referred to as learning ideas, usually problems or themes relevant to the employee. Participation in thematic learning activities will often lead employees to 'recall' experiences from the past that they deem relevant to their current learning path. They interpret and redefine their past experiences so as to fit with their current activities. In other words, when employees engage in intentional learning activities (e.g., self-study, training course), they usually think back to past experiences. They connect the latter to their current activities and, by so doing, integrate them in their learning path. Many trainers and educators also encourage this retrospective construction process (Yorks, 2005; O'Neil & Marsick, 2007). The creation of a learning path will also usually consist of learning activities more explicitly organized by employees themselves with a view to learning more about a certain topic improving a certain skill. Mostly, employees will alternate between integrating past experiences into their learning path and undertaking new activities to bring their learning path forward.

Employees can also participate in learning programs offered by educators (e.g., a professional development course or a supporting scheme to an organizational innovation). In participating in such programs, employees usually determine which parts of the course are most relevant to their own learning path. Certain parts of existing programs are more interesting to employees because they fit the learning paths that they are creating. The educator will notice this when employees drop certain parts of the program or ask for a more detailed elaboration of a certain topic. The extent to which the educator is able and willing to make such adaptations influences the benefit gained by individual employees with a view to furthering their learning path.

CONCLUSIONS AND IMPLICATIONS

This chapter set out to investigate the question of how social networks in organizations contribute to employee learning, which is a core issue in both notions of talent management and knowledge management alike. Based on the learning-network theory (Van der Krogt, 1998; 2007), which views organizations as networks and actors (cf. Sambrook, 2007; Garavan et al., 2007), we distinguished between two specific actor networks and corresponding processes especially relevant to individual learning. First, the work network, in which employees carry out and improve their daily work, which may lead to learning; and second, the learning network, where employees participate in specifically designed programs in order to learn. It was argued that their learning-relevant experiences gained in both processes can lead employees to create their own learning paths, that is, to make sense of the many learning-relevant experiences available with a view to bringing coherence and meaning to them. Individual learning paths are both employee-driven and affected by their work experiences and participation in learning programs. These work experiences and learning programs are, in turn, informed to a considerable extent by the particular work and learning networks that employees participate in.

Unlike many other network approaches, the learning-network theory refrains from seeing 'the' organization as 'a' network. Instead, it conceives of dynamic and diverse actor networks in an organization, each characterized by specific structural arrangements. The work network has different actor positions, power relations, and dynamics than the learning network, and both differ from the personnel allocation or HRM network (not discussed here; see Van der Krogt, 2007). Actors create these various networks and they then have to operate in what they have created. The focus here is on the various positions that employees have to negotiate in several different networks at the same time. The problems they experience in organizing their work, learning, and careers thus become surprisingly clear, as do the potential roles of managers and consultants in helping them cope.

For instance, think of an employee of a law firm who was trained as a lawyer but had to resort to a relatively low-profile job giving legal advice to one-off clients on the periphery of the firm. This employee really wants to become partner and needs the HRM (especially, career management) network, in which he (or she) has a weak position, to provide the necessary learning-relevant experiences. The work network does not give him the right experiences to convince the firm's partners to promote him to the next higher level. This employee will probably need the learning network (partially located outside the firm, in continuing legal education) to gain a better qualification in order to get promoted. If he is lucky, or a good negotiator, he can get his supervisor or a more experienced partner in the firm to mentor him, so that he can more easily integrate the learning-relevant experiences gained in the work, learning, and HRM networks into a coherent and meaningful learning path leading to his desired promotion.

One important question that needs to be answered by further research in this area is how the various networks created by actors are related. For example, is an organization with individual work more likely to have a loosely coupled than another type of learning network, as the learning-network theory would expect? Similar relationships are assumed between bureaucratic work and a vertical learning network, between organic work and a horizontal learning network, and between professional work and an external learning network. Clarifying these relationships can help employees better negotiate their positions in the various networks and thus optimize their learning paths.

Another characteristic of the learning-network theory that differentiates it from other network approaches is its position in the structure–agency debate. In his theory of structuration, Giddens (1984) distinguishes between structure (contextual conditions) and agency (actions undertaken by actors). He demonstrates how structures come into being over time as a result of agency and how, at the same time, agency is limited by existing structures. Although the tensions between these two principles are often mentioned in literature, it usually remains unclear how exactly actors can and cannot operate in the context of network structures. As we have illustrated in this study, the concept of an individual learning path, created in the context of work and learning networks, offers opportunities to provide more clarity about that question. Employees can take many opportunities to gain learning-relevant experiences (agency) from social networks, however which experiences and how many exactly depends on the types of networks in place (structure). These particular networks have come about, in the first instance, as a result of the actions of various actors over time. The concept of a learning path demonstrates how agency is both enabled and limited by particular types of structure (cf. Lin, 2002).

Structures in an organization, such as its social network, are often presented as inherently positive in their capacity to facilitate individual learning, work satisfaction, organizational commitment, and so forth. As far as learning is concerned, however, this chapter has argued that social networks can also restrict employees to a considerable extent. Depending on the type of network and organization and on the position of the individual employees therein, they may feel supported or inhibited to learn what they deem valuable to their work and their careers. Structure and agency should therefore be regarded in conjunction with one another and in terms of their meaningfulness to employees.

Important questions for further research in this area are how exactly employees create learning paths in the context of various social networks and what factors determine whether these structures support or inhibit them to do so. The learning-network theory offers a framework with which such research questions may be answered. It suggests that employees will be better able to create meaningful learning paths if they can exert a substantial influence on the primary work and learning-program creation processes in which they participate. This influence goes beyond having access to relevant information and communication channels; it means having enough power to be able to establish a better fit between work and learning programs, on the one hand, and their individual learning paths and professional development, on the other hand.

In terms of practical implications, this chapter demonstrates the relevance to organizational actors of various social networks for the individual learning paths of employees and, hence, for effective knowledge management through talent management. First, employees themselves who are interested in participating more actively in creating their own learning paths can use the framework presented in this chapter to reflect on the types of learning path they have created thus far and on other types available. They can also diagnose the types of work network and learning network that they participate in and see to what extent their learning paths are likely to correspond with existing network structures. This will give them an indication of the amount of energy to be invested in creating these learning paths—more energy is probably needed as correspondence decreases. The framework may thus be used as a tool for employees to analyze and further their own talent development.

Second, supervisors and managers who are serious about fostering employee learning can use the framework to create a better-fitting social environment for learning. Based on a diagnosis of the learning paths created or desired by their employees, managers can draw ideas from the framework about the types of work assignments and social support most conducive to the intended learning processes. They can also get ideas about the various ways available to organize their talent and knowledge management efforts. They may of course want to call in the help of an HR professional to facilitate these attempts.

Third, HR professionals can use the framework to better attune the learning and development programs that they design to the individual learning paths of the participants, which are strongly influenced by the work network in the first place. In general, the position of HR professionals in the relevant social networks is weak, possibly with the exception of their influence on the learning network of the bureaucratic organization. Managers and employees usually hold stronger positions and have more opportunities to exercise power and influence. The impact of HR professionals on the work network (and the HRM network) is modest, to say the least, and can only be attained through developing strong relationships with powerful actors in those networks, that is, with employees, supervisors, (HR) managers, and professional associations (including their own). They can, however, help these actors make sense of the relationship between social networks and learning paths, as the former will not usually have the expertise and energy to do so themselves.

Effective knowledge management requires ample attention to talent management. Employees (the talent pool of the organization) at all levels represent key agents of knowledge management in generating, acquiring, transferring, and applying important explicit and tacit knowledge (i.e., in learning). We have shown in this chapter how various social networks in the organization impact upon the core process of employee learning or, if you will, talent development. Organizations seeking to increase their competitive advantage should therefore take into account the crucial role of social networks.

REFERENCES

Argyris, C. and Schön, D. (1996). *Organizational Learning II*. Reading, MA: Addison-Wesley.

Billett, S. (2001). *Learning in the Workplace: Strategies for Effective Practice.* Crows Nest, NSW, Australia: Allen & Unwin.

Broad, M.L. and Newstrom, J.W. (1992). *Transfer of Training: Action-packed Strategies to Ensure High Pay-off from Training Investments*. San Francisco: Addison-Wesley.

Clardy, A. (2000). Learning on their own: Vocationally oriented self-directed learning projects. *Human Resource Development Quarterly,* **11**(2): 105–125.

Ellström, P.E. (2001). Integrating learning and work: Problems and prospects. *Human Resource Development Quarterly,* **12**(4): 421–435.

Fenwick, T.J. (2004). Towards a critical HRD. *Adult Education Quarterly,* **54**(3): 174–192.

Garavan, T.N., Gubbins, C., Hogan, C., and Woodlock, M. (2007). Transitioning to a Strategically Aligned HRD Function: The Case of a Health Services Organization. In Sambrook, S. and Stewart, J. (eds), *Human Resource Development in the Public Sector: The Case of Health and Social Care.* London: Routledge, pp. 40–79.

Giddens, A. (1984). *The Constitution of Society: Outline of the Theory of Structuration.* Berkeley, CA: University of California Press.

Hanson, E.M. (1979). School management and contingency theory: An emerging perspective. *Educational Administration Quarterly,* **15**(2): 98–116.

Kessels, J.W.M. and Poell, R.F. (2004). Andragogy, social capital theory, and implications for HRD. *Advances in Developing Human Resources,* **6**(2): 146–157.

Koslowski, S.W.J. and Salas, E. (1997). A Multilevel Organizational Systems Approach to the Implementation and Transfer of Training. In Ford, J.K. (ed.), *Improving Training Effectiveness in Work Organizations.* Mahwah, NJ: Lawrence Erlbaum, pp. 247–287.

Lin, N. (2002). *Social Capital: A Theory of Social Structure and Action.* Cambridge, UK: Cambridge University Press.

Mintzberg, H. (1989). *Mintzberg on Management: Inside our Strange World of Organizations.* New York: Free Press.

Mintzberg, H., Ahlstrand, B., and Lampel, J. (1998). *Strategy Safari: A Guided Tour Through the Wilds of Strategic Management.* New York: Free Press.

O'Neil, J. and Marsick, V.J. (2007). *Understanding Action Learning.* New York: AMACOM.

Poell, R.F. (2005). HRD Beyond What HRD Practitioners Do: A Framework for Furthering Multiple Learning Processes in Work Organizations. In Elliott, C. and Turnbull, S. (eds) *Critical Thinking in Human Resource Development.* London: Routledge, pp. 85–95.

Poell, R.F. and Van der Krogt, F.J. (2002). Using Social Networks in Organizations to Facilitate Individual Development. In Pearn, M. (ed.) *Individual Differences and Development in Organizations.* London: Wiley, pp. 285–304.

Roberson, D.N. and Merriam, S.B. (2005). The self-directed learning process of older, rural adults. *Adult Education Quarterly,* **55**(4): 269–287.

Sambrook, S. (2007). Discourses of HRD in the NHS. In Sambrook, S. and Stewart, J. (eds), *Human Resource Development in the Public Sector: The Case of Health and Social Care.* London: Routledge.

Storberg, J. (2002). The evolution of capital theory: A critique of a theory of social capital and implications for HRD. *Human Resource Development Review,* **1**(4): 468–499.

Streumer, J.N. (ed.) (2006). *Work-related Learning.* Dordrecht, Netherlands: Springer.

Tjepkema, S. (2003). *The Learning Infrastructure of Self-managing Work Teams.* Enschede, Netherlands: Twente University.

Tough, A. (2003). Episodes and Learning Projects. In Jarvis, P. and Grofin, C. (eds), *Adult and Continuing Education: Major Themes in Education* (Vol. II). London: Routledge, pp. 35–44.

Van der Krogt, F.J. (1998). Learning network theory: The tension between learning systems and work systems in organizations. *Human Resource Development Quarterly*, **9**(2): 157–178.

Van der Krogt, F.J. (2007). *Organiseren van leerwegen: Strategieën van werknemers, managers en leeradviseurs in dienstverlenende organisaties* [Organizing learning paths: Strategies of workers, managers, and consultants in service organizations]. Rotterdam, Netherlands: Performa.

Wenger, E. (1998). *Communities of Practice: Learning, Meaning, and Identity*. Cambridge, MA: Cambridge University Press.

Yorks, L. (2005). *Strategic Human Resource Development*. Mason, OH: Thomson South-Western.

6. The power of career counseling for enhanced talent and knowledge management

Ans De Vos and Nele Soens

INTRODUCTION

Practitioners and researchers generally agree that career management is an important part of an organization's talent management (Sullivan, 1999; Baruch & Peiperl, 2000; Baruch, 2004a; Rothwell et al., 2005). Over the past decades, changes in the socio-economic environment have dramatically altered the concept of a career and have contributed to the development of new models for career management (Arthur, Inkson, & Pringle, 1999; Baruch, 2004b). Central to the notion of the so-called 'new career' is the concept of organizations that can no longer offer their employees careers structured along a well-defined and fairly predictable upward trajectory, which parallels their increasing tenure within the organization (Hallier & Butts, 1999; Hall, 2002; Baruch, 2004b; Arthur, Khapova, & Wilderom, 2005; Feldman & Ng, 2007). In order to remain competitive in a business environment characterized by globalization and rapid technological innovations, hierarchical layers have been replaced by flatter and more flexible structures. In this new organizational setting, lateral or horizontal movements, temporary movements, and movement 'in place' by job enrichment are gaining importance as valid alternatives for the traditional linear career trajectory (Arthur et al., 1999; Currie, Tempest, & Starkey, 2006; Peiperl et al., 2000).

This evolution has important implications for both the demand and the supply sides of the internal labor market. On the supply side, this evolution is promising for those employees who value the development of their talent in directions that may deviate from the traditional predefined vertical career structures and who want to engage in a wide variety of challenges during their career. In the contemporary career environment, employees are seen as the primary actors responsible for their own employability, and mobility appears to be an ideal means to realize this: it allows employees to broaden their competencies, and hence, retain or improve their opportunities in both the internal and external labor markets. However, it also implies a changing attitude for those employees who would like the organization to take charge over their careers. How this individual responsibility might be facilitated is therefore an important challenge for organizations.

On the demand side, employers can benefit from a more flexible internal labor market characterized by increased mobility. Having 'the right person at the right place' in such a way that optimal performance can be delivered and competitive advantage can be realized is a central objective throughout all talent management strategies. In this context, career mobility offers the flexibility needed to respond to the changing needs for human resources. At the same time, supporting and stimulating mobility is an important tool for employee retention. Hence, the growing emphasis on career self-management does not mean that the role of the organization in managing careers has decreased. It has rather changed in content and approach, but its importance has not decreased. Moreover, in an economic era that requires organizations to be constantly on the look-out for improvements in order to remain competitive, knowledge management is crucial to ensure the efficiency of strategy realization. In this context, providing employees with opportunities for internal mobility can be an effective way to stimulate knowledge sharing both directly and indirectly, the latter by preventing employees (and thus the knowledge they have built) from leaving the organization due to a lack of career perspective.

In order to be successful in this challenge, organizations need a talent management approach that integrates different HR systems and processes and that actively involves employees in the management of their own careers. This requires that perspectives for (horizontal) mobility are accompanied by the right type of career support. Career counseling can be seen as a relevant instrument to realize this. Career counseling assists an employee in the process of self-reflection on personal strengths and weaknesses and in outlining a career path that matches his or her individual aspirations and competencies with the opportunities available within the organization. In this chapter, we discuss how an integrated process of career counseling can serve as a vehicle to stimulate career mobility and to improve the match between individual and organizational career needs.

This chapter is structured as follows. First, we discuss career mobility in the internal labor market. Next, we outline the implications for both the individual and the organization in terms of career development. This is followed by an elaboration of the role of career counseling as an instrument for stimulating mobility. We end with some reflections on the influence of organizational characteristics on the need and opportunities for mobility.

MOBILITY IN THE INTERNAL LABOR MARKET

Clarity about career pathways throughout an organization allows employees to understand their current position in the organization and their opportunities for future directions (Rothwell et al., 2005). Career structures in organizations have traditionally focused on advancing people on vertical ladders, in line with the traditional perception that a successful career involves successive linear movement up the organizational career ladder, gaining along the way additional increments in formal authority, prestige, and rewards (Garavan & Coolahan, 1996). In this traditional view, career success was evaluated based on the rate of upward mobility and external indicators of achievement. Stability of structure and clarity of career ladders implied unambiguous career paths, which were mostly linear and upward focused (Baruch, 2004a).

However, opportunities for advancement in terms of moving up the hierarchical ladder are becoming scarce. In flattening organizations, many intermediate layers of management have been eliminated, and more control is placed in the hands of frontline workers. With fewer mid-level management positions around, fewer opportunities exist for people to move up the traditional career ladder (Kaye & Farren, 1996; Baruch, 2004a; 2004b; Feldman & Ng, 2007). In view of these changes, organizations have focused on alternative ways to stimulate career mobility of the internal labor market.

Stimulating career mobility can be important for several reasons. First, the career perspective offered by the organization appears to have a significant impact on employee outcomes like commitment, satisfaction, and intention to stay (e.g., Steel, Griffeth, & Hom, 2002; Hsu et al., 2003). Second, from an organizational point of view, mobility can foster cooperation and information sharing between different units, departments, locations, or functional areas, since horizontal movements throughout the firm can decrease the borders that, especially in large organizations, often exist between these. Hence, the type of career perspective, and more specifically the opportunities for career mobility offered by organizations have important implications for knowledge management.

There are several types of non-vertical movements that organizations can offer as alternatives to the traditional vertical movement (Kaye & Farren, 1996). First, *lateral* or *horizontal* movements can be a relevant alternative. A lateral move involves a change in jobs but not necessarily a change in pay, status, or level of responsibility. Sideward, rather than upward, moves can broaden an employee's base of knowledge and skills and help develop new competencies (Schein, 1978; Kaye & Farren, 1996). In many flattening organizations, lateral movements are encouraged and even necessary as a means of acquiring the necessary broad experience before moving up the management ladder (Garavan & Coolahan, 1996). From a knowledge management perspective, horizontal movements facilitate the exchange of information. Employees entering a unit with a career history in other functional departments of the organization can bring in valuable knowledge. Consider, for example, a production engineer crossing over to marketing. In addition, these types of horizontal moves also have the benefit of enhancing more informal information exchanges between units, thanks to the development of social networks that traverse the borders of functional domains or geographical locations. For global organizations, offering international career steps is an important vehicle to stimulate knowledge across national borders.

Another career mobility option is often called 'growing in place', or 'job enrichment.' This refers to revitalizing people's interest in their work by replacing rigidly defined, overspecialized jobs with positions that enable them to exercise greater responsibility and autonomy. Job enrichment can be a relevant option for those employees who do not want to leave their current position or organization, by giving them the opportunity to expand their responsibilities in their current job in order to develop new competencies. Job enrichment enables employees to master important skills and build more productive relationships with colleagues and customers. These challenges can contribute to their career satisfaction and a sense of personal accomplishment. For example, the attitudes and behaviors of plateaued managers have been found to be significantly more positive when their job is richer and offers an opportunity to participate in decision-making (Tremblay & Roger, 2004). Job enrichment may include initiatives such as increasing an individual's responsibility for knowledge sharing, coaching of young employees or mentoring and, consequently, can also be seen as a relevant instrument for implementing effective knowledge management.

A third non-vertical career movement is the so-called *temporary movement* that people can make, for example, taking short-term job assignments or participating in project teams and task forces. This option is most recognizable in a project environment. It offers people the chance to explore what they are good at, and it might be a relevant option for those interested in variability and change throughout their career. By participating in temporary projects, employees can learn about themselves, and they can extend their network within the organization and their knowledge about the organization in a much broader way (Kaye & Farren, 1996). Obviously, by temporarily engaging employees in tasks that fall outside their core job or that involve the cooperation with colleagues from different units in project teams, knowledge sharing can be enhanced.

These alternative career moves concretize the notion of careers as 'life-long learning' experiences and respond to the idea that career success should be defined in terms of psychological success: the realization of one's individual career values and dreams, which can be much broader than moving up the vertical ladder (Eby, Butts, & Lockwood, 2003; Arthur et al., 2005). By offering alternative directions for making career moves, organizations can offer employees different options for realizing career success. It also provides a solution for the problem that if only vertical movements are structurally embedded in the organization, a career perspective is only created for those 'happy few' who are eligible for making vertical promotions, while the majority of people in the company might get frustrated by a lack of career perspective. In this sense, stimulating career mobility in other than upward directions fits within a talent management strategy that addresses all employees, not only those labeled as 'high potential'.

CAREER SELF-MANAGEMENT AND CAREER MOBILITY

This broad meaning of career mobility implies a stronger involvement of the individual employee in his or her career development. With fewer vertical and more horizontal opportunities for mobility around, employees are confronted with the challenge to outline their own career path in line with their own interests and to behave in such a way that they can realize their personal career goals. This has led organizations to stress the importance of career self-management. Career self-management refers to proactive behaviors that employees show with respect to managing their own careers (Orpen, 1994; Kossek et al., 1998), and it includes activities such as collecting information about existing or possible career opportunities, searching for feedback about one's performance and competencies, and creating career opportunities through networking and actions aimed at enhancing one's visibility. Career self-management, hence, involves those activities that allow individuals to make a realistic self-assessment of their own talents and capabilities in view of organizational career opportunities, and also concrete actions (e.g., networking, self-nomination, creating opportunities) undertaken to realize these ambitions (Noe, 1996; Sturges, Guest, & Mackenzie Davey, 2000; Sturges et al., 2002).

Even though career self-management is seen by many organizations as an important precondition for career success, empirical studies show large differences in the extent to which employees actively manage their careers. For instance, a recent study conducted among a representative sample of Belgian employees shows that only one out of three respondents engage in networking behaviors; only 50% regularly ask for feedback about their performance; and only one out of ten respondents engage in mobility-oriented behaviors (Verbruggen et al., 2005). These figures are substantially lower than the figures reported by Sturges et al. (2000) about the individual career management initiatives within a sample of UK graduates. Further analyses of the Belgian data based on socio-demographic factors show large differences between subgroups of employees. Employees with a higher educational attainment, young employees recently graduated from colleges and universities, and those at the higher ranks of the organization report more self-management activities.

However, these employees are often only a limited portion of an organization's workforce. This might not come as a surprise, but it holds a challenge for organizations who want to stimulate more career mobility among their total workforce. From a knowledge management perspective, stimulating knowledge exchange through mobility at all hierarchical layers is important since the importance of knowledge sharing is, in most organizations, not limited to specific subsets of employees or types of jobs. In this sense, career counseling can be viewed as a vehicle to stimulate career mobility by more actively engaging all employees in taking charge of their own career development. In this way career counseling is a relevant part of a talent management approach that addresses all employees working within the organization.

CAREER COUNSELING FOR STIMULATING AND SUPPORTING MOBILITY: AN INTEGRATIVE MODEL

The organization has a major role to play if it wants to stimulate career mobility: First, by establishing career structures and aligning different functional HRM areas within one consistent talent management strategy; second, by stimulating employees to reflect about their own career and to undertake actions to realize their career intentions and ensure their employability (i.e., the facilitation of career self-management).

The instruments that organizations can use for stimulating mobility in the internal labor market are, in the first place, a range of career management practices, such as career planning, job posting, assessment and development centers, competency management, career paths, and succession planning (Baruch, 2004b; Gutteridge, Leibowitz, & Shore, 1993a; Rothwell et al., 2005; Sturges et al., 2002). This wide range of practices can be grouped into two broad categories. The first category includes those activities that, from an organizational viewpoint, aim at ensuring the 'pipeline' of employees at different levels of the organization's hierarchical layers (e.g., job matching systems, succession planning, job posting). In the second category, those activities can be found that aim at providing employees with feedback and support they need to further develop themselves (career discussions, development centers, training sessions, etc.).

Organizational realities show that traditional career management practices such as job matching and training continue to predominate in many career systems (Gutteridge et al., 1993b; Bollen et al., 2006). In Belgium, for instance, internal job posting, reimbursement of participation in external training or workshops, and internal training and development programs continue to constitute the top three of most common practices (Bollen et al., 2006). While the same study showed a majority of organizations involving line management in holding career discussions, in most cases the outcomes of discussions are only weakly linked to other parts of their talent management strategy, with the exception of those employees targeted for succession management.

It is generally assumed that organizations need a mix of both types of career management initiatives in order to realize the idea of 'the right person at the right place.' However, the success of a bundle of career management practices used by an organization will depend on the extent to which there is a real *integration* of activities belonging to both categories. Career counseling can be regarded as a career management practice that explicitly aims at realizing this integration. It refers to those activities undertaken by the organization to assist employees in answering basic questions about their careers (What do I want? What am I good at? What type of person am I?); to link these answers to career opportunities available within the organization (e.g., perspectives for mobility); and to undertake actions in order to match their intentions with the latter (e.g., by following training courses, entering in a mentoring program, on-the-job learning).

Career counseling explicitly focuses on all talent (i.e., all employees in the organization), and should therefore be distinguished from succession management or other initiatives targeted at a specific group of 'key talent,' 'fast-track' management candidates, or 'high potentials' (even though it can be linked with initiatives for these target groups, as will be outlined further in this chapter). Hence, what constitutes career counseling in today's organizations is not the provision of isolated services but rather a specific integration of diverse career management practices. Moreover, it is linked with other HRM domains such as performance management and training. It is the integration of all these practices into a coherent system of career counseling that determines its effectiveness in stimulating mobility.

In what follows, we will elaborate on the objectives and the process of career counseling as an integrated combination of talent management practices, in which both the interrelatedness between career management practices and the relationship of career management practices with other HRM domains is discussed. This discussion is largely based on case study research and practical interventions that we have done in Belgian organizations.

The Purpose of Career Counseling

In general terms, the purpose of career counseling within organizations is to realize an alignment between the characteristics of the employees—their abilities, ambitions, and motivations—and the human resources needs of the organization, the latter being dictated by business needs. This is what Baruch (1999) refers to as the need for 'external integration,' that is, the fit between career systems and the organizational culture and strategy. For organizations that want to increase knowledge sharing between units, career counseling can thus be used to stimulate career mobility across units through different types of horizontal or temporary career moves.

From an organizational viewpoint, career counseling is an instrument of human resources planning that helps to assure steady succession and anticipate future personnel planning needs. By means of career counseling, organizations seek to orient their employees towards the job or position that delivers the greatest added value to the company. At the same time, however, organizations need to realize a balance between individual and organizational objectives. Bringing the issue of employee motivation into the picture, and its impact on employee performance, the job has to be aligned with the career aspirations and abilities of the person, and mutually satisfactory solutions have to be found.

Hence, the key motivation to invest in career counseling is better individual performance—and therefore improved business outcomes—achieved by having more satisfied employees. In short, career counseling allows the organization to have the right person in the right place, which is in the interest of both the individual and the organization. Finally, career counseling serves as an organization's retention tool, in the sense that investment in people's careers ties them to the company and increases the likelihood of the return on investment in career development.

The Process of Career Counseling: An Integrative Model

As outlined earlier, career counseling is a process that integrates several HRM systems and processes which fall under the term 'talent management.' In what follows, we consider a range of practices, processes, and techniques that constitute this career counseling process and unravel the way they are designed to be internally consistent and aligned with one

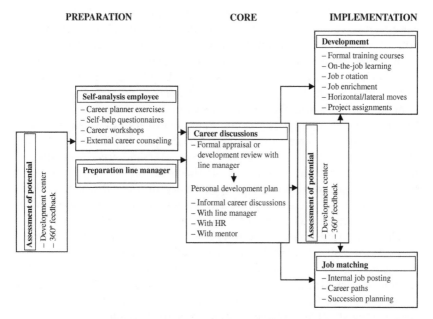

Figure 6.1 An integrative model for career counseling within organizations

another. This integrated process of career counseling is presented in the model in Figure 6.1. This model reflects what constitutes career counseling within organizations, how it is integrated with the broader organizational career management, and how it is intertwined with other HRM domains.

The core of career counseling

The essence of career counseling lies in the *formal appraisal or development review between a manager and an employee*, which takes place on a regular basis (annually, in many organizations). Whereas this formal discussion occupies the central place in career counseling, it does not mean that career counseling is being reduced to one (yearly) recurring moment. The role of the line manager as a career counselor also incorporates informal career support and developmental feedback, which turns career counseling into an ongoing communication. Next to formal and informal discussions with the manager, formal and informal *career discussions with a human resources professional* take a prominent place within career counseling. Contrary to the formal reviews that automatically cover the entire workforce, in most organizations, career discussions with an HR professional only take place at the employee's initiative.

Regarding the *content* of this formal review, organizations face the dilemma of combining versus separating the evaluative and developmental components. In practice, there are advantages and disadvantages to both options. On the one hand, combining evaluation of past performance and future career development may prevent the manager and the employee from having the discussion in an open way. Employees may be reluctant to be honest about their weaknesses and areas for development if they think this will damage their manager's evaluation of their performance. Furthermore, as many people do not have a clear idea of what they want to achieve in their career, and managers tend to avoid talking about complicated career issues, the career part may be overshadowed by the discussion about performance and reward. If this happens, the formal appraisal review cannot be considered a true opportunity for career discussion. These arguments against integrating career counseling with the appraisal review stand in contrast to its benefit of providing a reality check. Future career development needs to be linked to past and current performance in order to set realistic objectives and make deliverable promises.

Evidence shows that most organizations tend to combine both reviews, for reasons of (lack of) time and the inability to schedule more than one formal meeting a year between manager and employee, and thus, career counseling is incorporated as a part of the appraisal process. This implies the challenge for HR to ensure that the career discussion part of the performance review is taken seriously by both the employee and the line manager. As we will outline further in this chapter, this requires—in addition to clear communication—substantial support offered both on the 'input' side of the discussion (preparation) and on the 'output' side (career initiatives taken).

Supporting the need for preparation
For the formal appraisal review to be considered as true career counseling, the manager has to go beyond merely 'listening' to the outcome of the employee's self-reflection. In their role of career counselor, line management truly has to 'assist' and 'guide' employees in their self-analysis. In this regard, the assistance provided by HR in preparing the formal review plays an important role. This preparation can range from requiring the employee to glance at the evaluation form to be filled out, to providing employees with all kinds of vehicles for career assistance, such as career planning exercises, self-assessment questionnaires, workshops, or external counseling. Organizations that restrict themselves to the first extreme provide the employee with the least guidance possible. They run the risk that employees only prepare the evaluation part of the discussion and skip the career issues, for reasons of not being able to deal with these on their own, or not believing in the necessity of defining career expectations. It is clear that organizations extending career advice with the tools mentioned above are more

likely to reach high-quality career counseling, and closely approach the type of career guidance provided by specialized, external career counselors.

Preparation might not only be supported on the employee side. For managers to be prepared for the career discussion part, it is important that they also receive a structured document or tool that would help them to reflect in a more structured way about the career development of their employees. When managers only prepare the performance evaluation and goal-setting part, they run the risk of being unable to engage constructively in a discussion about career development or give relevant feedback on the concerns or expectations brought up by the employee. HR plays an important role in this preparation stage, by offering relevant tools for self-assessment, providing structured preparation guidelines, and creating awareness among employees and managers about the importance of the preparation. However, the extent to which the career discussion is really valued will depend strongly on what happens with its outcomes.

Follow-up of the career discussion
For career discussions to be acted upon, it is important that intentions expressed during the discussion are written down and linked with a concrete action plan. In many organizations, this is done by working out a *personal development plan*. In order for this personal development plan to be effective, two major points of attention should be taken into consideration: the quality of the plan and a way to follow up on what is articulated in it. Regarding its content, one of the major problems associated with personal development plans is the narrow-mindedness regarding what 'development' means. When drawing a development plan, managers and employees often limit their thinking to traditional, classical training courses, without addressing on-the-job development initiatives such as job rotation, job enrichment, participation in projects, or cross-functional or cross-departmental experiences, which may be more appropriate in view of an individual's development needs.

Furthermore, line managers often lack the competencies to define exactly an employee's developmental needs. Yet the more precise the developmental need can be identified, the better the proposed training or development initiatives can target that need. Follow-up of the implementation of the development plan is a second point that deserves explicit attention. In many organizations, what's expressed in the development plan is not monitored afterwards, often leading to a situation in which the writing of the development plan becomes considered as the final goal rather than the start of concrete actions. This can be overcome by formally checking whether the development initiatives that were agreed upon during the previous career review have been put into practice by the employee before starting a new career discussion. Another option is to build in checkpoints during the course of the year. HRM has an important role to play here, by informing both managers and employees about the purpose and application of personal development plans and by preparing line managers for this role through training or coaching.

The Periphery of Career Counseling

The above-mentioned formal and informal career discussions between the manager and the employee (or between an HR professional and the employee) are at the core of career counseling. However, in order to be successful in realizing its objectives, career counseling needs to be integrated with other talent management practices.

Assessment of employee potential

First, within the scope of career management, many organizations provide assessment tools like development centers, 360° feedback, or self-evaluation tools to measure employee potential. These assessment tools can be used either before or after the formal career discussion. As outlined before, it can help employees in the self-analysis when preparing for their career discussion. Also, line managers can use the report of a development center, for instance, to structure the career discussion. Moreover, tools for the assessment of employee potential can help in measuring the employee's abilities more precisely and identify the needs for development more sharply in the personal development plan.

Job matching systems

Assessment of the employee's career expectations on the one hand (self-analysis and career discussions) and the employee's capabilities and potential on the other (assessment tools and development plan) is a central component of career counseling, but not the only one. Instruments relating to 'job matching' are needed in order to relate the career discussion and personal development plan to concrete outcomes in terms of career perspective. This is a necessary link in order to ensure that both employees and managers take the career discussion seriously. This implies that the internal labor market and the possible career steps within this labor market need to be clarified in order to frame the discussion about the employee's career expectations. In this respect, it is essential for organizations to offer employees a realistic picture about different career paths that are possible and to provide them with a clear idea of what career mobility can encompass. This information is important for employees, in order to have realistic expectations and to develop their competencies in line with the conditions stipulated for moving.

For line managers, it is important to have an insight into possible career paths, especially when these paths cross the borders of their own department or business unit. Providing both employees and line managers with this information is an important task for HRM. It is here that career counseling can support internal mobility by introducing opportunities for lateral or temporary moves within the organization. In large organizations, this might sometimes require active involvement of HRM in the counseling process when the organization's size or structure make it impossible for line managers to be aware of all possible moves employees with a certain profile can make. Internal job posting is one frequently used practice to communicate about possible career directions, but postings need to be accompanied by clear support from the organization for employees to apply for internal vacancies.

Moreover, if organizations want to encourage internal mobility, they might not want to limit themselves to internal job posting. Actively matching individual aspirations with opportunities might be an important role for HRM in this regard. Even though the outcome of this job matching process might indicate for some employees that there is no appropriate perspective within the company that matches their career aspirations, doing this exercise as explicitly as possible is important for building loyalty and commitment. In these cases, providing a perspective in the current job through job enrichment initiatives may stimulate employee retention and avoid demotivation.

Training and development
Career counseling implies a close integration with training and development, in order to equip employees with the necessary skills and abilities to develop their career in the desired direction. This implies that intentions for development, as stipulated in the personal development plan, are translated into concrete initiatives. This requires a link between an organization's career system and the training and development function. As outlined earlier, it is important that development is not only defined in terms of following a training course, but that other initiatives (e.g., coaching, on-the-job learning, temporary assignments) are also considered.

Integration of job matching with training and development
If organizations want to stimulate mobility by offering career counseling, it is crucial for them to integrate job matching with development initiatives. In many organizations, this lack of integration is the major problem that prevents talent management from being effective. The integration of job matching with development is crucial from a retention perspective, but it is also a necessary condition for ensuring that knowledge management is enhanced by internal mobility. Organizations that offer opportunities for

mobility, for example, through job matching systems, without providing the necessary developmental support (e.g., training, coaching), put their employees at risk by letting them evolve towards business domains for which they do not have the necessary competencies or background. Organizations who invest in development without linking this to a career perspective might lose the talent in which they have invested because employees might compensate for the lack of opportunities in the internal labor market by a search for opportunities in the external labor market. To sum up, as depicted in Figure 6.1, career discussions with line management and/or HR are at the core of career counseling. Career workshops, external counseling, self-analysis tools, and the like, support the individual preparation of the discussion. The outcome of the formal appraisal is a personal development plan. As the formal career discussion is integrated as a component of this review, career counseling and performance management cannot be seen as separate HR practices. This means that career counseling does not involve an isolated activity. Moreover, these career discussions are integrated with a broad range of career management practices. Assessment tools are introduced into our integrative model both in preparation of and in addition to formal career reviews. Initiatives within the scope of job matching and development are essential to turn the career review outcomes into concrete actions. Finally, in order for career counseling to enhance and support employees' career development in ways that fit the organization's strategic objectives, a total reward system is needed that supports career moves that do not involve a step on the hierarchical ladder. For instance, skill- and knowledge-based pay systems are needed in order to make lateral movements more rewarding and acceptable.

Parties Involved

As it might have become clear from the previous paragraphs, the responsibility for career counseling is shared by three parties: employee, line manager, and the HR department. Regarding the employee, there is a clear consensus emerging from the career literature that employees are expected to take responsibility for their own career development. A variety of ways in which the organization can promote self-responsibility and encourage initiative exist, ranging from single, narrative injections in socialization programs that are free of engagement, to signing a deal that makes explicit both the employer's and the employee's responsibilities and obligations with regard to career management. It is obvious that the latter is more effective and stimulating.

The *line manager* plays a major role in the implementation of career counseling. The advantages of having line managers act as career counselors are many. Since their relationship with the employee is very close, they can stay in touch with the employee's development and career aspirations, and they are in the best position to have an accurate perception of individual performance and potential. Furthermore, the frequent interaction between employee and manager allows informal career discussions to become a regular feature of career counseling. Finally, line managers have adequate information about the opportunities in the organization, which helps to avoid unrealistic expectations and undeliverable promises.

However, among these same strengths, several weaknesses are situated, which should be addressed if an organization wants to ensure the effectiveness of the career counseling process. First, employees may be reluctant to be completely open with their manager and may avoid revealing their long-term aspirations for fear of seeming uncommitted. Managers, on their behalf, often feel uneasy about engaging in career discussions that may need to dig deep into personal matters, since they often do not have the skills to talk about complicated career issues. A key success factor of career counseling within organizations is hence the involvement and training of line management in supporting employees in identifying their career goals, strengths, and weaknesses. Whereas many organizations formally acknowledge this need, in practice the ability of line management to do so often remains the weak spot in the system. In addition, the term 'training' has many overtones. Many companies restrict these trainings to a general education in holding performance and career development reviews, whereas true career guidance goes far beyond that, in terms of in-depth support in self-reflection and analysis.

Time is a second problem when putting line managers in the role of career counselor. In reality, career discussions between line manager and employee are often constrained by day-to-day demands and work pressures. Line managers often perceive career counseling as a distraction from running their business, and informal career discussions are skipped because of lack of time. In operational environments, this problem can be solved by giving resources to cover the absence of both first-line supervisor and operator. Another way to stimulate management commitment for their responsibility as career counselor is to include managers' ability to provide career counseling as a criterion in their own performance evaluation. To make this work, managers' objectives need to reflect this responsibility, their performance appraisals need to deal with it, and management training needs to equip them with the right skills to be able to do it. This again implies a strong integration of career counseling with other HRM domains, including leadership development.

Finally, we elaborate on the responsibility of the HR function, which is twofold. First, HR needs to put in place systems and processes, and provide managers as well as employees with access to relevant sources like career workshops, development centers, training, and external coaching. Second, HR serves as a point of contact for both line managers and employees. Regarding the former, the role of HR is one of actively supporting line managers in their role of career counselor. In particular, this means equipping managers with the right skills, training them to use tools like personal development plans or self-analysis questionnaires in an appropriate way, and providing them with the necessary information on development and progression opportunities within the organization.

As far as employees are concerned, they can also turn to HR or the talent manager for discussing career issues, either on the advice of the direct supervisor or not. For instance, when the line manager lacks the skills or information required to answer the employee's career question, he or she may refer the employee to HR. On the other hand, employees can also bypass their direct supervisor and directly address HR themselves. Reasons for doing so might be a lack of trust between employee and supervisor or reluctance or inability on behalf of the employee to be completely open to the manager.

To conclude, career counseling involves a three-way partnership between employee, line manager, and HR professional. The key relationship is between employee and manager, assisted by HR as a facilitator and backup.

IMPACT OF ORGANIZATIONAL CHARACTERISTICS ON DESIRED CAREER MOBILITY

A final aspect that should be mentioned in the discussion about mobility is the impact of the organization-specific context, such as its strategic direction, size, structure, and industry. These types of characteristics affect the type and scope of career mobility that can be realized, as well as the need for investing in career mobility as a vehicle to enhance knowledge management.

First, an organization's decision about whether to encourage mobility and in which directions should be closely linked with corporate strategy. An organization's strategic direction, including choices regarding globalization, delocalization, restructuring, or downsizing, affects the structure and hence the opportunities for mobility in the internal labor market. For instance, globalization might lead to a stronger need for international mobility to support knowledge sharing across borders. Moreover, external conditions might play a role, such as the impact of economic growth versus decline. Stimulating mobility for enhancing knowledge sharing might be a good option in times of economic growth, but might become too expensive in times of restructuring or economic downturn.

With regard to the organization's size, its implications for both the need for knowledge sharing and the available opportunities for mobility are clear. The larger an organization is, the more knowledge management might become strategically important, and the more opportunities for both vertical and horizontal movements can be offered. In smaller organizations, internal mobility might not be the most valid type of initiative to be included in knowledge management. Depending on the organizational size, career counseling should focus more or less on mobility options versus options for job enrichment and the opportunities for strengthening the linkages throughout the (small) organization based on informal and formal project work.

Within flat organizations, stimulating horizontal mobility might not only be a means for stimulating knowledge management, but it can also compensate for the lack of vertical opportunities. For organizations working within a functional structure, however, the extent to which career mobility is needed will strongly depend on the strategy for developing specialists as opposed to generalists. A functional structure that builds on the specialization of employees might at the same time raise the need for knowledge management but risk creating too many generalists. This requires the organization to think carefully about opportunities for mobility that are in line with the need for specialization. Examples are international mobility or mobility within the field of expertise but across business units, or part-time involvement in cross-functional projects. Here, defining what type of mobility is strategically relevant might require an answer that is strongly dependent on the organization's size and activity range.

Finally, the industry in which an organization operates affects the opportunities for mobility. For instance, a high-tech organization might be forced to buy state-of-the art knowledge by hiring external recruits, thereby limiting the opportunities for horizontal mobility. Involvement in project work might be a valid option here to provide expert employees with a perspective and at the same time enhance knowledge sharing.

In turn these strategic and morphologic characteristics of an organization impact the focus of career discussions to be held during the career counseling process, as well as its outcomes in terms of development and mobility.

CONCLUSION

In an economic era that requires organizations to be constantly on the lookout for improvements to remain competitive, knowledge management is crucial to ensure the efficiency of strategy realization. In this context, providing employees with opportunities for internal mobility can be an effective way to stimulate knowledge sharing directly and indirectly, the latter by preventing employees (and hence the knowledge they have built) from leaving the organization due to a lack of career perspective. At the same time, however, in order to be successful in this challenge, organizations need a talent management approach that integrates different HR systems and processes and that actively involves employees in the management of their own careers. In this chapter, we have introduced career counseling as a vehicle to realize this. This chapter went beyond a one-sided focus on career counseling as a separate type of career management practice by both exploring how career management practices are internally consistent and aligned with one another, and looking at career counseling in conjunction with other HR practices.

Our research about the process of career counseling within organizations reveals that its core is situated in the formal, often yearly appraisal or development review taking place between a manager and an employee, complemented with informal career discussions with manager or discussions with an HR professional (see Figure 6.1). These core career counseling practices are open to all staff. In the periphery of career counseling we found, on the one hand, instruments that support employees in self-analysis of career expectations and abilities, like career workshops, self-help questionnaires, external counseling, and development centers. On the other hand, we link career counseling to job matching and development practices, which should facilitate the concrete implementation of personal development plans. Contrary to what constitutes the core of career counseling, peripheral practices are often not available to all staff, but depend on the target group. For instance, in many companies, external career counseling or development centers are reserved for the higher management levels or high potentials.

Key success factors for an effective career counseling process are the buy-in and the competencies of management to support employees properly in outlining their careers; the quality and follow-up of personal development plans; the active encouragement of individual initiative; and the alignment of development initiatives with career perspectives. From HR, this requires active initiatives for motivating line management and providing them with sufficient support in order to play their role of career counselor properly.

As far as the role of the employee is concerned, organizations should be cautious about relying on their employees. Career counseling practices that leave the initiative to the employee, such as informal career discussions with managers or HR, run the risk of not being used at all, and might create a gap between those (often ambitious and high-potential) employees actively managing their career and those that take a passive stance. If, for the latter group, line managers fail to address properly the issue of career development in the formal review, a great majority of (non-proactive) employees is at risk of being forgotten, with negative implications for their employability in the long run. For this reason, organizations must be cautious about building their career counseling system solely on individual initiative. The value of the career counseling model presented in this chapter lies in offering concrete ways to promote proactive behavior. We can conclude that in the current career landscape, where responsibility for career management is shared by employee and employer, organizations are going to need to dedicate more resources to career counseling in order to upgrade the quality of the guidance and to widen its access to all employees, with a final view to achieving the best fit between individual and organizational needs.

REFERENCES

Arthur, M.B., Inkson, K., and Pringle, J.K. (1999). *The New Careers: Individual Action and Economic Change*. London: Sage.

Arthur, M.B., Khapova, S.N., and Wilderom, C.P.M. (2005). Career success in a boundaryless career world. *Journal of Organizational Behavior*, **26**(2): 177–202.

Baruch, Y. (1999). Integrated career systems for the 2000s. *International Journal of Manpower*, **20**(7): 432–457.

Baruch, Y. (2004a). *Managing Careers. Theory and Practice*. London: Pearson Education.

Baruch, Y. (2004b). Transforming careers: From linear to multidirectional career paths. Individual and organizational perspectives. *Career Development International*, **9**(1): 58–73.

Baruch, Y. and Peiperl, M.A. (2000). Career management practices: an empirical survey and implications. *Human Resource Management*, **39**(4): 347–366.

Bollen, A., Christiaens, J., De Vos, A., Forrier, A., Sels, L., and Soens, N. (2006). Loopbaanbegeleiding in bedrijfscontext. De rol van organisatie, individu en overheid. [Career counseling within organizations: The role of the organization, the individual and the government]. Research report. Gent: Vlerick Leuven Gent Management School.

Currie, G., Tempest, S., and Starkey, K. (2006). New careers for old? Organizational and individual responses to changing boundaries. *International Journal of Human Resource Management*, **17**(4): 755–774.

Eby, L.T., Butts, M., and Lockwood, A. (2003). Predictors of success in the era of the boundaryless career. *Journal of Organizational Behavior*, **24**(6): 689–708.

Feldman, D.C. and Ng, T.W.H. (2007). Careers: Mobility, embeddedness, and success. *Journal of Management*, **33**(3): 350–377.

Garavan, T.N. and Coolahan, M. (1996). Career mobility in organizations: Implications for career development—Part 1. *Journal of European Industrial Training*, **20**(4): 30–40.

Gutteridge, T.G., Leibowitz, Z.B., and Shore, J.E. (1993a). *Organizational Career Development. Benchmarks for Building a World-class Workforce*. San Francisco: Jossey-Bass Publishers.

Gutteridge, T.G., Leibowitz, Z.B., and Shore, J.E. (1993b). A new look at organizational career development. *Human Resource Planning*, **16**(2): 71–84.

Hall, D.T. (2002). *Careers In and Out of Organizations*. Thousand Oaks, CA: Sage Publications.

Hallier, J. and Butts, S. (1999). Employers' discovery of training: Self-development, employability and the rhetoric of partnership. *Employee Relations*, **21**(20/21): 80–94.

Hsu, M.K., Jiang, J.J., Klein, G., and Tang, Z. (2003). Perceived career incentives and intent to leave. *Information & Management*, **40**(5): 361–369.

Kaye, B. and Farren, G. (1996). Up is not the only way. *Training & Development*, **50**(2): 48–53.

Kossek, E.E., Roberts, K., Fisher, S., and Demarr, B. (1998). Career self-management: A quasi-experimental assessment of the effects of a training intervention. *Personnel Psychology*, **51**(4): 935–962.

Noe, R.A. (1996). Is career management related to employee development and performance? *Journal of Organizational Behavior*, **17**(2): 119–133.

Orpen, C. (1994). The effects of organizational and individual career management on career success. *International Journal of Manpower*, **15**(1): 27–37.

Peiperl, M., Arthur, M., Goffee, R., and Morris, T. (2000). *Career Frontiers: New Conceptions of Working Lives*. Oxford: Oxford University Press.

Rothwell, W.J., Jackson, R.D., Knight, S.C., and Lindholm, J.E. (2005). *Career Planning and Succession Management*. Westport: Praeger.

Schein, E.H. (1978). *Career Dynamics*. Reading: Addison Wesley.

Steel, R.P., Griffeth, R.W., and Hom, P.W. (2002). Practical retention policy for the practical manager. *Academy of Management Executive*, **18**(2): 149–169.

Sturges, J., Guest, D., and Mackenzie, D.K. (2000). Who's in charge? Graduates' attitudes to and experiences of career management and their relationship with organizational commitment. *European Journal of Work and Organizational Psychology*, **9**(3): 351–370.

Sturges, J., Guest, D., Conway, N., and Mackenzie Davey, K. (2002). A longitudinal study of the relationship between career management and organizational commitment among graduates in the first ten years at work. *Journal of Organizational Behavior*, **23**(6): 731–748.

Sullivan, S.E. (1999). The changing nature of careers: A review and research agenda. *Journal of Management*, **25**(3): 457–484.

Tremblay, M. and Roger, A. (2004). Career plateauing reactions: The moderating role of job scope, role ambiguity and participating among Canadian managers. *International Journal of Human Resource Management*, **15**(6): 996–1017.

Verbruggen, M., Forrier, A., Sels, L., and Vandenbrande, T. (2005). Marktonderzoek naar de vraag naar loopbaanbegeleiding in Vlaanderen [Market research about the demand for career counseling in Flanders]. Research Report. Leuven: KULeuven, Department of Applied Economic Sciences.

7. Accelerated development of organizational talent

Konstantin Korotov

Organizations in many parts of the world are experimenting with ways to speed up the development of their management and employee talent in order to respond to current and anticipated pressures from the market-place. They aim to equip organizational members with the skills, knowledge, attitudes, and behavioral patterns necessary for success in future roles and tasks. Those future roles and tasks are perceived to be more challenging and important than the ones currently held by the accelerated development program incumbents. At the same time, preparation for the next steps in one's career is combined with the expectation of ongoing success in one's current position. Stepping up to the next level is contingent upon doing extremely well in the current role, (over-)achieving the targets set, and demonstrating readiness for the next challenge. Accelerated development may also take place as part of the organization's succession management efforts. In preparation for an expected promotion of an executive, knowledge needs to be transferred to his or her potential replacement, and the latter needs support in preparation for the new job. Thus, in effective accelerated development and broader succession planning and implementation efforts we can see an essential link between talent management and knowledge management.

Following Abel (2005), the challenge of a person going through a high-speed developmental journey in modern organizations is in the dual requirement of being excellent in the current job while preparing to take a significantly more challenging responsibility ahead. A person put on some kind of an accelerated program, at the time of being nominated for it, is often judged based on his or her professional and/or managerial potential and the degree of fit with the role ahead. However, while undergoing the developmental effort, he or she is most likely to be judged simultaneously on current successes and failures, and will be constantly reassessed in terms of the fit for the future expected position. The challenge for the organization is to make sure that individuals are supported in their current jobs and in preparation for the new roles. In a clear fusion of talent and knowledge management, these organizations need to manage transfer of knowledge within the talent pool in the most effective and efficient way.

The meaning of the word 'accelerated' is that such development takes place at a pace that is significantly faster than that of 'traditional' development that allows an individual to learn the intricacies of the current job, observe incumbents in a higher-level position (usually, one level up), practice elements of the boss's job when being delegated tasks, undergo formal training, or benefit from the knowledge accumulated by others and codified in the knowledge management systems. Accelerated development means, contrary to the usual, more traditional developmental path, bypassing traditionally expected career steps, learning opportunities stretched over a longer period of time, and/or age-related developmental progression. Accelerated development is a necessity for organizations facing unprecedented growth, lack of qualified individuals in the internal or external labor markets, and significant pressures from other organizations that are ready to 'poach' talented executives and employees and offer them even higher levels of responsibility and remuneration. Organizations also respond with accelerated development initiatives to the individuals engaged in career entrepreneurship, that is, those who make alternative career investments in order to enjoy quicker returns in terms of career growth and progression (Korotov & Khapova, 2007).

A recent discussion with a leader responsible for the lifelong learning and development of Europe-based partners in a global professional services firm has underscored the accelerated talent growth challenge faced by this organization and its direct competitors. In talking about challenges of managing partner development across many countries, she mentioned that in some markets where this global firm operates, partners in the national leadership positions are in their late fifties, which is a traditional age to make it to the top at a national level in that type of organization, while in a number of markets, particularly those that are characterized by dynamism and unprecedented growth, national practice leaders nowadays often get to that level in their mid- to late thirties (the age when in 'traditional' economies people are often only considered to be put up for a partnership vote). If people rise to the top significantly earlier, and if their respective organizations encourage (or are forced to tolerate) such quick rises, there is simply no time for a traditional, 'slow' career development path and growth time. In another professional services organization, a competitor of the firm mentioned above, a partner responsible for talent development commented, for example, that his organization needed to find new ways of growing and developing partner candidates and young partners, as some of them made partner in their late twenties! Many of them started to work early, when still in college, and, given the professional opportunities of quickly growing markets, they managed to gain success and quick career progression very early. The young age of the partners, however, made the organization face new and previously unknown challenges about personal maturity of the young partners, the issues of wisdom, client relationships, and so forth.

In a different setting, leaders of a global FMCG (fast-moving consumer goods) company were concerned that their Asia-Pacific operations continued to depend heavily on the expatriate pool generated in Europe or North America to run its business in the region. The company's leadership established it as a target to increase significantly the number of local nationals in the top-tier regional management positions within a short period of time. The leadership team defined the time as two years. The challenges faced by the organization (and, by extension, the executives in the human resources and learning and development functions) were twofold: on the one hand, to truly equip candidates for the top positions with the competencies necessary for success; on the other, to convince the rest of the organization, including top decision-makers worldwide, that the local talent was ready for the job. In addition, it was considered necessary to make sure that the regional talent also saw themselves as capable of taking over the top leadership jobs in the region and succeed in them.

Learning and development at a pace that is faster than usual is not completely new to organizations. Quite a few companies have long been experimenting with so-called 'fast-track' or 'high-flyer' development programs for specially selected cohorts of fresh college graduates or newly-minted MBAs. Incumbents in such programs would typically be recruited with a specific expectation that they would reach management positions in a shorter period of time than would be the norm for non-fast-track people. During a usually two-year-long program these management trainees would be put through a series of rotations through different organizational functions and/or geographical locations, to enable them to master various managerial competencies. It appears that with programs like these, some modern organizations are responding to the growing number of young people who are looking for accelerated development opportunities and want to bypass traditional career steps and do not want to take a traditional path to their career development. For example, in various countries, Unilever, for the past 40 years, has run a special accelerated development program—Unilever Graduate Recruitment and Development Program (UGRDP). Recently, Unilever Russia put on its website information about Maxim Popov, the youngest of the participants in such a program. At the time of writing this chapter, Maxim was only 20 years old. However, in two year's time, after going through an accelerated learning and development program involving rotation through different organizational functions and locations, he was expected to become a manager in one of Unilever's operations in Russia or in Europe (www.unilever.ru/ ourcompany/careers/Work_for_graduates/UGRDP2006.asp [in Russian]).

Companies that have formally structured opportunities for accelerated development of young candidates for managerial positions, usually pay very careful attention to the selection of participants in such programs, design structured training programs, ensure on-the-job exposure of incumbents to important organizational issues and opportunities to work with experienced mentors, manage rotation through various job posts and geographical positions, and, eventually, ensure a careful placement of program graduates in their first independent 'post-developmental' management roles.

Programs for high-flying graduates and their challenges have received attention in organizational literature. Larsen (1996; 1997), for example, asserts that such programs, in their traditional format, often end up being a tool for participants' individual career development and fail to respond to the strategic needs of the organization. Kovach (1986) discusses potential negative outcomes for graduates of high-flyer programs who may learn behaviors that are conducive to success at early stages in their careers, but which are potentially detrimental as they move to executive positions. Viney, Adamson, & Doherty (1997) stress that, initially, high-flyer programs were seen as pure learning opportunities for their incumbents with no expectation from the latter to contribute in a significant manner to the organization's results. With increasing competition, however, in many organizations those arrangements changed: companies started to expect business results from their management trainees relatively early on, leading to the paradox of having to cope successfully with tasks that are still being learned.

Larsen (1996) calls for a link between career, organizational development, and competitive advantage of organizations. The accelerated development programs should not be restricted to initiatives for quicker advancement of fresh graduates but should look to a broader pool of management talent. Companies, as mentioned above, use accelerated development programs as ways of coping with market pressures. They look at various cohorts of managers, and not just newcomers. Importantly, there is not just transfer of knowledge to the incumbents; the latter also have to transfer their knowledge to other people in the organization. Such programs often involve a component that deals with helping the incumbent develop his or her subordinates or prepare a successor before they can move to the next position.

It should also be noted that the opportunities and challenges of accelerated development of talent are not only important for organizations that are developing elite candidates for the management ranks; they are also important when considering developmental opportunities for rank-and-file employees who need to be prepared for changing requirements of the marketplace or evolving needs of clientele. For example, Kets de Vries et al. (2004) describe entrepreneurial efforts of new business leaders in Russia. A founder of a consulting company engaged in the field of enterprise resource planning (ERP) systems was initially forced to hire her employees among university students, as she couldn't afford to pay people who had already completed their degrees. Although the student-employees had sufficient technical knowledge (as they were coming from very good technology-oriented schools), they completely lacked business acumen, social skills necessary for dealing with clients (and co-workers), and even an under-standing of their own personal or career development. With the expansion of what became a very successful business, increased complexity of con-sulting activities, growing sophistication of clients, and a bigger emphasis on the bottom-line results, the organization's founder had to start thinking about quickly developing her existing staff to meet the competencies short-age challenges. Ironically, coming from a purely scientific background, she herself had to learn quickly about management and leadership, and about how to support the development of others. It should be noted, however, that in the majority of cases organizations are referring to preparation of people for higher levels of management and leadership responsibilities when they talk about accelerated development.

Methods of accelerated development differ significantly from company to company and country to country. For instance, in Russia's Gazprom, one of the world's largest and most successful corporations, about 1200 university graduates begin their careers every year. Their socialization into the company and their whole development process in very many cases starts with a blue-collar position, where newcomers with five or six years of uni-versity studies behind them do work that typically requires only a couple of months of on-the-job training. If successful in one of the blue-collar posi-tions, employees may be selected for white-collar jobs and later for further growth and development opportunities managed through the corporate university (Shevelkova, 2007). British American Tobacco has traditional high-flyer programs for university graduates and, at the same time, accel-erated growth programs for managers, where the focus is on executive com-petencies and leadership skills (Taylor, 2006). Ernst & Young, in some markets, has programs for partners that are geared at equipping them with the competencies needed to manage their respective practices and become leaders among very successful partners.

DEVELOPING A NEW IDENTITY THROUGH ACCELERATED DEVELOPMENT PROGRAMS

A critical issue in the process of accelerated development is not just a set of skills or knowledge that a participant in such a program has to master, but also the development of a new identity, a new sense of self that is claimed by the person him- or herself, and that is supported by the organization and people around the individual. Preparing for a new role (e.g., that of a manager instead of an individual contributor, that of a partner instead of an employee, or that of a national business leader instead of a top manager) has been shown to require a significant change in one's professional identity (e.g., Hill, 1992). Kovach (1986) notices that failure to manage transitions and learn how to deal with the changing expectations of the organization as one moves to the next career level often leads to derailment of fast-track employees.

New levels of responsibility, being in charge of other people, stepping into the shoes typically reserved for more 'mature' people, requires certain changes in one's view of oneself. Thus, accelerated development programs, if they are to prepare people for a new role that requires a new identity, need to create opportunities and provide support and resources for crafting this new sense of self that is associated with the new role. When working on a new identity, as suggested by Ibarra (2003; 2004), individuals need to start doing new things, start developing new networks, and start telling a new story about themselves.

Starting Doing New Things

While doing one's job today, participants in accelerated development initiatives in organizations have to learn the intricacies of their future job. They have to cope with today's responsibilities and simultaneously be successful in taking on pieces of work that are not typical for their current organizational position and level of responsibility. To be truly developmental and to contribute to the necessary perception by the organization of the manager going through accelerated development as a successful process, such projects need to be closely tied to the real business needs of the organization, and they need to be highly visible to organizational members. Organizations and their leaders (and not just HR professionals) need to identify real projects or processes that bring with them important opportunities for the organization. The projects or work on processes need to have a powerful sponsor at the top of the organization who is interested in the success of the project and people involved in its implementation, and who has the time and energy to spend with the members of the project team (many or all of whom may be involved in the accelerated development program). In order to succeed in both their current job and the new project, participants on the accelerated track need to have enough time and other resources and visible support, including ongoing mentorship from committed experienced leaders.

The projects need to be perceived as important not only by the organizational leadership, but also by other managers and often even the rank-and-file employees in the organization. If the accelerated development program reaches its goals, its participants will eventually gain higher-level positions quicker than normally expected by the organizational members. These executives must be able to claim their psychological right to such a position. In their turn, managers and employees need to 'accept' the person who has received his or her promotion by the means of accelerated development as a legitimate incumbent in the new position in order for him or her to be successful in the new role. In Bartel & Dutton's view (2001), new identity has to be claimed by the individual and granted by people in his or her surroundings, which requires identity work from all those involved.

In addition to the project work, participants in accelerated development programs have to demonstrate that they are doing new things in their daily interactions with colleagues. For example, they are expected to delegate more of their tasks to subordinates, give them more feedback and coaching, while simultaneously clearing more time for themselves in order to engage in new activities. Obviously, this is easier said than done. Managers on the accelerated track usually need support in learning to delegate tasks to their employees and guide them through their work without micromanagement. Such support involves formal training in delegation skills, introduction to coaching techniques for managers, and mentoring from more experienced colleagues or help from an executive coach.

With an increased move in the direction of knowledge work, designing and developing accelerated development programs needs to take into account the specifics of today's knowledge workers. Davenport (2005) defines knowledge workers as individuals with high degrees of education, experience, or expertise involved in jobs that create, distribute, or apply knowledge. One of the first fundamental features of knowledge work is its lower propensity to being structured, thus leading to a need for higher autonomy of the employee engaged in such work. Autonomy is particularly important in the way the work is organized, how people work towards their targets. Such a feature of knowledge work may become a particular difficulty for both people undergoing accelerated development and those around them. On the one hand, people on the accelerated track may be 'clinging' to their field of expertise or the competencies that they have developed and displaying those they feel confident and comfortable with. On the other, individuals around them may not easily accept the move of the incumbents into new territories. Organizations also need to make sure that the knowledge that is required for the incumbent's current role gets passed on to those who will take over when the person under development moves on; there is a need to capture his or her current knowledge and pass it to other people. At the same time, there is also a need to identify the patterns of behaviour that the incumbent needs to 'unlearn,' or to stop relying on, that are no longer appropriate when the move to the next level is made.

Those on the accelerated track need to delegate tasks and transfer knowledge to their subordinates, and simultaneously they also need to be delegated new responsibilities and be given new opportunities. This requires readiness from the people above and around the talented manager or employee. Top executives need to be ready to share responsibility and accountability, resources (including the knowledge accumulated in their position), contacts, and so on, with the incumbents of accelerated development programs. Davenport (ibid.) argues, however, that for knowledge workers, sharing is unnatural, especially today when there is an ever-increasing fear of competition from all quarters, and individuals on the accelerated track may be perceived as explicit competitors. Thus, in companies that use, for example, fast-track graduate development schemes, there may be open or subtle resistance on the part of the employees to share their knowledge with the trainees who could eventually become their bosses without a long-term organizational tenure. As expressed by an HR executive, sometimes the trainees are at fault: they create the impression of an air of superiority due to 'having been selected,' and, as a result, fail to gain cooperation and support from the people who have the necessary knowledge that needs to be shared. This concern about the negative side of the elitist nature of high-flyer programs is also documented in the literature (see, for example, Larsen, 1997). Obviously, working on the right attitude comes as part and parcel of the overall accelerated development approach. Gaining cooperation from the organizational members and learning how to elicit knowledge from the people who have it thus becomes a critical competence on the way to acquiring skills and competencies for the higher-level job.

Developing New Networks

Following Ibarra (2003; 2004), a new identity requires a new network—a new circle of professional and sometimes social contacts that will allow a participant in an accelerated development program to establish a new sense of self and gain confirmation of the acceptance of this new sense of self from colleagues and clients. An accelerated development effort, therefore, should include opportunities for meeting new people and learning to establish a new set of relationships at a different, usually higher level in the organization and its surroundings.

For an incumbent in an accelerated development program to be successful in the development of the new network, again, time, resources, and commitment from mentors or program sponsors are necessary. One of the critical resources is the desire of the person above the incumbent (e.g., his or her boss, mentor, program sponsor, etc.) to offer him or her access to their own networks, introduce them to new people, communicate the expectations the organization has of that particular individual, and so forth. New contacts and relationships involve higher-level management, executives from a different part of the organization (e.g., from another country's operations or global headquarters), clients, suppliers, government contacts, professional bodies or industry associations, academics, journalists, and so on.

An introduction to a new network, however, is not sufficient. The incumbent needs to learn to use the network productively: to contribute to the well-being and success of the others involved in order to be able to rely on the contacts when needed. As people vary in their abilities to establish relationships, additional support may need to be provided to the incumbents. This support can be in the form of training, mentoring, or coaching. Sometimes, sharing with the incumbent the mentor's experience in developing professional networks serves as a powerful motivational input for the incumbents of accelerated development programs. At times, support from a more experienced and established mentor or sponsor is necessary in order to help others accept the incumbent as a worthy addition to one's network. Kets de Vries et al. (2004) describe how a talented and competent, but young (in his early twenties) consultant from a new generation of Russians faced the challenge of non-acceptance from a 'traditional' Soviet-type director who would simply refuse to talk to him and demand the presence of the General Director of the consulting company to discuss the issues that the consultant was perfectly competent in.

Developing a New Story about Self

Ibarra (2003; 2004) and Ibarra & Lineback (2005) suggest that making a transition to a new identity is not possible without having developed a new story about oneself. What and who a person is, gets communicated to self and the people around through the narratives developed by people taking on a new identity. The narrative about oneself is accepted by the protagonist and then transmitted to the organizational members and other stakeholders in the accelerated development process. In order for the message to be effective, the protagonist, obviously, has to believe in the logic of the new story about him- or herself. Development of such a story may take time, as normally the sense of who we are develops with the experiences, reflections, dramas, and successes we go through over the years. The challenges in the accelerated development program are to make sure that this story, developed over a significantly shorter period of time, has enough substance in it to be credible, and is structured in such a way that the 'audiences' of the story accept the expected wealth of experience, skills, competencies, and so forth as legitimate despite the time constraints in developing them.

Working out a new story about self (e.g., that of a manager, and not a fresh university graduate; a leader of a professional services practice, and not a tax expert; a manager of managers, and not a manager of a team, etc.) often requires a push and enough support. Usually, it involves iterations of trying and getting feedback, and then trying and getting feedback again and again. Obviously, for such an interactive process a relatively safe environment and qualified feedback-providers, guides, and helping 'ears' may be required.

The tasks listed above are not for the faint of heart. Given the challenge of doing one's current job and being successful in it, while simultaneously preparing for a new one, and showing consistent progress and signs of success, may be daunting. Among those who are selected for accelerated development programs there are often those who Kets de Vries (2005) calls sufferers of the 'impostor syndrome,' 'fake syndrome,' or insecure over-achievers. People suffering from impostor syndrome are often driven by a fear that at a certain moment the organization is going to recognize that they are not as good as they seem to be. Usually, accelerated development programs attract a lot of attention from people at different levels in the organization. Under such increased scrutiny, the challenge of dealing with impostor syndrome becomes even more acute. As a result, the insecure overachievers impose extremely high demands on themselves and others, and sometimes overstretch themselves and the people around them. It is important, then, that as a result of the accelerated program, participants have a realistic view of themselves, a positive outlook on their competencies, and readiness to accept whatever limitations they may have. The learning aspect of a development program suggests that people make mistakes as they do new things, establish new networks, or tell new stories about themselves. Organizations need to be prepared to let some of the mistakes happen without the drastic consequences for the incumbent of an accelerated development program. However, as mentioned in an official description of such a program in a global company, participants are constantly under observation and constantly judged with respect to how well they meet the organization's expectations.

The issue of understanding (and sometimes accepting) one's limitations is equally important for the roles the incumbents prepare themselves for. One of the ways of avoiding potential disappointment associated with the new roles (which for quite some time probably seem to be an important objective for the incumbents) is through realistic job previews (Wanous, 1992). Although future positions may look attractive to an organizational member, he or she should also be aware of the challenges associated with the new job. For example, leadership positions in general have been shown to carry with them a number of psychological burdens. Thus, people who have made it to a position of significant responsibility often face the burden of loneliness of command, fear of envy, the 'what now?' syndrome, being constantly under scrutiny, feelings of personal guilt, an ever-steeper learning curve, and so on (Kets de Vries et al., 2007). As part of the accelerated development, individuals getting ready for these roles need to learn how to prepare for facing the situations (and their own feelings about the situations) that they are not yet familiar with. The principle of realistic job previews is based on the idea that people receive accurate information about their future role(s) that covers both the sources of satisfaction and dissatisfaction for role incumbents. Getting realistic information about the future role helps employees make a better decision about accepting the opportunity, and serves as a form of inoculation against future dissatisfaction. Besides, Wanous (1992) suggests that realistic job previews serve as mechanisms of anticipatory socialization and help individuals develop coping mechanisms, which eventually contribute to success on the job.

Realistic job previews can be viewed as a way of transferring knowledge about what the job really entails in order to increase the effectiveness of the future incumbent when he or she moves into a new position. Obviously, despite the generic attempts of codifying such knowledge (e.g., the above-mentioned challenges of becoming a leader in general (Kets de Vries et al., 2007)), the bulk of the knowledge remains organization- and position-specific. The transfer of such knowledge is then possible only through specific intra-organizational efforts. One of the ways is the mentoring of incumbents by more experienced organizational members. Similarly, knowledge about organizational politics, social networks, interaction patterns, and personal likes and dislikes gets transferred either through informal channels or mentoring efforts, requiring special effort and readiness from both the mentor and his or her protégé.

ACCELERATED DEVELOPMENT PROGRAMS AS IDENTITY LABORATORIES

All of the above considerations suggest that an accelerated development program is a multifaceted undertaking on the part of the organization with clear implications for a solid commitment to effective knowledge management. An accelerated development program effort also requires various skills and inputs from all the people involved: the incumbents, program organizers, sponsors, mentors, and others. Moreover, an accelerated development program has multiple learning outcomes that go beyond the more or less obvious functional knowledge and skills and understanding of how the organization functions. These learning outcomes include, but are not limited to, the following elements:

- ability to learn new identities;
- ability to deal with impostor syndrome (Kets de Vries, 2005);
- realistic job preview and sense of the reality of the roles ahead;
- ability to experiment and cope with both success and disappointment and failure;
- development and management of new networks;
- design of a new 'story' about self and the people around;
- acceptance of the incumbent in his or her new role by the organization.

All the above suggest that in order to be successful, an accelerated development effort has to lead to a transformation of its participants and their emergence with a new identity within the organization. But how can organizations create opportunities and conditions for such transformations? Recently there has been a renewal of interest in the potential offered by the psychodynamic concept of transitional space (Winnicott, 1953) and the anthropological concept of liminality (from the Latin word *limen* meaning 'threshold') (van Gennep, 1909) in exploring ways of how people achieve personal and professional transformation.

In one model of the identity transition process associated with radical career change (Ibarra, 2003; 2004), for example, there is special room given to liminal experiences and transitional phenomena. Liminal (in-between) experiences are traditionally characterized by a feeling of being between identities, being suspended, being in no-man's-land, and the awkwardness of being in the middle (Ebaugh, 1988; Ashforth, 2001). Nevertheless, regardless of their possible negative aspects, such experiences are also thought to give motivation and opportunities for people to imagine new alternatives to their current situation, with failure to do so often being the biggest stumbling block on the road to personal and professional transformation (Ibarra, 2004). Transitional phenomena (i.e., phenomena similar to transitional objects in their functions (Winnicott, 1953)) are conceptualized to provide resources and conditions for people to put identities into play (in other words, opening existing identities up to change and trying out new possible selves). Recent literature on transitions draws researchers' and practitioners' attention to the concept of transitional spaces, or special privileged areas that are set apart from mainstream activities and have a legitimate status as a place for experimentation and creativity (Amado & Ambrose, 2001; Ibarra, 2004; Korotov, 2005; 2006).

Transitional spaces create opportunities for play and experimentation, help the people inside them overcome change-related anxieties, offer novelty that gives an extra boost to desire for changing the self, impose certain rules and structures that are counter-normative to what exists in the world beyond the transitional space, set psychological, temporal, and spatial boundaries, and offer a menu of guiding figures to people inside the space. All these elements together create the potential for identity experimentation and renewal. There have been specific indications in literature and in practitioners' work that adult education and development programs can create spaces conducive to identity exploration and experimentation and provide elements of transitional space and liminal experiences (Ibarra, 2003; 2004; Korotov, 2005; 2006; Kets de Vries, 2006; Kets de Vries & Korotov, 2007).

To be successful, an accelerated development program has to have elements of an identity laboratory, because, as mentioned above, it is expected to lead to a change in one's identity in quite a short period of time. Identity laboratories can be conceptualized as special transitional environments demarcated temporarily, spatially, and psychologically from the rest of the identity-granting world. They provide the conditions for practicing elements of the new identity in a safe environment within the laboratory boundaries, and at the same time take some of the experimental outcomes into the real world of work and life. The laboratory is 'equipped' with identity exploration and experimentation opportunities, guiding figures or facilitators, and tools, such as transitional objects that participants need to learn to use to go through the laboratory productively. An identity laboratory environment is suitable for people who are in a liminal stage in their identity change process, that is, 'neither here nor there' (Ebaugh, 1988): in the process of disengaging from the old identity without having fully left it, and in the process of developing a new one, without yet having fully embraced it. The above-mentioned duality of the position of the person in an accelerated development program (e.g., being both under observation for success in the current role and constant assessment of the fitness for the future role) makes it safe to say that an incumbent of such a program is in a 'neither here nor there' position. More exactly, he or she is actually both 'here and there,' in the present and in the future.

To truly turn their accelerated development program into identity laboratories, organizations need to take into account that participants need to learn to benefit from the opportunities of experimenting with a new sense of self. Previous research (Korotov, 2005; 2006; Kets de Vries, 2006; Kets de Vries & Korotov, 2007; Kets de Vries et al., 2007) suggest that an identity laboratory experience usually has a number of important elements in it. These elements include pre-entry experience, initial surprise of getting into the accelerated program's environment and learning to use it, engaging in identity exploration through examining past and present identities, staging identity experiments, and, finally, stepping out of the program into the real world.

Pre-entry Experience

Before admittance to the accelerated programs, participants usually engage in a heavy dose of assessments and competition, or, as a minimum, discussions with their mentors or bosses. Officially designed to assess the fit between a candidate and the future role requirements these pre-program activities per se trigger some of the initial learning that will later grow to a full-fledged dimension as the program unfolds. The selection process reveals some of the elements of the future roles and the accelerated development path and triggers potential participants' curiosity about themselves and their future. The selection activities can serve as sampling of the unusual nature of the developmental path and as a rule-setting mechanism, the start of individual psychological contracts and commitments to future actions such as readiness to engage in the accelerated development program at cognitive, behavioral, and emotional levels required for a true identity transformation (Kets de Vries & Korotov, 2007).

The pre-entry experience, apparently, is important for accelerated talent development programs in order to contribute to the formation of the incumbents' expectations and fantasies about their forthcoming learning and experimentation experience, including the initial feeling of psychological safety of experimenting during the program. It also gives participants a preview of what is going to lie ahead of them in the program, as well as the rules in the program. As shown by research on transformational executive programs, participants' learning often starts before their official start in the program, namely, during the selection and preparation stages (ibid.).

Surprise and Learning to Use the Space of the Accelerated Talent Development Program

Despite the development of preliminary expectations, the actual initial program experience frequently turns out to be different from both the expectations and any kind of previous developmental experience participants have had. The beginning of the program normally brings about surprise (cf. Louis, 1980). Major dimensions of surprise are about the experimental nature of the program and opportunities and challenges that are perceived to be opened by it, as well as the need to explore and engage in one's own identity transformation process. The programs and the developmental assignments often make people realize that their organizations consist of people who should be viewed 'not as rational agents, as passive functionaries, as economic beings or as cogs on a machine, but as distinct individuals, with emotional and fantasy lives, with histories and pasts, diverse emotions and developing identities' (Gabriel & Carr, 2002: 354–355).

After realizing the novelty, unusualness of their situation of being put on an accelerated development path, which per se is a factor conducive to identity experimentation (Yost, Strube, & Bailey, 1992), participants need to learn how to use this new environment. Organizational members engaged in the accelerated development program need to master:

- managing the boundaries of transitional space of the program;
- identifying resources and instruments available to them and learning to use them;
- figuring out the rules of behavior, given their fast-track status, and the limits of those rules.

Organizations may provide incumbents with a lot of resources and opportunities, as well as establish expectations and rules of behavior. However, participants may not necessarily be familiar with those. Besides, many of the instruments provided by accelerated development programs require learning to use them. Thus, working with mentors or coaches, often a new experience for participants, demands learning what can be expected from such an opportunity and how best to use it. In line with the above, Lombardo & Eichinger (2000) suggest that participants in such programs need to be effective learners. Success of an accelerated talent development program may require special efforts in helping participants learn how to use the program in the best possible way.

Identity Exploration: Examining Past, Current, and Future Identities

An important part of the participants' experience in accelerated talent development programs is self-exploration, which happens both through structured activities included in the program by design, as well as through individuals' exposure to new tasks, roles, networks, and opportunities. People also engage in identity exploration through the overall process of being in an unusual group, going through new types of work activities, getting external and internal feedback (cf. Ibarra, 1999; 2003), self-reflection, and interactions with other members of the class. The self-exploration process, if we truly expect development of a new identity in participants of the accelerated program, needs to be built into the program as one of its core elements.

The process of exploration often becomes a multidimensional journey, as various aspects of identities, beyond the professional ones, become salient and become intertwined in the process. Participants also get a chance to compare their current view of self with that expected in their future possible role and to assess internally the fit and possible developmental routes. Identity exploration opportunities may come up in various forms during an accelerated development program: assessments and self-assessments, work with mentors and coaches, engagement in group discussions and debriefing or developmental experiences, self-reflection, interviews with incumbents of higher-level roles, and so on. Based on our knowledge of transformational programs for experienced executives (e.g., Kets de Vries & Korotov, 2007), identity exploration opportunities are often viewed as premium features of an executive course. Such opportunities should be promoted and included in accelerated development program philosophy and design.

Identity Experimentation

Participants engage in identity experimentation both through mental experiments, where they are trying to see themselves in a new role or with a new identity or identities, and in more tangible activities associated with experimenting with new possible identities. An important feature accompanying experiments staged by participants in the program is the perceived psychological safety of engaging in such experimentation. A lot of experimenting requires preliminary discussions and getting 'permission' to experiment from the guiding figures, the role of whom is primarily vested with the program sponsors and participants' mentors. Although at certain points other participants may become able to play the roles of sounding boards, advisors, and peer coaches, in many cases endorsement for identity experimentation should come from the mentors who guide the participant through the accelerated program.

Experimentation in the course of an accelerated development program involves both professional and personal aspects. It often includes playing with options unthinkable or unimaginable before the program, such as moving into a new functional field or living in a new geographical location. As one of the outcomes of the program should be the placement of the incumbent into a role that best fits his or her talents and interests as well as organizational needs, the accelerated development effort should provide the program incumbent with the opportunities to try to estimate the potential fit with the new identity and discuss it with the organization.

Stepping Out of the Executive Program

The ending of the accelerated development program means a certain turning point for both the participants and the organization. The end result is the perceived readiness for taking the new role, demonstrated through results achieved in the process of work during the program (doing new things), a set of new contacts and relationships (new networks), and a new view of self communicated to organizational stakeholders (new story).

The program should terminate with another important feature—realization of the importance of the process that the participants have been subjected to for their continuous development in the future. An important take-away from the program, a learning outcome, should be the ability to keep developing oneself, keep looking for new opportunities for self, one's team, and the organization. Hall (2002) calls this a metacompetency of identity learning. Such a metacompetency becomes the foundation for the future growth and development of the talented individual for personal success and the success of his or her organization.

CONCLUDING REMARKS

New roles require new identities associated with them. Preparing talented individuals for the new tasks in an accelerated fashion often requires people to develop a new view of themselves significantly ahead of the 'normal' course of one's life and career development. Taking into account this challenge means that the designers of the accelerated programs need to focus not only (and maybe not so much) on the technical aspects of the new roles (e.g., professional skills and knowledge), but also on what it takes to be ready to succeed in the new role, to be accepted as a legitimate incumbent in the role, to be able to view oneself as someone who enjoys the role, and who wants to be productive and successful in it. This valuable new role information represents a critical content form for knowledge management processes, and again demonstrates the vital link of comprehensive knowledge management in effective talent management.

REFERENCES

Abel, D. (2005). Leadership education as a moving target. *International Journal of Leadership Education*, 1(1), 9–21.

Amado, G. and Ambrose, A. (2001). *The Transitional Approach to Change*. London: Karnac.

Ashforth, B.E. (2001). *Role Transitions in Organizational Life: An Identity-based Perspective*. Mahwah, NJ and London: LEA Publishers.

Bartel, C. and Dutton, J. (2001). Ambiguous Organizational Memberships: Constructing Organizational Identities in Interactions with Others. In Hogg, M. and Terry, D. (eds) *Social Identity Processes in Organizational Contexts*. Philadelphia, PA: Psychology Press, 115–130.

Davenport, T. (2005). *Thinking for a Living: How to Get Better Performance and Results from Knowledge Workers*. Boston, MA: Harvard Business School Press.

Ebaugh, H.R.F. (1988). *Becoming an Ex: The Process of Role Exit*. Chicago: The University of Chicago Press.

Gabriel, Y. and Carr, A. (2002). Organizations, management, and psychoanalysis: An overview. *Journal of Managerial Psychology*, 17(5): 348–365.

Hall, D.T. (2002). *Careers In and Out of Organizations*. Thousand Oaks, CA, London, and New Delhi: Sage.

Hill, L. (1992). *Becoming a Manager*. Boston, MA: Harvard Business School Press.

Ibarra, H. (1999). Provisional selves: Experimenting with image and identity in professional adaptation. *Administrative Science Quarterly*, 44(4), 764–792.

Ibarra, H. (2003). *Working Identity: Unconventional Strategies for Reinventing Your Career*. Boston, MA: Harvard Business School Press.

Ibarra, H. (2004). Identity Transitions, Possible Selves, Liminality, and the Dynamic of Career Change. INSEAD Working Paper 2004/98/OB.

Ibarra, H. and Lineback, K. (2005). What's your story? *Harvard Business Review*, 83(1): 65–71.

Kets de Vries, M. (2005). The dangers of feeling like a fake. *Harvard Business Review*, 83(9): 108–116.

Kets de Vries, M. (2006). *The Leader on the Couch: A Clinical Approach to Changing People and Organizations*. Chichester: John Wiley & Sons.

Kets de Vries, M. and Korotov, K. (2007). Creating transformational executive education programs. *Academy of Management Learning and Education*, 6(3): 375–387.

Kets de Vries, M., Korotov, K. and Florent-Treacy, E. (eds) (2007). *Coach and Couch: The Psychology of Making Better Leaders*. Houndmills and New York: Palgrave.

Kets de Vries, M., Shekshnia, S., Korotov, K. and Florent-Treacy, E. (2004). *The New Russian Business Leaders*. Cheltenham, UK and Northampton, MA: Edward Elgar.

Korotov, K. (2005). Identity Laboratories. INSEAD PhD Dissertation.

Korotov, K. (2006). Identity Laboratories: The Process of Going through an Executive Program. In Weaver, M. (ed.) 2006 Academy of Management Annual Meeting Best Paper Proceedings, 11–16 August, 2006, Atlanta, GA, ISSN: 1543–8643.

Korotov, K. and Khapova, S. (2007). Career Entrepreneurship. Paper presented at the 23rd European Group for Organizational Studies Colloquium. Vienna, Austria, 5–7 July, 2007.

Kovach, B. (1986). The derailment of fast-track managers. *Organizational Dynamics*, 15(2): 41–48.

Larsen, H. (1996). In search of management development in Europe: From self-fulfilling prophecies to organizational competence. *The International Journal of Human Resource Management*, 7(3): 657–676.

Larsen, H. (1997). Do high-flyer programs facilitate organizational learning? From individual skills building to development of organizational competence. *Journal of European Industrial Training*, 21(9): 310–317.

Lombardo, M. and Eichinger, R. (2000). High potentials as high learners. *Human Resource Management*, **39**(4): 321–330.

Louis, M.R. (1980). Surprise and sense making: What newcomers experience in entering unfamiliar organizational settings. *Administrative Science Quarterly*, **25**(2): 226–251.

Shevelkova, O. (2007). Vverkh Po Trube (Up the Pipe) [Electronic Version]. *SmartMoney Russia*, **14**. Retrieved 26 April 2007 from http://www.smoney.ru/article.shtml?2007/04/16/2730 (in Russian).

Taylor, J. (2006). Predvidet, Vovlekat, Vdoknovlyat, Focusirovat (To foresee, involve, inspire, and focus). *Harvard Business Review Russia*, August, 20–21 (in Russian).

van Gennep, A. (1909). *The Rites of Passage*. Chicago: University of Chicago Press.

Viney, C., Adamson, S. and Doherty, N. (1997). Paradoxes of fast-track career management. *Personnel Review*, **26**(3): 174–186.

Wanous, J.P. (1992). *Organizational Entry: Recruitment, Selection, Orientation, and Socialization of Newcomers*. Reading, MA: Addison-Wesley.

Winnicott, D. (1953). Transitional objects and transitional phenomena. *International Journal of Psycho-Analysis*, **34**(1953): 89–97.

Yost, J., Strube, M. and Bailey, J. (1992). The construction of the self: An evolutionary view. *Current Psychology*, **11**(2): 110–121.

PART 3

Performance management

8. Reward and recognition concepts that support talent and knowledge management initiatives

Nancy A. Inskeep and Bettie Hall

In 1900, over 96% of the world's population performed manual labor and lived within populated areas of less than 100 000 people. Then, the average work lifespan was 25 years. By the end of the century, only 25% of the world's working population performed manual labor, child labor was curtailed in most developed societies, and 50% of the world's population lived in cities with populations over 100 000. To support these changes, the average work lifespan rose to 50 years (Drucker, 1996). By 2007, people are now aware that they will probably work up to or past that 50-year milestone. How do you make working attractive when even people in well-paying jobs want to leave them? How do you attract, retain, motivate, recognize, and reward a diverse workforce that is geographically scattered and working in the electronically connected e-world? One answer is to provide sincere, valued, and well-managed reward and recognition (R&R) programs that attract and retain talented individuals, develop and share their knowledge, and motivate them to continue specific behaviors and actions.

THE ORGANIZATIONAL NEED FOR R&R PROGRAMS

Well-defined and supported talent and knowledge management programs are strategic imperatives for success in today's global business environment. Products do not get developed, customers do not get served, sales do not get signed, and accounting does not collect revenues unless someone somewhere has used their talent on behalf of the organization. Organizations regardless of size now operate on a global basis by accessing labor, markets, and suppliers throughout the world. All governments, societies, and organizations are vying for these limited resources and face similar challenges. Common labor challenges involve aging populations, unqualified job candidates, immigration and emigration controls, outsourcing and offshoring (Jamrog, 2004; Favell, Feldblum, & Smith, 2007; Lavenex, 2007). Both consumer and business markets are now global in nature, with regulations and commoditization continuously changing and impacting operations. Sources and channels of supplies are constantly being assessed to provide the best solution for the organization based on a myriad of factors such as strategic partnerships. The issues surrounding labor, markets, and suppliers are often interrelated, as with the rising popularity of diaspora networks that connect immigrant workers back to their established or ancestral homelands, often coordinating business opportunities and organizing supply and distribution channels between their home and adopted lands (Whiting, 2006; Zhang, 2006).

R&R programs need to be defined to support the organization's mission and strategic objectives, yet flexible enough to provide real meaning and value to its workforce regardless of that workforce's location. People can no longer assume that they will have a stable work location and be physically near everyone with whom they need to interact to accomplish their work successfully. Managers within the organization may find themselves supervising personnel across time zones, borders, or continents. Employees may find themselves reporting to someone that they have never met and with whom they can only establish a virtual relationship (Hildebrand, 2007). R&R programs need to recognize these disparate situations and deliver not only the appropriate rewards and recognitions, but also mechanisms that communicate the program's features, functions, and choices (Human Resource Institute, 2004).

Organizations need the right person with the right skills at the right place performing the right actions at the right time. Ideally, organizations want to manage strategically across the globe, yet appreciate and implement on a local basis. To this end, organizations are beginning to define the 'global talent' that leads its 'global workforce,' where global talent consists of highly skilled people who prefer to work outside their home countries, manage the organization's local workforce at a global location, and nurture that local workforce and its potential leaders. Thus, global talent specializes in establishing and guiding the organization's international business, while the global workforce is charged with managing that business within their home country (Zingheim & Schuster, 2001).

Talent management (TM) is a core business practice that identifies, acquires, and retains the skill sets that are necessary to achieve the organization's business objectives. A successful organization must have a solid foundation of labor, be it a few people or thousands. TM programs oversee the human capital of the business enterprise, balancing the decision of who among the labor base is worthy of the organization's time, effort, and investment against the realities of keeping that labor base engaged and motivated enough to attach itself to and remain with the organization.

An organization's human capital holds that organization's knowledge assets within its collective mind and determines the competitiveness, innovativeness, and survival of that organization. Knowledge management (KM) programs are designed to capture, document, and communicate that organizational knowledge. A solid KM program establishes a shared infrastructure for the collection and assessment of current knowledge, the enhancements that arise from expanding that knowledge, and the building of new creative constructs that link known elements of information and experience with the uncertainty of thoughts and concepts. Robust TM and KM programs that motivate the workforce provide a competitive advantage to that organization and are strong foundational elements of the R&R structure.

THEORIES OF MOTIVATION FOR TALENT AND KNOWLEDGE MANAGEMENT WITHIN R&R PROGRAMS

A formal R&R program enables organizations to attract, develop, and retain talented employees. It consists of monetary rewards, non-monetary rewards, and organized processes surrounding the circumstances under which such rewards are distributed (Armstrong, 2002). A formal rewards system reveals a belief structure about why people engage in work and what they should be able to expect as a result of their work activities in a given organization. While this belief structure cannot be easily quantified, it can and does emerge in behaviors that can be observed, documented, and analyzed (Frey & Osterloh, 2001). It can and does also emerge in the organization's established processes and the systems that actuate these processes. Because beliefs about what work is and why people do it can vary among cultures and continents, planning a global R&R program that is relevant and meaningful to all employees is no easy task. It requires basic understanding of the knowledge accumulated over the years about what motivates people to come to work, to develop expertise, and to become and stay productive.

What people view as a reward or incentive is grounded in their individual values, beliefs, and attitudes (Eisenberger et al., 1997; Dulebohn & Martocchio, 1998; Green, 2000). These underlying qualitative influences often subvert attempts to objectively capture, quantify, and systematically represent any sort of incentive program that will meet with unanimous approval and support. Recognizing the existence and influence of these hidden influences and understanding the emotions that can invade or erupt during the formulation of incentive plans is necessary to create a formal R&R program that can be successful across many different kinds of boundaries, both geographical and cultural. To gain that understanding, it is useful to review the basic theories that provide the basis for R&R programs.

Founding Theories

One of the more recognizable motivation theories in the Western world is Abraham Maslow's 'Hierarchy of Needs.' This theory categorizes human needs into levels, beginning with lower-level, physiological needs such as the requirement for water and safety, and progressing upwards through higher-level, intellectual needs such as self-actualization. The theory argues that these needs drive people to work and engage in comparable social activities and that people must satisfy lower-level needs before they can move on to satisfy higher-order ones (Maslow, 1943). This theory provided the foundation for numerous subsequent scholars of human behavior and motivation such as Clayton Alderfer.

Alderfer extended Maslow's theory by postulating that people could and did have more than one level of need operating at any given time and that there was no orderly progression through levels of need. His 'Existence-Relatedness-Growth' (ERG) needs theory categorizes people's needs as existence, relatedness to others, and personal growth. Using this theory, focusing on just one area of need would not suffice in motivating workers (Alderfer, 1969). Instead, people could derive numerous satisfactions from their work all at once, and thus rewarding them would involve recognizing multiple avenues of motivation.

While these theories were generally applicable to human behavior, David McClelland's 'Acquired Needs Theory' examined human motivation in relation specifically to work. People are not born with, but acquire reasons for working, according to McClelland. These reasons could be classified as achievement, affiliation, and power. The need for achievement might manifest itself in a person trying to improve a process or to master a complex skill. The need for affiliation could be observed in an employee's desire to work cooperatively with others, while the need for power might be detected through a person's desire to control or influence others. The theory acknowledged that people are not motivated by needs alone, but also by such factors as values, habits, and skills (McClelland, 1962).

Frederick Herzberg's 'Two Factor Theory' classified motivation into motivational and hygiene factors. Hygiene factors relate to the work environment, such as wages and office layout, and do not necessarily encourage anyone to perform better; rather, they are utilized to maintain performance and retain talent. Motivational factors, on the other hand, increase a person's satisfaction with their employment and can lead to greater productivity. Such factors include public recognition, formal advancement, or added responsibility. Herzberg argued that none of these factors were operating in isolation, but in combination with each other such that a kind of balancing act could be achieved to encourage and retain top performance (Herzberg, Mausner, & Snyderman, 1959).

Douglas McGregor's 'X/Y Theory' presented an entirely different kind of proposition. This theory presents management as either authoritarian or participative. The authoritarian relies on rewards and punishments to control employees because people do not really enjoy working and must therefore be made to do so. The participatory manager assumes that people enjoy working, seek responsibility, and want to excel at their jobs. The two views can be used as a scale to determine which is the more dominant in an organization (McGregor, 1960).

William Ouchi's 'Theory Z,' which can be viewed as a mixture of Japanese and US management, proposes that organizations do best when they offer their workers stable employment combined with collective decision-making, individual accountability with informal control, and incentive systems that involve not only the employees but also their families and communities (Ouchi, 1981).

Victor Vroom's 'Expectancy Theory' argues that employee performance is determined by such variables as an individual's personality, experience, skills, and abilities. Expectancy theory incorporates three key concepts: valence, expectancy, and instrumentality. Valence is the level of desire a person has for a reward. Expectancy is the confidence a person has regarding what is achievable. Instrumentality refers to a person's belief that a desired outcome will actually result from the achievement of performance, which relies on a high degree of trust between the organization and its workforce (Vroom, 1964).

Finally, Robert House's 'Goal-setting Theory' focuses on managers as the critical factors in motivating workers. To attract, retain, and motivate top achievers, managers must be clear, consistent, and reliable in communicating how, when, and to what extent the achievement of goals will be rewarded. Managers are also responsible for removing contextual obstacles to achievement, such as personality conflicts within a team and office politics. This theory incorporates four types of behaviors a manager can offer employees to either encourage or inhibit the achievement of goals: directive, supportive, participative, or achievement-oriented (House, 1971).

Using R&R Concepts to Motivate Individuals and Teams

Many of the common theories regarding motivating a workforce are founded in common sense and have generated practical advice as to how individuals and teams can be motivated to achieve their greatest potential. There is an old saying that if you look for the bad in a person, then you will surely find it; the same holds true when looking for weaknesses in an employee. What makes a leader great is to recognize, address, and change a weakness into a strength. Walters (2001) identified common and practical techniques for nurturing and motivating individuals, while Grazier (1998) identified common characteristics of teams that display high levels of motivation (see lists below). Both practitioners relied on the application of incentive and recognition concepts:

Individuals

Techniques for nurturing and motivating individuals (Walters, 2001) include the following:

- Provide positive recognition and feedback to the person in a well-considered, specific, illustrative, and behavior-based manner that will reinforce that recognized behavior.
- Identify a person's skills and qualities and then recognize and apply them as a new strength; for example, a highly detail-oriented person might make an excellent project manager.
- Ask the person what they like to do and why, then provide opportunities for those types of activities.
- Gather feedback and thoughts from the person's co-workers using a formal 360° assessment, or by informally sharing within the business environment positive compliments, kudos, or thank-you messages about that person.
- Look back regarding why you hired this person, then determine how to tap into those skills and qualities.
- Enable the person to learn more about other roles and positions through shadowing, coaching, mentoring, or interning programs.
- Reassess what you perceive as a weakness by looking at the function or process that the weakness is currently supporting; for example, if a person has uninteresting writing but excellent proofing skills, then that person may be an excellent quality control or testing associate.

Teams

Techniques for nurturing and motivating teams (Grazier: 1998) include the following:

- Recognize that the needs for sustenance, safety, security, belonging, recognition, growth and achievement are motivational drivers.
- Understand the factors that influence an individual's decision to become a voluntary and active team member such as the team's purpose, membership, and management.
- Realize that motivation will only occur if the individual's wants and needs are aligned with the team's wants and needs.

- Assess what the individual defines as a challenge such as the level of difficulty, a positive learning curve, or learning a new skill.
- Establish opportunities to socialize and fraternize with team members that will not only motivate individuals, but will also create new communication channels, positive reinforcement among peers and mutual support.
- Expose the team to controlled or managed situations dealing with negative people, difficult circumstances, operational problems, or outright disasters or errors.
- Provide the team with both authority and responsibility.
- Support the team members' efforts to enhance their skills and qualities.
- Identify the team's comfort zone, both as a team and individually and encourage the team members to grow outside of these parameters.
- Create opportunities for the team and its members to display their leadership skills.

THE IMPACT OF MOTIVATION ON R&R PROGRAM DEVELOPMENT AND MODELS

Globalization places new demands on R&R programs to ensure consistency across organizational, cultural, and value and belief system boundaries. What is a reward to one group may not constitute a reward for another. Numerous internal factors affect how individuals can be motivated. These factors are dependent not only on culture, context, attitudes, and beliefs, but also on past experience, personality traits, personal preferences, work history, and life events. External factors can also affect motivation, such as reinforcements, rewards, feedback received, career expectations, job status, and seniority, as well as the employee's age, education, income bracket and level of responsibility. How an individual defines a reward as being valuable is very personal, and this valuation is not always apparent to external view. The costs of not adequately rewarding an organization's talent include high turnover, low productivity, missed deadlines, absenteeism, disruptive office politics, low quality, poor customer service, and theft or pilferage. Since these costs may be hidden, they are often attributed to other factors. Lawler (2005) found that a lack of job security and career path negatively impact motivation. However, organizations can no longer promise lifelong employment, secured retirement plans, and standardized career paths. Long-term relationships built upon trust, loyalty, and mutually implied promises of support have been replaced with transaction-based relationships that rely on the mutual exchange of services for value-perceived benefits and rewards.

Organizations build reward, recognition, and incentive plans utilizing varying levels of compensation, perquisites or 'perks,' and benefits. The process involves understanding the organization's strategic plans and goals, identifying the desired skills and competencies needed to achieve those strategic initiatives, and clarifying which of the skills and competencies are available within the organization's resources and which are not. To align the organization's goals with its human capital requires that those goals be well defined and measurable, clearly communicated, and able to identify and reinforce the desired behaviors and actions that should be recognized and rewarded. A basic tenet is to link pay to performance. However, egalitarian pay systems are still commonplace and do not relate pay to performance, economics, or some other objective criteria (Baker, Jensen, & Murphy, 1988). Instead R&R elements of compensation, perks, and benefits are often standardized within pay ranges, incentives are scaled to promotion or management levels, and poor performances are not addressed. The lists below present several innovative models that illustrate a holistic approach to R&R planning by offering monetary and non-monetary elements that provide meaning and value to the workforce:

Traditional Compensation Packages

Compensation packages for non-executives include pay in the forms of wages and salaries, as well as benefits (George, 2002):

- health benefits of various types of insurance and disability coverage;
- some type of personal or self-funding retirement account match;
- education and training;
- stock purchase plans;
- company-paid communications for one's residence;
- professional certification reimbursement;
- stock options;
- club or organizational memberships such as health clubs or professional associations;
- company car or car allowances;
- mass transit travel reimbursements;
- parking reimbursements;
- vacation options such as buying additional or selling unneeded days;
- leave options such as sabbaticals or family leaves;
- day care or day-care subsidies, for both one's elders and one's offspring.

Executive Compensation Packages

These packages are intensely negotiated remuneration agreements that yield all manner of rewards (Bebchuk & Fried, 2006; Conyon, 2006):

- signing bonus, known as the 'golden hello';
- goodbye payments, known as a 'golden parachute,' that may result from one's voluntary or involuntary separation;
- annual base salary;
- annual bonus plan that is linked to achieving financial objectives;
- stock options, which are a right to purchase corporate stock for a designated price (called the 'strike price') at a designated time in the future with the expectation that 'ownership' of the organization will reinforce the executive's interest in performing;
- restricted stock, which are outright grants of stock that vest at some future date;
- long-term incentive plans, which are essentially employment contract bonuses that are granted if the executive commits to a long-term relationship with the organization;
- general benefits that may include retirement plans, medical coverage, low- or no-interest mortgages or loans, and practically anything else that can be named and agreed upon by the executive and the board negotiating the employment agreement.

Flexible Compensation

In addition to basic compensation, organizations may offer some flexible elements, or flexible compensation (Hoffman, 1999):

- commissions for referred or inside sales;
- flexible work schedules;
- flexible work locations such as choosing among available on-site locations;
- telecommuting or remote access, where one works off-site;
- time off for community service;
- job sharing, where two or more people share a full-time position;
- paid leave banks, where one receives a total number of paid days off per year to use as one sees fit in accordance to the needs of the business;
- professional development opportunities such as certification programs;
- career planning and counseling;
- internal promotion and advancement;
- phased retirement such as offering staggered work periods or reduced schedules;

- casual dress;
- clothing such as spirit or logo wear.

Perks

Some organizations are able to schedule group events or provide access to organizational assets and vendor agreements, or perks (Caggiano, 1997):

- access to organizational real estate such as meeting and vacation facilities;
- access to organizational licenses such as parking facilities, sports arena boxes, or theater seats;
- access to organizational agreements that pass pricing economies on to the workers such as travel agencies, car rentals, office supplies, and motor vehicle parts and service;
- discounted or free products and services made by the organization;
- subsidized or free cafeteria, vending, or other food and beverage services;
- on-site restaurants or food delivery arrangements;
- on-site access to professionals such as doctors, dentists, barbers, or cosmetologists;
- concierge services such as dry cleaning, shopping, and car detailing services;
- regularly scheduled afternoon breaks with food such as tea time or cookies and milk;
- afternoon events such as golf outings or movie matinees.

Informal Recognition

Informal recognition (Nelson, 1999) may include the following:

- Take a walk and personally say 'thank you.'
- Call the person and say 'thank you.'
- Write a handwritten note that says 'thank you'; it is more personal than e-mail.
- Join in and help when people are in need.
- Give a person a break when they need one; have them take a walk, take them out for coffee; do anything that breaks the cycle and allows the person some respite.
- Provide a change of pace and opportunity by inviting the person to an activity or on to a project that would interest them.
- Establish a method of visibly recognizing jobs well done, such as e-mail announcements explaining the who, what, and why of the job, and

immediately follow this up with an informal gathering or announce-ment of food placed in some central location as a 'thank you.'

- Use humor, if appropriate, for good performance: king for a day, queen for the week, or recipient of the magic wand for making the customer problem disappear.
- Forward all positive communications about a worker to that worker and their supervisor such as customer kudos, written notes or e-mails, or verbal comments.
- Sometimes a worker receives a compliment from a customer, but the worker did not follow the expected process or procedure that man-agement expects to be followed; under these circumstances let the worker know that the customer was satisfied but explain to the worker that the correct procedure should be followed in the future.
- Praise in public; criticize in private; never criticize or reprimand a worker in front of a group.

Formal Recognition

Formal recognition (Grazier, 1995; Wong, 1998; Henneman, 2005) may include the following:

- Begin by identifying the problem or issue that you are trying to address.
- Identify the undesired actions, behaviors, and perhaps attitudes that cause or reinforce the problem or issue.
- Identify the desired actions, behaviors, and attitudes that will resolve or mitigate the problem or issue.
- Ensure that the management infrastructure is in place to support a 'positive' program; you want to align the recognition program with the management culture and strategic initiatives.
- Specify your expectations in terms of results: what do you want to happen?
- Build a development team that reflects a cross-section of the organ-ization and establishes credibility for the program and its efforts.
- Design a reward structure based on how the workers value certain rewards, such as cash versus non-cash; hold focus groups or use other mechanisms to elicit information that will help rate, rank, and value potential awards.
- Establish the recognition or nomination methodology defining how you will know that someone acted in a manner that deserves recognition.
- Develop specific criteria as to what actions and performance will be rewarded: the act, the circumstances, the recipients as individuals or

as teams, the timing in relation to the act, the ceremony or lack thereof, and the scheduling of rewards in terms of being planned or spontaneous.

- Brand the program to solidify what the program is and what it will do.
- Communicate the development of the program throughout the process.
- Support, assess, and revise the program once it is in production.
- Ensure that the program is used by eliciting nominations and examples of the desired actions and behaviors; be generous in a moderate way.
- Allow flexibility that supports the program's purpose: to reward and to recognize.
- Understand that recognition is often a balancing act of rewarding those who are worthy without making the reward process itself commonplace and meaningless.
- Understand and appreciate the nature of the reward's recipient; for instance, if the person is shy, present the reward to that person alone or in his or her immediate work group, not the entire department.
- Be tactful and use good judgment; for instance, if a group of 30 people was involved in the activity, reward all 30 with a nominal or less expensive award, and perhaps provide a verbal or less expensive recognition to key team members, but do not award only those key team members when the entire team contributed to the effort.

Special Considerations

Special considerations for recognizing international or global workforces (Speizer, 2005) may include the following:

- Recognize if managing international R&R programs is not your core competency.
- Know what is and is not valued, symbolic, or discussed within the society and culture of the workers such as death or illness.
- Understand the challenges of not only implementing a global program, but also supporting it, as with logistics, taxes, tariffs, and crossing international borders.
- Understand the cost-of-living and economic differences among your workforce; something as simple as a bicycle may be just recreation for one worker versus a major quality of life change by providing transportation to another.
- R&R programs should be tailored to the workforce's location to be effective and appreciated; rewards that are disproportionate to the locale may be misunderstood and embarrassing.

- The most common international awards are money, gifts, and travel.
- Outsource or contract for an online R&R program that operates in multiple languages, uses catalogs that are targeted at specific cultures, and relies on local fulfillment.

PLAN GLOBALLY, IMPLEMENT LOCALLY

Leaders in charge of devising an R&R program for a global organization cannot know what motivates each employee. Leaders can, however, begin building their approach on solid business and motivational principles, create open communication channels for feedback and recommendations from the organization's constituents, and refine and use the knowledge gleaned from their endeavors. Perhaps the most challenging part of building an R&R program that has TM as a key goal and which builds on the knowledge assets of the organization is integrating that program with the global strategic plans. The overarching strategic plans are centrally defined and developed by key leadership yet must be understandable and relevant to local workforces. It is a constant balancing act to plan globally and implement locally.

Local workers need to believe that they have a real opportunity to influence and to grow within the global organization. To this end, the local workers will provide their talents and share their knowledge. The foundation of any successful R&R program is to acknowledge sincerely and respectfully the workforce's contributions to the organization's ongoing existence and success. The burden is on human resources professionals and the organization's leadership to work closely with local management and employee representatives to determine what attitudes, behaviors, performances, and skills contribute to the organization's achievements and success. Management must take the time to establish strong relationships with its workers and use the knowledge gained from these associations to design, implement, and continually improve its R&R, TM, and KM programs.

CONCLUSIONS

The knowledge that comprises a knowledge-based system for an organization must contribute to performance support or improvement for it to have any value. This is not easy to accomplish for several reasons. It is often difficult to distinguish 'knowledge' from 'information.' Knowledge is shared, useful, reliable, valid, accessible, current, and useable, and building a repository of such knowledge is not a quick or easy task that can be assigned to a given department and forgotten. Knowledge is only as valid as the best available information at a given time, which can change constantly, requiring ongoing updates to any existing repository. Therefore, the culture of an organization needs to work with whatever technology is used to build, maintain, and appropriately share the knowledge. The rewards should be tied to performance, not title. Rewards that are tied to titles lead to entitlement, whereas rewards that are tied to performance should be available to everyone (Wilson, 2003). An organizational climate that provides rewards to human talent for sharing knowledge within the organization is as necessary as the technology selected to permit the storing and appropriate sharing of knowledge.

REFERENCES

Alderfer, C.P. (1969). An empirical test of a new theory of human need. *Organizational Behavior and Human Performance*, **4**(1969): 142–175.

Armstrong, M. (2002). *Employee Reward*. Trowbridge, Wiltshire: Cromwell Press.

Baker, G.P., Jensen, M.C., and Murphy, K.J. (1988). Compensation and incentives practice vs. theory. *Journal of Finance*, **47**(3): 593–616.

Bebchuk, L.A. and Fried, J.M. (2006). Pay without performance: Overview of the issues. *Academy of Management Perspectives*, **20**(1): 5–24.

Caggiano, C. (1997). Perks You Can Afford. Retrieved 15 January 2008, from http://www.inc.com/magazine/19971101/1359.html.

Conyon, M.J. (2006). Executive compensation and incentives. *Academy of Management Perspectives*, **20**(1): 25–44.

Drucker, P.F. (1996). The shape of things to come. *Leader to Leader*, **1**(Summer), 12–18. Retrieved 10 January 2008, from http://leadertoleader.org/knowledgecenter/journal.aspx?ArticleID=134.

Dulebohn, J.H. and Martocchio, J.J. (1998). Employee perceptions of the fairness of work group incentive pay plans. *Journal of Management*, **24**(4): 469–488.

Eisenberger, R., Cummings, J., Armeli, S., and Lynch, P. (1997). Perceived organizational support, discretionary treatment, and job satisfaction. *Journal of Applied Psychology*, **82**(5): 812–820.

Favell, A., Feldblum, M., and Smith M.P. (2007). The human face of global mobility: A research agenda, *Social Science and Modern Society*, **44**(2): 15–25.

Frey, B.S. and Osterloh, M. (eds) (2001). *Successful Management by Motivation: Balancing Intrinsic and Extrinsic Incentives*. Berlin/Heidelberg/New York: Springer.

George, T. (2002). Incentives Reward in Tough Times. Retrieved 15 January 2008, from http://www.informationweek.com/news/snowArticle.;html?articleID=6503562.

Grazier, P. (1995). Starving for Recognition: Understanding Recognition and the Seven Recognition Do's and Don'ts. Retrieved 15 January 2008, from http://www.teambuildinginc.com/article_recognition.htm.

Grazier, P. (1998). Team Motivation. Retrieved 24 August 2006, from http://www.isixsigma.com/offsite.asp?A=FrRUrl=http://www.teambuildinginc.com/article_teammotivation.htm.

Green, T. (2000). *Motivation Management: Fueling Performance by Discovering What People Believe About Themselves and Their Organizations*, Palo Alto, CA: Davis-Black Publishing.

Henneman, T. (2005). Recognition Do's and Don'ts: Eight Tips on Creating Effective Reward Programs. Retrieved 15 January 2008, from http://www.workforce.com/archive/feature/24/19/11/241916.php.

Herzberg, F., Mausner, B., and Snyderman, B.B. (1959). *The Motivation to Work* (2nd edition). New York: John Wiley & Sons.

Hildebrand, C. (2007). Cross-cultural collaboration. *PM Network*, **21**(3): 46–54.

Hoffman, R. (1999). It Takes More Than Pay to Keep Good Workers. Retrieved 15 January 2008, from http://www.inc.com/articles/1999/08/13723.html.

House, R.J. (1971). A path goal theory of leader effectiveness. *Administrative Science Quarterly*, **16**(3): 321–339.

Human Resource Institute (2004). The Future of Attracting, Retaining and Motivating Key Talent. Special Report from the Canadian Management Centre (CMC) by the Human Resource (HR) Institute presented September 2005.

Jamrog, J. (2004). The Perfect Storm: The Future of Retention and Engagement. Special Report from the Canadian Management Centre (CMC) by the Human Resource (HR) Institute presented September 2005.

Lavenex, S. (2007). The Competition State and Highly Skilled Migration. *Social Science and Modern Society*, **44**(2): 32–41.

Lawler E.E., III (2005). Creating high performance organizations. *Asia Pacific Journal of Human Resources*, **43**(1): 10–17.

Maslow, A.H. (1943). A theory of human motivation. *Psychological Review*, **50**(1943): 370–396.

McClelland, D. (1962). Business drive and national achievement. *Harvard Business Review*, **40**(4): 99–112.

McGregor, D. (1960). *The Human Side of Enterprise*, Columbus, Ohio: McGraw-Hill.

Nelson, B. (1999). Personalizing Recognition. Retrieved 15 January 2008, from http://www.inc.com/articles/1999/05/16635.html.

Ouchi, W.G. (1981). *Theory Z: How American Management Can Meet the Japanese Challenge*. Reading, MA: Addison-Wesley.

Speizer, I. (2005). Good Intentions, Lost in Translation. Retrieved 15 January 2008, from http://www.workforce.com/archive/feature/24/22/42/index.php.

Vroom, V.H. (1964). *Work and Motivation*. New York: John Wiley.

Walters, J. (2001). How to Uncover Employee Potential. Retrieved 10 January 2008, from http://www.inc.com/articles/2001/03/22371.html.

Whiting, S. (2006). Harnessing international brainpower. *Expatica HR*. Retrieved 9 March 2007 from http://www.expatica.com.

Wilson, T.B. (2003). *Innovative Reward Systems for the Changing Workplace* (2nd edition). New York: McGraw-Hill.

Wong, N. (1998). Tips for Creating and Maintaining an Informal Recognition Program. Retrieved 15 January 2008, from http://www.workforce.com/archive/feature/22/17/08/223428.php.

Zhang, K. (2006). Recognizing the Canadian Diaspora. Canada Asia, **41**(March). Retrieved 10 January 2007 from http://asiapacific.ca/analysis/pubs/pdfs/commentary/cac41.pdf.

Zingheim, P.K. and Schuster, J.R. (2001). How you pay is what you get. *Across the Board*, **38**(5): 41–44.

9. Talent management, performance management, and the management of organizational knowledge: the case for a congruent relationship

Patrick F. Schutz and Donald A. Carpenter

INTRODUCTION

The relationship between talent management (TM), performance management (PM), and knowledge management (KM) may be elusive and often confusing. Perhaps the reason for the confusion is because management practitioners in each of the three disciplines tend to become somewhat myopic in their areas of specialization. Managers spend countless hours attempting to determine how to improve their employees' performance— always seeking the kind of practice or system that may encourage workers toward higher levels of self-motivation and productivity. Talent managers, performance managers, and knowledge managers alike are primarily concerned with accomplishing their tasks within their own environments and time constraints. Understandably, managers tend to seek answers to *their* questions, *their* challenges; as a result they tend to work in parallel universes—within the same organization. Hence, the reason for continual seminars and innumerable symposia intended to bring the practitioners of the various disciplines together to gain knowledge and share their experiences in an attempt to advance the common comprehension of what works in management and what does not. More frequently however, talent managers, performance managers, and knowledge managers choose to attend meetings and seminars that are in their own respective fields, rather than spend their limited, scarce, and valuable time discussing and learning about the *potential* benefits that may be derived from the creation of congruent and synergistic connections between their disciplines. Yet, human resource managers, work supervisors, department heads, and executive officers from all functional areas of the organization seem to have a strong need to share their expertise as well as their challenges, problems, and solutions. A symbiotic connection exists whether or not managers are willing to admit it.

The creation of well-functioning, dynamic organizational cultures and distinct competitive advantages seem to demand that connection.

Specialists are even more separated from the opportunities to share and learn from people in other disciplines. Not surprisingly, specialists are inclined to be most comfortable and motivated when they are working on those things that interest them and with which they are most familiar. To illustrate the typical lack of communication and knowledge sharing between disciplines, quite often specialists from diverse fields within the organization have to be intentionally brought together for the purpose of lending their particular expertise in a group effort to solve some problem or to invent some creative product or innovative approach. Given the opportunity, many of us would choose to operate at a high level of performance—in our own area of specialization. So, it is not surprising that the relationship between talent management, performance management, and knowledge management can be elusive and occasionally confusing.

Nevertheless, a relationship does exist. As discussed in Chapter 2, which dealt with the broad function of HR planning, all three are related via the duty and responsibility of designing and implementing policies, procedures, and practices that are intended to enhance the inimitable competitive advantage gained by the organization through strategically directing the activities of its human resources. However, agreement among the players about the relationship between these three disciplines does not necessarily imply that there is widespread collaboration.

As we discussed earlier with regard to HR planning, TM serves as an essential cultural and philosophical foundation for high-performing organizations. TM is the universe within which PM and KM can operate most effectively and efficiently. PM and KM are both subsets of TM. However, none of the three systems will thrive and yield optimal organizational performance unless they are congruent and interconnected. If your assessment at this point is that this is merely a case for enhanced communication among departments and functions, you would be partially correct. It is more than that, however; it is communication by design. By designing a TM culture where both PM and KM become active participants in decision-making at all levels, all members of the organization are required to share pertinent information and seek workable and synergistic solutions, with the ultimate result being the accomplishment of the overall organizational goals and objectives.

The crux of this chapter is the manner in which this collaboration can be orchestrated. Research of current literature will be presented in reference to the three disciplines, and arguments will be presented in favor of the necessity of coordinated interaction between them. Some typical barriers to interaction and coordination among the three disciplines will be discussed. Finally, a case example will be presented to illustrate the value-added properties of such coordination by using the potential connection between KM and performance appraisal systems (a subset of performance management).

PERFORMANCE MANAGEMENT: AN ORGANIZATIONAL IMPERATIVE

According to our understanding, performance management is a subset of talent management. As discussed in a popular HRM text:

> Performance management consists of all organizational procedures that determine how well employees, teams, and ultimately, the organization performs. Every HR function contributes to this performance. The process includes HR planning, employee recruitment and selection, training and development, career planning and career development, and compensation. (Mondy & Noe, 2005: 252)

Den Hartog, Boselie, and Paauwe (2004) state that:

> clearly, the process of performance management involves managing employee efforts based on measured performance outcomes. Thus, determining what constitutes good performance and how the different aspects of high performance can be measured is critical to the design of an effective performance management process. (p. 556)

Kirchoff (2006) drew the following conclusions from the work of Blair and Cochran and Kaplan and Norton: 'In 1982, it was reported that 38% of value in organizations consisted mainly of intangible assets and 62% of tangible assets. In 2002, 80% of value in organizations consisted of intangible assets compared to 20% of the value from tangible assets' (p. 1). This dramatic change is somewhat the result of the emerging knowledge economy and perhaps somewhat the result of a growing awareness on the part of firms that their employees are their most important asset.

For further proof of this trend we need only witness the plethora of books, articles, training programs and seminars designed around TM, and the managing of the performance of that organizational talent. Often due to the unique and dynamic job descriptions that have evolved because of, or emerged as a result of, the new knowledge economy, employers recognize that their employees are largely responsible for their organizations' successes and/or failures. The attempt by companies to utilize their employees' performance and overall characteristics (traits, skills, and aptitudes) to create an inimitable competitive advantage is illustrative of the attention being paid to designing processes to establish, measure, reward, and record (via KM) employee performance.

There are numerous connotations of the term 'performance management.' Williams (in Clive, 2001) defined three such models: 'Performance management as a system for managing an organization's performance; performance management as a system for managing employee performance; performance management as a system for integrating the management of organizational and employee performance' (p. 473). These distinctions are important for researchers, and it is good for the practitioner who reads that research to know the PM perspective of the writer. But, for our purposes in this discussion, PM is viewed in a general context similar to Williams' third, integrative definition relating to those systems that are designed to enhance the performance of the employee and thereby positively affect the overall performance of the firm. Under these circumstances, the performance of each employee is significant, and when the performance of all employees is aggregated, overall organizational performance is impacted. Our view of PM closely resembles, and has been informed by, Gilley and Maycunich (2000) and their defining work on the developmental organization:

> Traditional organizations fail to have or embrace a comprehensive performance management process instrumental in bringing about the performance achievements needed to secure desired business results. Consequently, traditional organizations' strategic business goals and objectives are often unrealized . . . traditional organizations believe that their employees are easily replaced; thus policies and procedures demonstrate a revolving-door philosophy toward human resources. (p. 279)

These authors cite several insightful reasons why employers are not successful in achieving business results. Inadequate job design, poor managerial practices, inadequate training and development, inappropriate corrective strategies, and inefficient and ineffective compensation and reward programs. Understandably then, Gilley and Maycunich recommend that at the organizational level, firms should:

1. Conduct stakeholder valuations of both external and internal clients to ascertain their needs and thereby establish organizational goals and objectives.
2. Link job design directly to strategic goals, including business processes, performance outputs, standards and activities, and competency maps (a comparison of competencies that are needed for a specific job and the competency level of an employee in that job, which helps to ascertain individual and overall gaps).

3. Establish synergistic relationships between managers and subordinates.
4. Conduct developmental evaluations or performance reviews on a frequent basis.
5. Create developmental growth and development plans in such a way that employees are able to transfer learning to the job. These plans are created in tandem with both the manager and the employee directing their efforts toward identifying and promoting knowledge, skills, competencies, and behaviors that are necessary to improve individual performance, which will 'enhance their developmental readiness, and allow the firm to continuously renew itself' (p. 289).
6. Link compensation and rewards to performance growth and development, which is critical to improving employee loyalty, commitment, and motivation.

Writing about organizations that desire to be performance-driven, Stiffler (2006: 1) suggests that a performance-driven firm must connect:

> the objectives of the organization with the goals of its individuals; the budgets and resources of the organization with the objectives of the organization; the measurement of past performance with adjustments of the future direction; the information in finance with the information in human resources; and the pay of each person in the organization with that individual's performance.

These linkages should serve to bring together the employee-centered and the organization-centered models in one, integrated approach to PM.

As is the case with TM, some believe that PM is also a nuclear component of organizational culture, and indeed could become a culture in its own right. Stiffler (ibid.) refers to a performance-driven organization; ostensibly a performance culture is the eventual outcome of that initiative. Graham (2004) asserts that a performance-based culture includes components at both the organizational and individual level, respectively. PM at the organizational level is focused on results that are directly confederated with the mission and core values of the organization and driven by goals that cascade according to the strategic plan. Performance measures and targets are actively promoted. A critical juncture is reached at the point where PM at the individual level meets the organizational level. An overall strategic plan, based on performance, is only as effective as the managers who are charged with the responsibility of ensuring that the goals and strategies do indeed cascade to all departments and individuals. This second-level cascading process is critical for achieving desired organizational outcomes, and it involves effective TM at its core.

Of course, there is always the danger that an organization may *think* that it has effective PM processes and practices when in reality it does not. This condition relates precisely to the need for the firm to make certain that goals not only cascade, but are truly understood in order for practice to be successful. A Watson Wyatt study (in Hansen, 2005) indicated that the devil may in fact be in the details, in this instance. This study gave credence to numerous other studies suggesting that employees don't necessarily concur with management that they (the employees) understand the goals that they are supposed to achieve. Employees also, according to these studies, sometimes take exception to management statements that they are evaluated and rewarded based on their performance in achieving those goals. Results of the Watson Wyatt study, for example, display striking dissimilarities between managerial and employee perceptions of significant PM activities. With respect to the organization's provision of goal-setting's linkage to the business objectives, 91% of the employers answered in the affirmative, while only 58% of their top performers agreed and 31% of their poor performers agreed. Providing coaching and feedback is an integral aspect of any successful PM initiative. In this study, 91% of the employers stated that their company provided coaching and feedback, 64% of their top performers agreed and 38% of their poor performers were in agreement. Regarding formal annual performance reviews, 98% of employers said that their companies provided them, 75% of top performers and 57% of poor performers agreed. On pay linked to annual performance review results, 92% of employers agreed that pay was linked to annual reviews, 64% of top performers and 40% of poor performers agreed. When asked if the organization provided career development, 82% of employers said yes, and a slight 36% of top performers and 23% of poor performers agreed (Hansen, 2005).

If this study can be generalized to a greater population, and similar research seems to verify that it can, it seems that either companies are not monitoring their PM component activities and making corrective adjustments, or employees are not aware and/or intelligent enough to recognize a PM component activity when they see it (i.e., annual performance reviews), or both. Why might there be such striking discordance between employer perceptions of their PM systems and those held by their employees—and particularly their top-performing employees? Certainly, it may be that the PM system is faulty in one or more of its components. Our view is that there still exists a significant lack of understanding of PM and its purpose. We believe that an increased communication of the various PM system components is critical to assisting the company in successfully implementing its PM. Each PM component would need to be addressed on both the organizational and the individual level with the intent of defining and describing its primary function and the correct methods for implementing the PM component with each and every employee in mind. Linking the PM system with the TM system accomplishes this important communication, at least partially, through the use of effective and creative IT and knowledge management (KM) systems, processes, and procedures.

Jason Averbrook of Knowledge Infusion (HR and TM technology consultants) asserts that a more effective approach to PM consists of 'intertwining performance management with other talent management functions' (Ruiz, 2006: p. 47). Ruiz suggests that:

> The ideal of performance management—clear lines of sight between each employee and the larger organizational goals, frequent feedback and performance evaluations that are tightly integrated with compensation, succession planning and retention, to name but a few—is unlikely to emerge unless companies incorporate automation and drop ineffective processes. (ibid.)

Ruiz's comments are in conjunction with her reporting of the findings of a *Workforce Management* magazine and IDC (a global market intelligence firm) survey of 218 HR leaders at companies of 2500 or more employees in relation to the level of automation utilized in their PM processes at their companies. The findings indicate that most firms are still operating their PM systems without much automation, and 'Goals are being cascaded from the top of the organization, but technology tools are largely absent from the process, meaning that the links between individual goals and corporate goals are likely to elude many employees' (ibid.).

Finally, taking into consideration all of the time and creative effort necessary to design, implement and maintain an effective PM process, one might question whether or not it is worth the expense. Can the ROI (return on investment) of a practical and creative PM system be justified? Kirchoff (2006) cites an 11-year study of more than 200 companies that clearly indicated that those organizations that had a PM cultural approach (our assertion of a strong TM cultural context) 'significantly outperformed' organizations without a PM cultural approach to managing with respect to financial and operational measures. In a delightfully succinct and condensed manner, Kirchoff explains the relationship between individual performance and overall organizational performance: 'Individual performance drives departmental performance, departmental performance drives business unit performance, and business unit performance drives overall company performance' (p. 1). If we nurture our employees and give them the direction and resources they need to become high performers, and if we install automation to aid in collaboration among the human resource functions, the business bottom line should be positively impacted. Similarly, succession planning would be more seamless because attrition would be less of an issue, recruitment efforts would be more fruitful, and organizational knowledge would be more readily accessible and robust.

GENERAL TM/PM/KM RELATIONSHIP

As mentioned before, in the authors' earlier chapter (Chapter 2) related to HR planning, we recommend that TM be considered as the larger environment within which PM and KM reside. If an organization fully accepts TM as a philosophy and standard operating culture, then the importance of the roles played by PM and KM are more easily understood. The TM culture will, by its very nature, drive the organization to find ways to attract, develop, and retain their most valuable resources—their people. Embracing TM as a primal cultural value therefore causes the organization to continually seek avenues by which their valuable human resources can become the firm's inimitable competitive advantage. For instance, recruitment and selection of high-quality employees become not only the work of the HR department, but also the responsibility of supervisors, managers, and peers. The HR staff may help in the design and implementation of recruitment and selection, but they will not be doing so in isolation, and synergistic outcomes should ensue. In the same manner, all of the various activities aimed at developing and maintaining a motivated, high-quality workforce are also approached in this holistic fashion. Exit interviews, performance appraisal, succession planning, training and development programs, safety, compensation, and employee relations all become the work of the entire organization.

In its early years, an organization often adopts a TM approach out of necessity; it will do this to survive regardless of whether or not the firm realizes that it is following what we would call a TM approach. Ironically, organizations begin the first stage of their life cycle in a fully integrated manner, albeit initially without the benefit of more formal KM. Later in its lifespan the organization may elect to expend time, money, and effort and create PM processes to train and develop some of their top performers, and to attempt to elevate employee productivity and motivation. Still later, the organization may choose to hire a consultant, or direct an in-house employee, to design and install some KM processes to help staunch the loss of knowledge experienced as a result of high turnover. This is what we mean by systems operating in isolation. Unfortunately, in this case (see Figure 9.1) the old expression, 'The left hand doesn't know what the right hand is doing,' is particularly appropriate. It should be obvious from Figure 9.1 that there is no interaction (communication/knowledge sharing) among the three systems in this scenario. They are truly independent of each other. Rarely does this scenario occur as a planned approach by management.

In the case of performance appraisal (PA), the PM system is often operating on its own. In this instance, the process of PA could conceivably be less useful than desired. Supervisors are usually given a format for evaluating employee performance, the supervisor performs the task well or poorly,

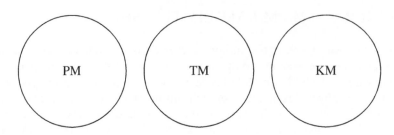

Figure 9.1   Independent systems

according to his/her level of knowledge about the process and personal motivation; the employee receives and signs the appraisal document; and the form
is then sent to HR where one copy is filed in the employee's personal file and
another may be given to the payroll supervisor for compensation purposes.
It is important to note that Figures 9.1 to 9.4 relating to relationships between
the three management approaches are intended to illustrate only a few of the
possible connections and interactions between and among those approaches.
There are, of course, an infinite number of potential combinations.

As an organization matures, situations will undoubtedly arise where
some degree of cooperation between these three systems and their components will become essential, or simply emerge, as shown in Figure 9.2. Here,
existing PM and KM systems, TM and PM systems, and TM and KM staff
members collaborate on one or more projects or ongoing operations so that
both will benefit. For example, recruiters may collaborate with and inform
compensation staffers of their inability to attract much-needed talent. With
collaboration, PA usage may be expanded by an IT program or even a full-
blown KMS to assist in more clearly determining from PA results valuable
knowledge gained by the employee, and transferring this information to the
supervisor and elsewhere within the organization.

Figure 9.3 represents a degree of integration of all three systems.
Although we assert that TM should be ubiquitous, for purposes of illustration, it is shown here to represent TM's primary functions of employee
attraction/recruitment, development, and retention. PM and KM also
retain their primary purposes. In this situation, each of the approaches is
somewhat integrated and some of their functions become synergistic. This
is a significant level of development whereby each of the approaches col-
laborates to some degree in some areas of management. Using our example
of the PA process, the danger in this scenario is that PA may not be one of
the areas of collaboration among the approaches. The lack of input of PA
is especially regrettable since this function represents a potentially valuable
source of information to fill KM processes, and provide input that can help
guide future key KM activities such as recruitment, selection, and training.

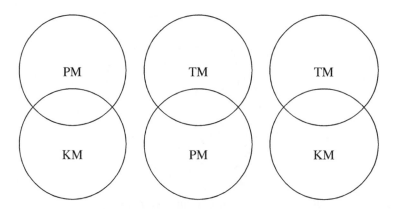

Figure 9.2   Partially integrated systems

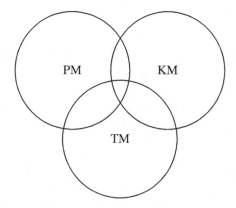

Figure 9.3   Fully integrated, loosely coupled systems

Figure 9.4 displays a very high degree of integration of the management systems. Activities employed by the three management systems intersect (collaborate) on multiple levels. TM, PM, and KM still maintain distinct roles in the organization, but the opportunity is there for all of them to combine forces whenever such joint action would positively enhance a process or procedure. For example, in this figure, PA is shown as a point where all the approaches focus on one system. In this instance, KM might be the catalyst for the collection, interpretation assistance, and dissemination of aggregate PA results (especially in the case of lessons learned) to not only the supervisor, but also the employee, the training staff, the supervisor's manager, the manager's manager, the succession planning incumbent, the recruiters, the employee selection authority, the job

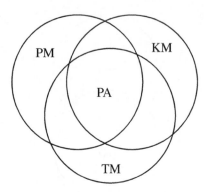

Figure 9.4   Fully integrated, tightly coupled systems

analysts and job designers, the compensation staff, and on and through-out the organization.

KNOWLEDGE MANAGEMENT APPLIED TO PERFORMANCE APPRAISAL

Effective KM and knowledge management systems (KMS) are largely dependent upon successful talent management for input. TM and the various previously mentioned components of PM provide the substructure upon which effective KM systems can be built. The strategies and methods of PA, an important component of PM, are integral to effective TM and PM. Once the money and efforts have been expended to attract, assess, and select the most qualified individuals for our jobs, it is essential that the organization designs and implements fair and inherently motivational practices for appraising and rewarding performance. It is widely accepted that PA systems that identify and reward appropriate behaviors, and provide a framework for planning future performance standards, tend to correlate positively with employee motivation and retention. If the motivation and retention of talent are at least partially due to successful PA, and if PA is an essential element of an effective TM and PM system, and if KM systems are subsequently built upon a TM and PM platform, then the PA component should necessarily be robust, organic (animate), and practical in terms of proprietary organizational needs.

Our organizational talent is largely responsible for the degree and scope of our organizational knowledge. It is therefore appropriate to assume that the retention and motivational levels of our talent (via PA) are at least partially responsible for creating the conditions upon which the formation of an effective, efficient, and desirable KM system can be devised. We now return to the discussion about the inter-relationships between TM, PM, and KM to establish a background for our illustration of the benefits that can be reaped from integrating KM into the TM/PM operating environment. We will use PA as an example of how a PM function can become much more effective as a result of integrating KM into the process.

Knowledge Management Support for Performance Appraisal

As illustrated in Figure 9.1, TM, PM, and KM can exist as separate systems in an organization, Figure 9.2 shows the partial integration of any two of those three sets of activities. Figures 9.3 and 9.4 indicate more fully integrated approaches, with TM, PM, and KM interacting at varying levels of coupling. In the most highly coupled integration of the three areas, KM can provide important, even critical support for PA. Figure 9.5 illustrates that various PA techniques and processes differ from each other in terms of the proportion of subjectivity or objectivity required to implement the particular technique. Of course, multiple techniques can be blended, which might alter their position on the scale in Figure 9.5. Furthermore, in the hands of a particular appraiser, a given technique might be more or less subjective than if the same technique is applied by a different appraiser.

In most uses of PA within organizations subjectivity represents a significant problem in search of a solution. The subjectivity of a particular PA technique is accompanied by the ambiguity of its results. The more subjective, the more room there is for interpretation of the results. The greater the possibility of interpretation, the greater the chance there is for misinterpretation.

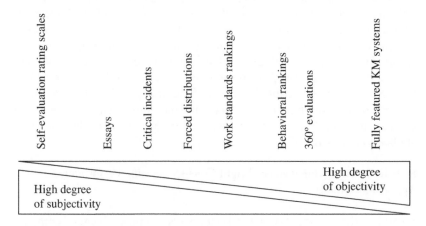

Figure 9.5   Comparison of performance appraisal systems

PA is a form of decision-making. In decision science, there are many strategies for removing the amount of risk from the decision at hand. Risk, in the instance of PA, often stems from ambiguity. Consequently, subjectivity yields ambiguity and risk. Conversely, objectivity results from more information being available. A complete set of information, that is, 'perfect information,' means there is no risk and there is no ambiguity. Yet even in the more objective PA techniques in Figure 9.5, there is still a significant degree of subjectivity. KM can support PA by helping with the reduction of ambiguity and risk of misinterpretation.

Consider, for example, the critical incident technique of PA. It has the potential to be the richest form of appraisal—assuming that *all* critical incidents have been tracked and recorded. Unfortunately, in many organizations, all that are recorded are the negative critical events, such as customer complaints or supervisor reprimands. Given a fully featured KMS, all critical events could be recorded. In the ultimate scenario, there could be a record of each time an employee did anything that affects, positively or negatively, any progress toward achievement of any corporate goal or objective. Consequently, all activities of an employee could be critical incidents. Hence, a complete recording is possible, thereby removing one of the many problems with the critical incident method of PA. Furthermore, the KM system could have reported the ultimate impact of each critical incident. It also could have provided a cumulative scorecard of the employee's net impact on the condition of the company. Therefore, such an ultimate system would eliminate subjectivity and ambiguity as there would be no need for human interpretation. In a decision-making sense, there would be no risk as the information would be perfect.

Having laid out that scenario, the authors hasten to add that such an ultimate system is only hypothetical. Moreover, there would be huge challenges to implement such a system. Not the least of those challenges is the privacy issue, as complete and continuous monitoring would be required to record all possible critical incidents. Nevertheless, the above scenario serves the purpose of illustrating the potential of KM to improve PA. Even a KM system that provides a minimal amount of additional information could result in reduced subjectivity and ambiguity. Any one of the PA techniques and processes included in Figure 9.5 can benefit from wise application of KM.

How Knowledge Management Might Enhance Specific Performance Appraisal Methods

Several of the classical PA methods share a common problem of comparison to preset measurements. Included in this category are rating scales, work standards, and, to some extent, behavioral anchors. In each case, measurements need to be established, which itself can be a subjective process. Then a supervisor needs to judge the employee against the measurement, inducing more subjectivity. Questions arise such as 'How do we know that terms such as "satisfactory," "proficient," "highly proficient," and "excellent" are appropriate for measuring a task?,' 'How do I determine if this employee is "highly proficient" rather than "excellent"?,' 'How do we know a particular standard, such as a sales quota, is set at a proper level?,' or 'How do we know a particular behavior is desirable and advances corporate goals?'

A KMS could assist in this process by setting the measurement level or category or standard based on an examination of relevant knowledge at hand. For example, the KMS could examine dynamic characteristics of sales territories, such as changing population demographics and competitive activity, to set sales quotas. Or the KMS could analyze cases wherein specific employee behaviors are tied to success or failure of the company reaching its objectives. Those behaviors could then be categorized as desirable or not, or could even be differentiated by nuances, allowing behaviors and rating scales to be integrated.

Other performance evaluation methods that could be improved through use of KM are ranking and forced distributions. These share the measurement challenge described above, but also the challenge of determining the right distribution into which to force employees. If a company uses a stratified method whereby a certain number of employees must fit into each stratum, how does the company know what the strata boundaries should be and what the right numbers of employees are within each stratum? If a company uses a normal distribution, how does it know how the measurement is normally distributed?

Again, KM can come to the rescue. A KMS could examine the relevant data and fit it to multiple distributions to discover the proper one to use. True, a statistician could do the same thing. But the KMS could continuously reevaluate the knowledge it applies to the task and a continuously refit the distribution. In this illustration, KM makes the use of a particular distribution more defensible. That, in turn, reduces subjectivity.

Even a 360° process, viewed by some as the thoroughbred of the performance evaluation methods, can be improved by application of KM techniques. The title of this PA method means that an employee's performance evaluation is a synthesis of multiple evaluations. In the case of professional workers, for example, the total evaluation could be comprised of self-evaluation, peer evaluation, supervisor evaluation, and client evaluation. Subjectivity is reduced by the combining of the results of all the evaluations. However, each of those component evaluations relies upon one or more of the performance evaluation methods described above. Consequently, applying KM as appropriate to each of the component evaluations reduces the subjectivity of that component and further reduces the subjectivity of the entire 360° process.

KM Software for Integrating PM and TM

The authors know of no prewritten KM software packages that specifically address PA. That does not mean that such software is non-existent; it only means that perhaps it has escaped our scrutiny. This section will provide an overview of a few PA systems that provide some of the capabilities described herein.

SuccessFactors (performance and talent management solutions) notes that its web-based software 'automates many of the historically time-consuming processes: a writing assistant helps you articulate goals, a legal scan quickly highlights non-compliant language and an audit trail tracks the entire review process from start to finish and automatically routes the final product to HR' (SuccessFactors, 2007). The company boasts 1300+ business customers ranging from small to Fortune 500 size, such as PepBoys Auto Parts.

Halogen eAppraisal is also a web-based package that 'can align and track employee goals, measure employee performance, complete training and development plans, keep employee journals, review real-time reports and more!' (Halogen Software, 2007). The software is used by nearly 1000 client organizations and includes 360° multi-rater capability. The package features an executive dashboard featuring graphs and charts, which tracks real-time data and allows for drilling down through the source data.

Profiles International offers CheckPoint 360°, which 'surveys 70 specific job skills, which fall into eight universal management and leadership competencies and 18 skill sets. Multi-rater feedback surveys are completed by managers, their bosses, their peers, and the people who report to them. The data are compiled into thorough and concise reports for managers to see how their job performance is evaluated by the full circle of people who observe it. CheckPoint 360° reports include recommendations for professional development to enhance each manager's job performance' (Profiles International, 2007).

The above sampling of performance appraisals is not intended to be exhaustive. The reader can explore those and other examples (e.g., Bowland Solutions, 2007; Grapevine Surveys, 2007) and arrive at his or her own evaluation. There are also many generic knowledge management software packages that might be adaptable to PA purposes (e.g., Qlikteck, 2007).

CONCLUSION

Talent management, performance management, and knowledge management are management approaches that share the common goal of establishing effective systems, processes, procedures, and decision rules intended to achieve both individual and organizational goals. We have attempted to make the case for the potentially synergistic outcomes that may result from integrating these three approaches. It is our belief that smart talent managers will seize every opportunity to do so.

REFERENCES

Bowland Solutions (2007). Web-based HR and research solutions. Retrieved 13 June, 2007 from www.bowlandsolutions.com.

Clive, F. (2001). Performance appraisal and management: The developing research agenda. *Journal of Occupational and Organizational Psychology*, **74**(4): 473.

den Hartog, D., Boselie, P. and Paauwe, J. (2004). Performance management: A model and research agenda. *Applied Psychology: An International Review*, **53**(4): 557.

Gilley, J. and Maycunich, A. (2000). *Beyond the Learning Organization: Creating a Culture of Continuous Growth and Development Through State-of-the-art Human Resource Practices*. Cambridge, MA: Perseus.

Graham, J. (2004). Developing a performance-based culture. *Journal for Quality and Participation*, **27**(1): 4.

Grapevine Surveys (2007). Performance evaluations. Retrieved 13 June, 2007 from www.grapevinesurveys.com.

Halogen Software (2007). eAppraisal. Retrieved 13 June, 2007 from www.halogen-software.com.

Hansen, F. (2005). Pushing performance management. *Workforce Management*, **84**(13): 22, 24.

Kirchoff, J. (2006). Why performance management improves human capital ROI. *SHRM Research Quarterly*. Alexandria, VA: Society for Human Resource Management.

Mondy, R. and Noe, R. (2005). *Human Resource Management* (9th edition). Upper Saddle, NJ: Pearson Prentice Hall, p. 252.

Profiles International (2007). CheckPoint 360°. Retrieved 13 June, 2007 from www.profilesinternational.com.

Qliktech (2007) QlikView. Retrieved 13 June, 2007 from www.qliktech.com.

Ruiz, G. (2006). Performance management under-performs. *Workforce Management*, **85**(12): 47, 49, 50.

Stiffler, M. (2006). Driving performance. *Workforce Performance Solutions Magazine*. Retrieved 16 January 2008 from http://www.wpsmag.com/content/templates/wps_articleid=508&zoneid=38.

SuccessFactors (2007). Performance and Talent Management. Retrieved 13 June, 2007 from www.successfactors.com.

PART 4

Organizational learning and development

10. Talent management and the global learning organization

Dennis Briscoe

The quality of a firm's talent is central to its ability to learn. The effective management of that talent is directly linked to the organizational learning that is so necessary in today's hyper-competitive global economy. This chapter addresses the nature of that linkage, first defining talent and 'talent management' and 'organizational learning' in the global environment and then describing how these concepts are so intricately connected, relying closely on each other. The success of these linkages goes a long way toward determining the global enterprise's competitive advantage and economic success.

TALENT MANAGEMENT—TERMINOLOGY AND DEFINITION

Reference to 'talent management' terminology and concept can be found today in many locations. The following quotes provide a short sample of the diversity of these references:

> It's no longer what you own or build; success is hinged to the resources and talent you can access. (*The Wall Street Journal*, quoted in Cascio (2005b))

> The war for talent is over (and the talent won!). (Title of a recent webcast by Lance Richards, Senior Director of International Human Resources for Kelly Services, hosted by the American Society for Human Resource Management, 14 September 2006)

> Companies have become much better at managing the traditional technologies of the workplace. Now we face the bigger challenge as managers of actively engaging the willing contribution and talents of all our people if we are to sustain long-term success. That doesn't happen by accident, intuition, or innate skill. It takes a determination to learn continuously and to create a community of interest within the organization, so that the full range of initiative can be released. Now more than ever, that is what creates the winning advantage. (Geoff Armstrong, President, Institute for Personnel and Development, United Kingdom, 1999)

It is interesting that with all the attention in the media and in the practitioner press to the central importance of talent management, definitions of the word 'talent' in this context appear only in Buckingham and Coffman (1999): 'a recurring pattern of thought, feeling, or behavior that can be productively applied' (p. 71) and in Michaels, Handfield-Jones, and Axelrod (2001): 'the sum of a person's abilities—his or her intrinsic gifts, skills, knowledge, experience, intelligence, judgment, attitude, character, and drive. It also includes his or her ability to grow' (p. xii). Thorne and Pellant (2007) discuss at some length what talent looks like—with terms like extraordinary individuals, a buzz, focused, and achievement oriented—yet still never offer a clear definition, with the exception of the *Concise Oxford* Dictionary's definition: 'a special aptitude, or faculty.' Thorne and Pellant (ibid.) don't think this definition does justice as a description of our most talented people (p. 7). Because of its encompassing coverage, however, it meets the needs of this chapter and text.

Two definitions of talent management were identified: 'the identification, development, and management of the talent portfolio—i.e., the number, type, and quality of employees that will most effectively fulfill the company's strategic and operating objectives' (Knez & Ruse, 2004: 231) and:

> a conscious, deliberate approach undertaken to attract, develop and retain people with the aptitude and abilities to meet current and future organizational needs. Talent management involves individual and organizational development in response to a changing and complex operating environment. It includes the creation and maintenance of a supportive, people oriented organization culture. (Stockley, 2006: 1)

Given the above definitions, a discussion of talent and talent management would seem central to any discussion of the role of HRM. But among the human resource and management textbooks reviewed, most don't even discuss the topic of talent management (for example, see Dessler, 2005; Fisher, Schoenfeldt, & Shaw, 2006; Mathis & Jackson, 2006; Redman & Wilkinson, 2006; Gomez-Mejia, Balkin, & Cardy, 2007; Mondy, Noe, & Premeux, 2008). Only one current reviewed human resource management textbook mentions talent and that was in an index (see Cascio, 2005a), and that was only to summarize the Buckingham and Coffman (1999) definition and usage (see above). The lack of usage of this theme in current college texts suggests that the topic of talent management is either such a new topic (at least with the use of this particular terminology) that academics (at least, textbook writers) see it only as a fad or a new term for old concepts or it has not yet made it into what they consider to be the relevant literature for discussion in their texts.

On the other hand, a reading of the more extensive practitioner literature not only provides the same shortage of definitions (it seems to be assumed that everyone understands what the terms refer to) but also suggests that there are many different usages of the word 'talent.' Usually, the term is used to refer either to 'top' management (in both the sense of those on top and those who are the best performers) or the top-performing employees, particularly those in technology-driven occupations. In addition, this literature uses many synonyms for the word talent (such as celebrated excellence, fast-trackers, high potentials, highly educated and highly skilled, a breed apart, IT specialists [scientists, engineers, designers, programmers, etc.], top leaders, top management, superkeepers, high-end employees, knowledge workers, etc.), but, again, with no definitions. That is, the terms 'talent' and 'talent management' are primarily used to discuss issues related to the attraction, development, and retention of critical and high-performing employees.

In the context of this chapter and this book, however, the term 'talent management' refers to management and human resource management decisions and practices that relate to and involve the entire workforce. The word 'talent' is used to apply to all employees: young, old, new, seasoned, those who work with their hands and those who work with their heads, blue-collar, white-collar, pink-collar, hourly, salaried, service workers, scientists, engineers, knowledge workers, physical laborers, and so forth. In today's fiercely competitive global and knowledge-based economy, the attraction, development, and retention of high-performing and high-potential employees in all positions, from the bottom to the top of the organization, seems absolutely critical.

Today, all employees have to bring their best creativity, passion, and service to the job, no matter what their levels in the organization or their job titles; so talking about talent management in the context of all of an organization's employees makes special sense. Organizations need them (talent) the talent doesn't necessarily need the employer. From the talent point of view, it is a seller's market. Employees can pick and choose where and when to work and employers must do everything they can think of (and more) to attract, develop, manage, and retain that talent. It is their sole source of sustainable, non-reproducible, global, competitive advantage.

THE WAR FOR TALENT

The term 'war for talent' was coined by McKinsey & Company in 1997, based on its large study of firms and executives (Michaels et al., 2001; Thorne and Pellant, 2007). Based on its five-year in-depth research surveys of 13 000 executives at more than 120 companies and case studies of 27 companies, McKinsey & Company identified five imperatives that firms need to act on if they are going to win the war for managerial talent and make talent a competitive advantage. The term evidently struck a strong chord with managers and human resource managers, who were experiencing this 'war,' but had not yet found a term to describe what they were experiencing. 'Overnight, it seemed, everyone was talking about the war for talent' (Michaels et al., 2001: 1).

The war for talent began in the 1980s with the birth of the Information Age (Michaels et al., 2001; Tulgan, 2002; Herman, Olivo, & Gicio, 2003). With it, the importance of hard assets—machines, factories, and capital—declined relative to the importance of intangible assets such as proprietary networks, brands, intellectual capital, and talent. The shift to the Information Age still continues and is far from over. Accordingly, the war for talent is far from over. As the economy and work become ever-more knowledge-based, the differential value of highly talented people continues to mount.

The economy was burning white hot in the late 1990s and companies were scrambling to hire and retain the people they needed (Michaels et al., 2001). Companies were offering large signing bonuses (e.g., while out jogging early one morning in San Diego, this author passed a billboard with the picture of a new US$60 000 BMW—with this caption: 'This can be yours for coming to work for . . . [a start-up high-tech firm whose name I had not seen before—or since].'), new employees were asking for raises three months after they joined, and headhunters were cornering hot recruits before they had even settled behind their desks. Many companies had hundreds of vacancies they couldn't fill, and some of the venerable bastions of talent (such as investment banks and consulting firms) were losing talent to dot.com start-ups. It was easy to see the war for talent raging in the recruiting and retention frenzy of the late 1990s.

Then the dot.com bubble burst, the Nasdaq crumbled, and fears of recession spread. As the economy cooled off it was easy to think that the war for talent was over. But it was (and is) not over. Today (and continuing into the foreseeable future) the causes of the shortage of talent are just as relevant as ever, as much due to the shifting demographics (a result of the low birthrates that have persisted in all developed economies, and some developing economies, since the early 1960s) and the changes in worker attitudes wanting more balance between work and home, as it is to the demand from companies and other types of organizations (such as governments and schools) for talent (due to their growth as well as to their aging and retiring workforces—with more employees retiring than there are new people entering the labor force to replace them) (Michaels et al., 2001; Herman et al., 2003; Burud & Tumolo, 2004).

Access to the best talent was always critical to the success of an enterprise. That's nothing new. But in the workplace of the past, employers could practically own their most valuable talent, monopolizing them through long-term employment relationships. That's no longer possible because employers can't offer long-term job security—they don't know what skills they will need even within the near future—and because more and more people are thinking like free agents—they choose and stay with jobs and employers as long as those jobs and those employers fulfill their interests (Tulgan, 2002). The new world of business—characterized by unrelenting global competition, rapid technology change, constant realignment of industries and skills, and aging populations—make it impossible for firms to continue to make long-term commitments to employees. Plus, the new generations that are joining the labor force bring a demand for a more balanced life—one where family and outside-of-work interests are just as important as career and work itself (Burud & Tumolo, 2004; Herman et al., 2003). New dual-focus workers don't want the work-only commitment and they seek work that is challenging and interesting while allowing the flexibility to live where and how they want.

Thus, the war for talent persists. In the new economy, every term of employment—schedules, location, assignments, co-workers, pay, and more—is open to negotiation, whether the organization likes it or not (Tulgan, 2002). The most valuable talent has the most negotiating power—and all talent at every level of the organization is valuable. Every employment relationship lasts exactly as long as the terms are agreeable to all parties.

In an extension of the earlier McKinsey study, Michaels et al.'s (2001) research found that what distinguished high-performing companies from average-performing ones was not better HR processes, but the fundamental belief in the importance of talent. Also important were the actions higher-performing organizations took to strengthen their talent pools. However, Michaels et al. were quite surprised by the general lack of focus on talent issues. Only one in four companies had made strengthening their talent pools a top priority. Even though they could prove analytically that better talent leads to better organizational performance, many companies were missing the opportunity (p. xi).

Collins (2001) similarly found that the critical variable for firms that were able to develop from being only good organizations to being great ones was attention to first hiring the right (and best) people. Berger (2004) also found the commitment to talent management was the defining variable in long-term, sustained, organizational excellence (see the summary at the end of this chapter).

As Michaels et al. (2001) found, almost all the managers they talked with recognized the benefits of strengthening their organizations' talent pools. However, many didn't know how to do it. They didn't know how to get the momentum of their organizations behind the effort. In many ways, this is what knowledge management and organizational learning is all about: finding or creating ways to leverage the talent of the organization. And in the international/global context, it is even that much more complicated and difficult. In Michaels et al.'s 2000 survey (reported in their 2001 book), 99% of the respondents said their management pool needed to be much stronger in the near future while only 20% agreed that they had enough talented leaders to pursue most of their companies' business opportunities (p. 4). And it seems reasonable to assert that this shortage of talent extended throughout the organization.

The rest of this chapter, then, extends the discussion of talent management to the concepts of knowledge management, organizational learning, and places these into a global context.

HUMAN CAPITAL

The key to winning the war for talent is the effective measurement and management of an organization's human capital (Baron and Armstrong, 2007). As stated in the second section of this chapter, we have moved from an industrial society, where the primary source of wealth was machinery and other physical assets, to a knowledge society, where the primary source of wealth is human capital. In the traditional accounting practices developed during the industrial era, organizational value was recognized as being comprised of three major classes of assets that are integral to the organization's ability to produce goods and services (Weatherly, 2003): financial assets (such as cash and marketable securities, often referred to as financial capital), physical assets (tangible assets such as property, plant and equipment, and inventories), and intangible assets (traditionally found on the balance sheet under headings such as customer goodwill, but now recognized more broadly to include human capital, customer capital, social capital, and structural capital, as summarized in Table 10.1). In today's knowledge-based economy, it is these intangible assets that create value, not the traditional financial and physical assets.

Up until the early 1980s, the book value (on the firm's balance sheet) of a company's 'tangibles'—the financial and physical assets—accounted for almost all of its perceived value, or its market capitalization. But during the 1980s, the market and book values of publicly traded companies began to deviate from past patterns and from each other (Schmidt, 2002a; 2002b; 2002c). Firms were generating earnings higher than would be normally expected based on their tangible assets alone. And the traditional guesstimate of 'customer goodwill' didn't seem adequate to explain the

Table 10.1   Sample elements of intangible capital

Human	Customer	Social	Structural
Tacit knowledge	Customer relationships	Corporate culture	Intellectual property
Education	Brands	Infrastructure assets	Patents
Vocational qualifications	Customer loyalty	Management philosophy	Copyrights
Professional certifications	License agreements	Management practices	Trade secrets
Work-related know-how	Business collaborations	Formal and informal networking systems	Trade marks and service marks
Work-related competence	Distribution channels	Coaching/mentor relationships	Design rights
Work-related experience	Customer lists	Knowledge management	

Source: Based on Weatherly (2003: 2).

difference. Eventually, the cause was realized to be the increasing import-ance of a firm's intangible assets, that is, the increasing importance of its human, social, customer, and structural assets.

Research evidence that supports the shift from tangible to the sorts of intangible assets shown in Table 10.1 appeared in a series of articles and presentations in 2002. Schmidt (2002a, 2002b, and 2002c), Schmidt and Lines (2002), Hurwitz et al. (2002), and Montgomery and Lines (2002) reported on their research at the major management consultancy, Towers & Perrin, which developed a way to show that intangibles are today the source of as much as 85% of a firm's revenues and profits, which relate directly to the public firm's market capitalization. For example, as early as 1996, Microsoft—an organization that clearly depends on its human capital, and that has a huge market value, relative to its revenues and number of employees—determined that the ratio of the value of its intan-gible assets to the value of its book (tangible) assets exceeded 11 to 1 (Dzinkowski, 2000). This kind of determination was made in spite of the current state-of-the-art inability to measure the value of these intangible assets. Microsoft may not be able to measure the real value of its intangi-ble assets (its human capital), but it is clear to the organization that those are the core sources of its corporate value.

The large HR consultancy, Hewitt Associates, has recently reported that 'the attraction and retention of pivotal employees play a critical role in increasing shareholder value' (Kanter & Zagata-Meraz, 2007, p. 1).

According to Hewitt's research, for the average Fortune 500 company, a ten-point increase in a company's 'Talent Quotient' score (a measure of a firm's flow of top-quartile employees into and out of the organization) adds approximately US$70–160 million to its bottom line over the following few years (ibid.). This sort of research has been performed in a number of settings, clearly illustrating the value of people (talent, human capital, management) in the performance of the firm that links directly to its performance in the stock market (see, for example, the research done at Sears [Rucci, Kirn, & Quinn, 1998]; also Pfeffer, 1998; Fitz-enz, 2000; Becker, Huselid, & Ulrich, 2001; Phillips, Stone, & Phillips, 2001; Kravetz, 2004; Baron & Armstrong, 2007).

In yet another major study, O'Toole and Lawler (2006) make the link directly to the workforce, the organization's talent: 'increasingly, the market value of a corporation reflects such "intangible assets" as its brand name, the organizational systems and processes it uses, and, perhaps most important, the quality of its workforce' (p. 34). This was true in both the high-involvement (HI) and global competitor (GC) companies (the two types of high-performing organizations that O'Toole and Lawler identified in their research) where managers had introduced practices specifically designed to develop and effectively utilize their human capital—HI companies with a focus on developing and involving their workforces, and GC companies with an eye on obtaining the best talent available to perform whatever work needs to be done at a specific time (ibid.).

All four aspects of the intangible assets listed in Table 10.1 are important to the success of today's enterprises. Clearly, brand names, customer loyalty, corporate culture and management ability, patents and trade secrets are critical to success in the global economy. Yet, central to all of these intangible assets (as the studies discussed above indicate) is the firm's human capital. An organization's human capital is the collective sum of the attributes, life experience, knowledge, inventiveness, energy, and enthusiasm that its people choose to invest in their work (Weatherly, 2003: 1). This is the source of the talent that creates organizational success.

THE LEARNING ORGANIZATION

Andrew Grove, ex-CEO of Intel, says, 'The ability to learn faster than your competitors . . . is the only sustainable strategic advantage.' In general, learning is the acquisition and application of new knowledge, skills, and experience that changes behavior, thought, and beliefs that results in improved performance and better adaptation to—or ability to take advantage of—the environment. This definition applies both to individuals and to the teams and organizations in which they work. This is the logic of the learning organization: the unpredictable and rapid pace of today's new world of business forces people and organizations to change in order to survive. Change implies doing new things in new ways and that requires purposeful learning. Learning can also occur via trial and error, but trial and error by itself does not guarantee helpful change or helpful learning. Those individuals and organizations that learn more quickly (and better) are more likely to be successful. Successful people and organizations are more likely to have developed and to use techniques and strategies to enhance the speed, quality, and quantity of their learning.

The leaders of today's organizations are increasingly aware that, in order to be successful in today's hyper-competitive global economy, they must turn their organizations into 'learning organizations.' And, as they are discovering, this is easier said than done. They are learning that learning itself must be an area (if not *the* area) of focus, of attention—not just one of the things that good management does, but the single most important thing: everything that organizations do is about learning, about improving, about getting better at everything they do.

We see comments in both the academic and practitioner literature to support this point. For example, the only route to sustainable success for any enterprise in today's global economy is to learn and innovate faster than its competitors. Talent management must be a key component of overall corporate strategy, in order to achieve competitive success. And, in our global economy, knowledge transfer and learning across national borders and organizational boundaries is necessary for success, since best practice and great ideas can come from anywhere.

Many books and articles have been published on the learning organization and its related themes in the last 20 or so years.[1] Many models have been developed to pull together the many sub-topics and themes or to focus on one or more particular component. The intent, here, is to provide only an overview of this broad and diverse literature.

For the purposes of this chapter, the process of organizational learning includes four steps:

- knowledge creation;
- knowledge saving;
- knowledge sharing;
- knowledge use.

All steps are critical. All steps are difficult and confront significant individual and organizational barriers. All steps are global. All steps require an enterprise culture that supports learning. And all steps require talent to implement. The rest of this section provides a short overview of each of these steps.

Knowledge Creation

There are a number of sources of learning and, thus, situations in which knowledge can be created. Each of these could be described in length, but are only listed here. A short description of these sources follows. These sources include self-learning (trial and error, reflection on experience); learning from individual, team, and organizational experience (through after-action reviews, recording the experience, and lessons learned); learning from experts, customers, and the competition; learning from the environment and the industry; learning from experimentation; and learning from creative thinking.

One of the most important of these sources of learning has been described by the Center for Creative Leadership (CCL) in its studies of thousands of executives as learning from experience, or the 'lessons of experience' (McCall, Lombardo, & Morrison, 1988; McCall, 1998; McCall & Hollenbeck, 2002). The most important experiences have been found to include challenging assignments, learning from others (as in critical understudy positions and from mentors and colleagues), learning from hardships (such as business mistakes and family difficulties), 'other events' such as course work and one's first supervisory assignment, and, in the international context, the experience of living in another national culture.

The specific tactics that have been found to enhance learning (at both the individual and team levels) include accessing other people (through networking and using the organization's knowledge inventories and expert directories), gaining assistance and support to solve problems through one's networks and organizational inventories, archives, and directories, then taking specific action to deal with the problems and challenges, and lastly, thinking and reflecting on the outcomes.

At the organizational level, learning occurs through collaboration (across functions and, indeed, across all borders), encouraging exploration and experimentation, identifying best practices, reviewing organizational experiences and practices, and updating organizational memory with new learning (or, as some have described it, keeping the recipe, or keeping track of how the organization has done things).

Some of the problems in identifying learning from experience and in recording it for future needs include the following:

- converting individual and team knowledge from internal knowledge, or tacit knowledge, to explicit knowledge, so it can be recorded, archived, examined, and improved;

- converting private knowledge to public knowledge;
- making knowledge that is for whatever reasons unavailable become available;
- converting knowledge that the 'owner' considers his or her own (i.e., personalized) to a form where it can be codified and thus saved and shared.

Every one of the sources of learning requires competencies that can be screened for during the recruiting and hiring processes as well as trained for after selection. That is, if talent management is to become truly a firm's first priority, then consideration of the talents related to the learning processes must be a key component of those activities.

Knowledge Saving

Knowledge by itself has a limited value. It must be available to people in the organization—and, ideally, available when and where they need it. Thus, the second step in knowledge management and organizational learning is the saving of the information and knowledge, the saving of what the organization has learned from its many activities.

For example, a former CEO of Hughes Space Systems Division has commented on the organization's losing of what he referred to as the recipe for making satellites. That, is, they didn't record the steps they went through or the specific things they learned with each satellite they designed and built so that each successive satellite required the project team to start almost from scratch. They had not developed a 'learning organization' or 'knowledge management' mentality, and thus paid the price of having to re-create the needed knowledge on every new contract.

A similar example in a more 'low-tech' organization involved McDonald's (the world's largest hamburger fast food restaurant chain) also losing its literal recipe (Griesing and Kirk, 2004). Part of its famous advertising in the past was its reference to the 'special sauce' on its hamburgers. Evidently, in a cost-cutting move, they changed the formula for making the sauce. A couple of years ago, during a period of financial struggle, they brought back one of their retired CEOs, Fred Turner. In one of his moves to return the firm to financial health, he orchestrated the return to the old formula for their hamburger sauce. Except that he found that the firm had literally 'lost the recipe.' Thank goodness (if you love McDonald's hamburgers and their special sauce), he remembered the name of a supplier that had helped develop the sauce 36 years before. The supplier was able to recover the recipe.

The point in these examples is to show how important it is to save the 'learning' of the organization. If the key knowledge of the organization is not recorded, then when it is needed, at a later time, it is not available. And the organization either has to expend the time and money to recreate the knowledge, with the risk of never recovering it and/or losing the customer, or of losing so much money in the process that the firm cannot recover.

The key to learning more and better is 'sharing.' Every individual (and team) has information and knowledge unique to him/her/it. Others need that information and knowledge in order to most effectively do their jobs, to serve their customers. The one with the information/knowledge must share it with the ones without it (or, at least make it available to others). And the ones without it must be willing to learn from those who have it, to access the stored information and knowledge. And, in order to make this work, the organization must facilitate and encourage the storing and sharing of the knowledge.

Technology is very important in all fours steps of the learning and knowledge management process. But it is particularly important here. Many formats have been created for the purpose of recording knowledge, including archives, directories, and yellow pages. And many technologies have been applied to facilitate the saving of information and identifying who has the knowledge and where and how it can be located. Obviously, computer technology, intranets, and online communication all enhance the ability of employees and teams to develop, record, update, and access knowledge.

Many special concerns arise at this stage, including the willingness (or not) of employees (and, possibly, others as well, such as customers and suppliers) to participate in the initial creation, identification, and evaluation of the knowledge and in the posting of the information, as well as the later updating of it as new knowledge and experience is accumulated.

Knowledge Sharing

The third step in the organizational learning process is the sharing of the knowledge and information. Once experience is evaluated, the critical lessons are learned, and the knowledge is captured and saved, then such learning needs to be leveraged by making sure it is shared with the organization. The technology and infrastructure that 'houses' that knowledge must be open to everyone and everyone needs to be familiar with how to access it. If directories (that identify experts and experience throughout the organization) and archives (that house 'lessons learned') are not available to everyone, or the technology is not 'user friendly,' then the lessons learned are not available to people in the organization as they need it or want to use it. Thus, creativity is stifled and new customer questions and needs (that usually can be answered and met with earlier experience from meeting other customer's needs) cannot be satisfied, or at least not in a timely manner, as the customer service representative struggles with the new opportunity.

Even if locating experts and retrieval of knowledge is relatively easy and people know how to use the systems, if the organizational culture does not reward its use or the seeking of help from outside one's immediate resources (one's own knowledge base or one's immediate team or office) is frowned upon, then knowledge will not be shared and, again, the ability of the firm to learn faster than the competition will be greatly constrained.

Knowledge Use

The final, and maybe most important step in organizational learning is the willingness to use organizational and individual knowledge. People need to be willing to rely on the knowledge of others.

The objective of organizational learning and knowledge management is to create a motivated and energized work environment that supports the continuous creation, collection, use, and reuse of both personal and organizational knowledge in the pursuit of business success (Ahmed et al., 2002). Central to achievement of this objective are two fundamental assets: people (whose knowledge resides in their skill, expertise, experience, intuition, etc.) and organizations (whose knowledge is embedded within its culture, processes, and systems). How well these are capitalized determines the extent of the organization's competitive advantage.

The key (and, often most difficult) step in this process is to create a corporate culture that supports organizational learning, the sharing of knowledge, and the use of what is stored and shared. As Senge (2006) has indicated, the creation of this community of committed learners is typically the biggest stumbling block to successful organizational learning. Employees must recognize that today, given the rapid and revolutionary nature of change in every area of business, no one is an expert. People are only as good as their willingness to tap into a network of people who collectively have the expertise to solve the new problems that customers present.

As important as organizational learning and knowledge management is to the success of the organization, there are many barriers to its effectiveness. At the individual level, people don't listen well to others, they lack curiosity and inquisitiveness, their arrogance of assumed knowledge blocks out others' ideas, they take critical feedback personally, they tend not to admit they have a problem, their lessons are not made explicit, or codified, and their existing mental models block out the possibilities of other perspectives (Argyris & Schön, 1978; Argyris, 1999; Marquardt, 2002; Senge, 2006). Of course, there are also organizational barriers to learning, some of which include the arrogance of success that blocks continual screening of the environment for changes, organizational forgetting (not recording the lessons of experience, losing key people to turnover), lack of communication across functional boundaries, organizational politics and conflicting goals and objectives, stereotypes about customers and suppliers, and cultural misunderstanding (Marquardt & Reynolds, 1994; Bartlett & Ghoshal, 2002; Senge, 2006).

A learning organization is a firm that has an enhanced capacity to learn, adapt, and change. Its intellectual capital includes not only learning basic capabilities needed to perform current jobs, but also stimulating creativity and innovation plus motivating employees to acquire and apply new knowledge. It is an organization skilled at creating, acquiring, and transferring knowledge, and at modifying its behavior to reflect new knowledge and insights. And it is one that continually transforms itself to better manage and use knowledge for corporate success; it encourages and empowers people within and outside the organization to learn as they work, and it utilizes technology to maximize learning and productivity.

In summary, learning in organizations is:

- the most important source of sustainable competitive advantage and, thus, absolutely necessary for success in our turbulent, chaotic world;
- important at the individual, team, organizational, and inter-organizational (cross-border) levels.

And effective learning organizations are skilled at:

- problem-solving;
- experimenting with new ideas;
- learning from their mistakes;
- learning from the success (and failures) of others, as in examination of best practices; and
- transferring knowledge quickly and effectively throughout the organization.

THE GLOBAL LEARNING ORGANIZATION

The global learning organization has all the above characteristics except it is more complex. The global context (national cultures, national legal frameworks, varying local knowledge and practice) provides an overlay and filter through which all attempts at learning and knowledge management have to flow. Eventually, firms find that the players (in this case, the global talent) determine whether attempts to learn across borders work (Marquardt, 2002; Fink & Holden, 2005; Voelpel, Dous, & Davenport, 2005). And all of this takes place in an environment where firms of all types, in all sorts of industries, and from all countries have become aware of the need to gather talent (Wooldridge, 2006).

You have to have the right leaders (visionaries, people who can teach the vision, and people who know how to develop the culture of learning); the right local staff (who are adaptable and willing to learn from others in other parts of the organization—that is, willing to dispense with the 'I won't deal with it if it wasn't invented here' syndrome, and willing to share what they know); the right agents of transfer (expatriates, business travelers); the right technology (for capture and transfer of knowledge and learning—meaning everyone throughout the global operations has the same technology, but also has common knowledge about and the willingness to use the technology); and the right people at headquarters, who understand the impact of national culture and the difficulties encountered in transferring knowledge out from headquarters and in from the field.

During the dot.com boom and bust of the 1990s and now on into the new millennium, corporate executives are learning a lasting lesson: it takes extremely competent people to manage global organizations and to create and deliver the complex services and products that are keys to success in the global economy (O'Toole and Lawler, 2006). For global firms to be successful in the future they will need to develop systems and practices that attract, retain, and develop skilled, educated, and talented managers, professionals, and technicians, from all over the world. A person's country of origin will no longer be the overriding factor in hiring and retention. Now, the strengths and passion the person brings to the job will be the most important. 'We are, in fact, at the dawn of the Age of Human Capital' (ibid.: 35).

The shifts to services, high-speed product development, global operations, and higher-value-added activities by enterprises around the globe have led them to create ever-more complex organizations. And this creates the need for ever-more competent employees and executives. The HRM function and management in general are now under increasing pressure to acquire, develop, and retain the talent and to capture and use the learning that are critical to delivering the creativity, innovation, and customer service on a global level that is needed for sustained competitive advantage (see, for example, Ellerman, 1999; Moore and Birkinshaw, 1998; Tsang, 1999; Javidan et al., 2005; Lunnan, et al., 2005; Paik and Choi, 2005; and Voelpel et al., 2005).

LINKAGES BETWEEN TALENT MANAGEMENT AND THE GLOBAL LEARNING ORGANIZATION

In a 2005 special issue on global transfer of management knowledge in the *Academy of Management Executive*, the guest editors (Fink and Holden, 2005) demonstrated the important and necessary linkages between people and organizations in the global economy. As the title of the special issue indicated, it was about the transfer of management knowledge, but as has been suggested in this chapter and throughout this book, all levels of talent are important. The articles illustrated two main points. First, the special issue made the point that the global transfer of management knowledge (indeed, all kinds of knowledge) has to be seen as a form of experimentation with people and processes. In the early phases, newly introduced international knowledge transfer systems rapidly meet resistance. This can be followed by a period of socialization between expatriate top managers and local managers (getting to know each other). If there is also an opportunity to slowly replace local staff who could not or did not want to work under the new management practice by people with better cultural fit, there is a good chance that years later the originally intended management practice can be implemented. But this may require the remaining issues to be resolved in what might be called 'a space of social negotiation,' which could become a cross-cultural power game. The creation of a framework of intensive interaction between the key parties seems to be a precondition as it helps establishing cross-cultural trust, which is strongly emphasized as being decisive for a successful process of changing attitudes (p. 7).

The second point made is that people in 'remote regions' will not participate in knowledge management systems unless they feel trusted—and hence valued—by headquarters. So, attention by headquarters (central, regional, and country) to both developing this trust and identifying people who are willing to work in such an environment, goes a long way toward ensuring that transfer of knowledge can and will take place. And this transfer of knowledge ought to go in both directions, since best practice, best ideas, and best talent to implement such practices and ideas is as likely, today, in our 'flat world,' to be located in foreign affiliates and locales as it is to be located 'at home' in central headquarters and home country operations (Friedman, 2005).

In light of these points, in order for the MNE to become a global learning organization and, thus, to ensure its sustained competitive success, it must do the following:

- Adopt three parallel attitudes:
  - make talent management priority number one for management and HR (Cascio, 2005b);

- hire the right (and best) people—no matter where they are located in the world and great things will happen (Buckingham & Coffman, 1999; Buckingham & Clifton, 2001; Collins, 2001);
- implement the understanding that there is a direct (line of sight) link between positive employee attitudes and stock price (Rucci et al., 1998; Hurwitz, et al., 2002; Schmidt, 2002b).
- Attract and retain the best qualified talent it can to staff the MNE. These qualifications must include an ability and willingness to share what one has learned and to learn from others and must, therefore, be a part of the recruiting and hiring process as well as components of the training and development agenda (Briscoe, Schuler, & Claus, 2008).
- Attract and retain talent that is interested in and qualified for international assignments.
- Facilitate transfers between various employment locations, product and project assignments, and functional responsibilities within the MNE, wherever they are located around the globe.
- Establish global training and support programs that develop and enhance and provide opportunities for the organization's talent, wherever they are located.
- Establish and maintain a consistent and reasonable relationship between the compensation of employees of all affiliates, both at home and abroad.
- Maintain a reward system that is reasonable in relation to the practices of competitors around the globe while also providing the recognition and rewards that attract and retain the best global talent.

The survey of organizations that had survived and prospered over the last 25 years by the LBA Consulting Group (Berger, 2004), found that those organizations that achieved sustained excellence, first and foremost recognized the need for proactive talent management and developed systematic ways to accomplish it. They found that successful companies either directly articulated or intuitively focused on three outcomes (p. 4), which reinforces the work discussed in this chapter by Peters (1997), Buckingham and Coffman (1999), Collins (2001), and Burd and Tumolo (2004), among others, and provides a good summary of the importance of talent management in the global organization:

- The identification, selection, development, and retention of 'superkeepers' (that small group of individuals who have demonstrated superior accomplishments, and who embody the core competencies and values of the organization). Their loss or absence severely retards organizational growth because of their disproportionately powerful impact on current and future performance and their holding of the corporate memory. Bill Gates once said, 'Take our twenty best people away from us and I can tell you that Microsoft would be an unimportant company' (quoted in Berger, 2004, p. 4).

- The identification and development of high-quality replacements for a small number of positions designated as key to current and future organization success (commitment to succession planning and the development of people to fill key positions). Gaps in replacement activity for key positions are highly disruptive, costly, and distracting to the organization (and a sign, as discussed, of loss of organizational memory and knowledge).

- The classification of and investment in each employee based on his/her actual and/or potential for adding value to the organization (his or her strengths and talents, as described by Buckingham and Clifton, 2001). As Cascio (2005b) and Berger (2004) point out, talent management requires not only identifying the top performers at all levels, but also those who, for whatever reasons, cannot, do not, or will not meet organizational expectations, and must, therefore, be outplaced.

CONCLUSIONS

My first task in this chapter was to define who it is we are talking about managing when we talk about 'talent management.' In this book and chapter, organizational talent pertains to all employees performing organizational tasks, including contingent employees. Second, I provided a description of 'learning in organizations' and knowledge management and their desired result, 'the learning organization.' As far as I can tell, no researchers have connected the topics of talent management and organizational learning—or the learning organization. I therefore attempted in this chapter to draw some parallels between talent management and learning in organizations (through critical processes of knowledge management), and to demonstrate how the achievement of organizational excellence and success is reliant on both these issues. Indeed, organizations cannot achieve one without achieving the other. Third, I put all of this information into a global context, describing why talent management now is by necessity a global concern, and why talent and its organizational learning, coordinated through effective processes of knowledge management, must be managed from a global perspective.

NOTE

1. This is meant to be only a sample of some of the best of the multitude of references on these topics over the last ten years: Ahmed, Kok, and Loh (2002); Argyris (1999); Baird and Henderson (2001); Barnes (2002); Berry (1998); Brown and Duguid (2000); Choo (1998); Davenport (2005); Davenport and Prusak (1998); Davenport (1999); DiBella and Nevis (1998); Dotlich and Noel (1998); Easterby-Smith, Burgoyne, and Araujo (1999); Fuller (2002); Fulmer and Keys (1998); Garger (1999); Hansen, Nishria, and Tierney (1999); Kleiner and Roth (1997); Lei, Slocum, and Pitts (1999); Liebowitz and Beckman (1998); Lubit (2001); Marquardt (1999; 2002); McKenzie and van Winkelen (2004); Roth and Kleiner (1998); Senge (1990; 2006); Sparrow, 1998; Stewart (1994; 1997); Townsend and Gebhardt (1999); and Webber (1999).

REFERENCES

Ahmed, P.K., Kok, L.K, and Loh, A.Y.E. (2002). *Learning Through Knowledge Management.* Oxford/Woburn, MA: Butterworth-Heinemann Publishers.

Argyris, C. (1999). *On Organizational Learning* (2nd edition). Malden, MA: Blackwell Publishers.

Argyris, C. and Schön, D.A. (1978). *Organizational Learning: A Theory of Action Perspective.* Reading, MA: Addison-Wesley Publishing.

Baird, L. and Henderson, J.C. (2001). *The Knowledge Engine: How to Create Fast Cycles of Knowledge-to-Performance and Performance-to-Knowledge.* San Francisco: Berrett-Koehler Publishers.

Barnes, S. (ed.) (2002). *Knowledge Management Systems.* London: Thomson Learning.

Baron, A. and Armstrong, M. (2007). *Human Capital Management: Achieving Added Value Through People.* London/Philadelphia: Kogan Page Limited.

Bartlett, C.A. and Ghoshal, S. (2002). *Managing Across Borders: The Transnational Solution* (2nd edition). Boston: Harvard Business School Press.

Becker, B.E., Huselid, M.A., and Ulrich, D. (2001). *The HR Scorecard: Linking People, Strategy, and Performance.* Boston, MA: Harvard Business School Press.

Berger, L.A. (2004). Creating a Talent Management System for Organization Excellence: Connecting the Dots. In Berger, L.A. and Berger, D.R. (eds) *The Talent Management Handbook.* New York: McGraw-Hill.

Berry, M. (1998). Learning 'next practices' generates revenues. *HRMagazine*, **43**(7): 146–152.

Briscoe, D.R., Schuler, R.S., and Claus, L. (2008). *International Human Resource Management* (3rd edition). London/New York: Routledge.

Brown, J.S. and Duguid, P. (2000). Balancing act: How to capture knowledge without killing it. *Harvard Business Review*, **78**(3): 73–80.

Buckingham, M. and Clifton, D.O. (2001). *Now, Discover Your Strengths.* New York: The Free Press.

Buckingham, M. and Coffman, C. (1999). *First, Break All the Rules: What the World's Greatest Managers Do Differently.* New York: Simon & Schuster.

Burud, S. and Tumolo, M. (2004). *Leveraging the New Human Capital.* Palo Alto, CA: Davies-Black Publishing.

Cascio, W.F. (2005a). *Managing Human Resources* (7th edition). Boston: McGraw-Hill Irwin.

Cascio, W.F. (2005b). *Yahoo! Fueling the Talent Engine* (DVD). Alexandria, VA: The Society for Human Resource Management.

Choo, C.W. (1998). *The Knowing Organization*. New York: Oxford University Press.

Collins, J. (2001). *Good to Great*. New York: HarperCollins.

Davenport, T.H. (2005). *Thinking for a Living: How to Get Better Performance and Results from Knowledge Workers*. Boston, MA: Harvard Business School Press.

Davenport, T.H. and Prusak, L. (1998). *Working Knowledge: How Organizations Manage What They Know*. Boston, MA: Harvard Business School Press.

Davenport, T.O. (1999). *Human Capital*. San Francisco: Jossey-Bass Publishers.

Dessler, G. (2005). *Human Resource Management* (10th edition). Upper Saddle River, NJ: Pearson Prentice Hall.

DiBella, A.J. and Nevis, E.C. (1998). *How Organizations Learn*. San Francisco: Jossey-Bass Publishers.

Dotllich, D.L. and Noel, J.L. (1998). *Action Learning: How the World's Top Companies are Re-creating Their Leaders and Themselves*. San Francisco: Jossey-Bass Publishers.

Dzinkowski, R. (2000). The measurement and management of intellectual capital: An introduction. *Management Accounting* (UK), **78**(2): 32–36.

Easterby-Smith, M., Burgoyne, J. and Araujo, L. (1999). *Organizational Learning and the Learning Organization*. London: Sage Publications.

Ellerman, D.P. (1999). Global institutions: Transforming international development agencies into learning organizations. *Academy of Management Executive*, **13**(1): 25–35.

Fink, G. and Holden, N. (2005). Introduction: The global transfer of management knowledge. *The Academy of Management Executive*, **19**(2): 5–8.

Fisher, C.D., Schoenfeldt, L.F., and Shaw, J.B. (2006). *Human Resource Management* (6th edition). Boston: Houghton Mifflin Co.

Fitz-enz, J. (2000). *The ROI of Human Capital: Measuring the Economic Value of Employee Performance*. New York: American Management Association.

Friedman, T.L. (2005). *The World is Flat*. New York: Farrar, Straus and Giroux.

Fuller, S. (2002). *Knowledge Management Foundations*. Boston, MA: Butterworth-Heinemann.

Fulmer, R.M. and Keys, J.B. (1998). A conversation with Peter Senge: Developments in organizational learning, *Organizational Dynamics*, **27**(Autumn): 33–42.

Garger, E.M. (1999). Goodbye training, hello learning. *Workforce*, **78**(11): 35–42.

Gomez-Mejia, L.R., Balkin, D.B. and Cardy, R.L. (2007). *Managing Human Resources* (5th edition). Upper Saddle River, NJ: Pearson Prentice Hall.

Griesing, D. and Kirk, J. (2004). McDonald's finds missing ingredient. *Chicago Tribune*, 24 June.

Hansen, M.T., Nohria, N., and Tierney, T. (1999). What's your strategy for managing knowledge? *Harvard Business Review*, March–April: 106–116.

Herman, R., Olivo, T., and Gioia, J. (2003). *Impending Crisis: Too Many Jobs, Too Few People*. Winchester, VA: Oakhill Press.

Hurwitz, J., Lines, S., Montgomery, B., and Schmidt, J. (2002). The linkage between management practices, intangibles performance, and stock returns. *Journal of Intellectual Capital*, **3**(1): 51–61.

Javidan, M., Stahl, G.K., Brodbeck, F., and Wilderom, C.P.M. (2005). Cross-border transfer of knowledge: Cultural lessons from Project GLOBE. *Academy of Management Executive*, **19**(2): 59–76.

Kanter, M. and Zagata-Meraz, S. (2007). Hewitt Associates' research shows impact that pivotal employees have on business results. Retrieved 15 January 2008 from http://www.hewittassociates.com/intl/NA/en-US/AboutHewitt/Newsroom/Press ReleaseDetail.aspx.

Kleiner, A. and Roth, G. (1997). How to make experience your company's best teacher. *Harvard Business Review*, September–October: 172–177.

Knez, M. and Ruse, D.H. (2004). Optimizing your Investment in your Employees. In Berger, L.A. and Berger, D.R. (eds) *The Talent Management Handbook*. New York: McGraw-Hill.

Kravetz, D.J. (2004). *Measuring Human Capital: Converting Workplace Behavior into Dollars*. Mesa, AZ: Kravetz Associates Publishing.

Lei, D., Slocum, J.W., and Pitts, R.A. (1999). Designing organizations for competitive advantage: The power of unlearning and learning. *Organizational Dynamics*, **27**(3): 24–38.

Liebowitz, J. and Beckman, T. (1998). *Knowledge Organizations*. Boca Raton, FL: St. Lucie Press.

Lubit, R. (2001). Tacit knowledge and knowledge management: The keys to sustainable competitive advantage. *Organizational Dynamics*, **29**(3): 164–178.

Lunnan, R., Lervik, J.E.B., Traavik, L.E.M., Nilsen, S., Amdam, R.P., and Hennestad, B.W. (2005). Global transfer of management practices across nations and MNC subcultures. *Academy of Management Executive*, **19**(2): 77–80.

Marquardt, M.J. (1999). *Action Learning in Action: Transforming Problems and People for World-class Organizational Learning*. Palo Alto, CA: Davies-Black Publishing.

Marquardt, M.J. (2002). *Building the Learning Organization* (2nd edition). Palo Alto, CA: Davies-Black Publishing.

Marquardt, M. and Reynolds, A. (1994). *The Global Learning Organization*. Burr Ridge, IL: Irwin.

Mathis, R.L. and Jackson, J.H. (2006). *Human Resource Management* (11th edition). Mason, OH: Thomson South-West.

McCall, M.W., Jr. (1998). *High Flyers: Developing the Next Generation of Leaders*. Boston, MA: Harvard Business School Press.

McCall, M.W., Jr. and Hollenbeck, G.P. (2002). *Developing Global Executives: The Lessons of International Experience*. Boston, MA: Harvard Business School Press.

McCall, M.W., Jr., Lombardo, M.M., and Morrison, A.M. (1988). *The Lessons of Experience: How Successful Executives Develop on the Job*. New York: The Free Press.

McKenzie, J. and van Winkelen, C. (2004). *Understanding the Knowledgeable Organization: Nurturing Knowledge Competence*. London: Thomson Learning.

Michaels, E., Handfield-Jones, H., and Axelrod, B. (2001). *The War for Talent*. Boston, MA: Harvard Business School Press.

Mondy, R.W., Noe, R.M., and Premeux, S.R. (2008). *Human Resource Management* (10th edition). Upper Saddle River, NJ: Pearson Prentice Hall.

Montgomery, W. and Lines, S. (2002). Evolution of the HR lexicon: The intangibles value chain. *CRNnews*, **7**(6): 1, 25.

Moore, K. and Birkinshaw, J. (1998). Managing knowledge in global service firms: Centers of Excellence. *Academy of Management Executive*, **12**(4): 81–92.

O'Toole, J. and Lawler, E.E., III (2006). *The New American Workplace*. New York: Palgrave Macmillan and Alexandria, VA: Society for Human Resource Management.

Paik, Y. and Choi, D.Y. (2005). The shortcomings of a standardized global knowledge management system: The case study of Accenture. *Academy of Management Executive*, **19**(2): 81–84.

Peters, T. (1997). *The Circle of Innovation*. New York: Alfred A. Knopf.

Pfeffer, J. (1998). *The Human Equation: Building Profits by Putting People First*. Boston, MA: Harvard Business School Press.

Phillips, J.J., Stone, R.D., and Phillips, P.P. (2001). *The Human Resources Scorecard: Measuring the Return on Investment*. Boston, MA: Butterworth-Heinemann.

Redman, T. and Wilkinson, A. (2006). *Contemporary Human Resource Management* (2nd edition). Harlow, UK: Prentice Hall/Financial Times.

Roth, G. and Kleiner, A. (1998). Developing organizational memory through learning histories. *Organizational Dynamics*, 43–60.

Rucci, A.J., Kirn, S.P. and Quinn, R.T. (1998). The employee-customer-profit chain at Sears. *Harvard Business Review*, Jan–Feb.: 82–97.

Schmidt, J.A. (2002a). Best practices in human resource management: New perspectives—the strategic importance of human capital. (Keynote presentation) *CRNnews* Conference, 20 September, San Diego, CA.

Schmidt, J.A. (2002b). How much is goodwill worth? *MWorld*, American Management Association, **1**(1): 23–28.

Schmidt, J.A. (2002c). Measuring, managing the intangible: Taking stock of human and organizational strategy, *CRNnews*, **7**(3): 1, 25, 31.

Schmidt, J.A. and Lines, S. (2002). A measure of success. *People Management* (UK), **8**(9): 32–34.

Senge, P.M. (1990). The leader's new work. *Sloan Management Review*, **32**(1): 74–92.

Senge, P.M. (2006). *The Fifth Discipline: The Art & Practice of the Learning Organization*. New York: Doubleday/Currency.

Sparrow, J. (1998). *Knowledge in Organizations*. London: Sage Publications.

Stewart, T.A. (1994). Your company's most valuable asset: Intellectual capital. *Fortune*, October: 68–73.

Stewart, T.A. (1997). *Intellectual Capital: The New Wealth of Organizations*. New York: Doubleday/Currency.

Stockley, D. (2006). Talent management concept—definition and explanation. Retrieved from http://derekstockley.com.au/newsletters-05/020-talent-management.html, 16 January 2008.

Thorne, K. and Pellant, A. (2007). *The Essential Guide to Managing Talent*. London/Philadelphia: Kogan Page Limited.

Townsend, P.L. and Gebhardt, J.E. (1999). *How Organizations Learn*. Crisp Publications.

Tsang, E.W.K. (1999). Internationalization as a learning process: Singapore MNCs in China. *Academy of Management Executive*, **13**(1): 91–101.

Tulgan, B. (2002). *Winning the Talent Wars*. New York: W.W. Norton & Co.

Voelpel, S.C., Dous, M., and Davenport, T.H. (2005). Five steps to creating a global knowledge-sharing system: Siemens' Share Net. *Academy of Management Executive*, **19**(2): 9–23.

Weatherly, L.A. (2003). Human capital—the elusive asset. *SHRM Research Quarterly*. Alexandria, VA: Society for Human Resource Management.

Webber, A.M. (1999). Learning for a change (interview with Peter Senge). *Fast Company*, **24**(May): 178–188.

Wooldridge, A. (2006). The battle for brainpower [a series of articles on the global war for talent]. *The Economist*, 7 October: 3–24.

11. Social capital: bridging the link between talent management and knowledge management

Rhonda Jones

INTRODUCTION

There have been hundreds of books, articles, and research papers published regarding knowledge management. A search of Amazon.com and ScienceDirect will yield at least 1100 books with 'knowledge management' in the title, and 5500 articles that have the phrase in the title, abstract, or keywords. What is knowledge management and why are so many people writing about it?

Many definitions of knowledge management exist, with there being no one explanation that is universally accepted. In this chapter, knowledge management is referred to as 'the strategies and processes of identifying, capturing, and leveraging knowledge to enhance competitiveness' (University of California, Berkeley, 1999) and 'the ability to develop, share, deposit, extract, and deliver knowledge such that it might be retrieved and used to make decisions or to support the [organizational] processes' (Nakra, 2000: 54). The topic is of interest because, generally, the consensus has been that efficient and effective knowledge management leads to a more competitive organization through, among other things: better decision-making (Kridan & Goulding, 2006), improved customer service (Laycock, 2005), lower transaction costs (Silvi & Cuganesan, 2006), and increased product innovation (Tsai & Ghoshal, 1998).

In the same vein, talent management has become a popular buzzword in the management literature. Although not yet as prolific a topic as knowledge management, a recent search of Amazon.com and ScienceDirect yielded more than 800 books and articles with 'talent management' in the title, abstract, or keywords. Using the definition of talent management 'broadly defined as the implementation of integrated strategies or systems designed to increase workplace productivity by developing improved processes for attracting, developing, retaining and utilizing people with the required skills and aptitude to meet current and future business needs' (Lockwood, 2005), the case has also been made that implementing well-designed talent management processes will lead to increased organizational competitiveness through a reduction in turnover and heightened employee satisfaction and commitment (Heinen & O'Neil, 2004; Farley, 2005; McCauley & Wakefield, 2006).

An interesting question that results from an initial investigation of these two topics is what, if any, is the connection between knowledge management and talent management? Can a firm use one to influence the other? A careful review of the literature implies that there is a way for talent management to impact knowledge management. It is through the use of activities that enhance social capital, which is 'broadly defined as an asset that inheres in social relations and networks' (Leana & Van Buren, 1999: 538).

This chapter will briefly discuss the three main concepts that have already been introduced (talent management, knowledge management, and social capital), outline how they are linked in organizations, and summarize practical steps that managers and HR practitioners can take to enhance all three, which should lead to increased competitiveness.

KNOWLEDGE MANAGEMENT

Separate from data, which is simply 'raw or unabridged descriptions or observations about states of past, present, or future worlds' (DeLong & Fahey, 2000:3), knowledge is a product of human reflection and experience. It resides at both individual and collective levels, is communicated through language, stories, rules, and actions, and can vary according to the specific environmental context (ibid.).

Knowledge has been recognized as one of the keys to organizational survival. Further, as the pace of change in business increases, it becomes imperative for an organization to increase its ability to capture, organize, and disseminate its collective knowledge in order to maintain its competitive advantage. 'In today's global economy, which is characterized by shorter product life cycles, increased employee turnover, and ubiquitous information technologies, an organization's ability to manage knowledge may be the only remaining source of competitive advantage' (Vincent, 2006: 1). As stated by Thomas and Allen (2006): 'In an economic system where innovation is critical, the ability to increase an organization's sources of innovation from all forms of knowledge becomes a key capability' (p. 136). The implication for the organization is that it is increasingly difficult to attain and sustain a competitive advantage through the reallocation of financial capital and other tangible assets. Instead, an organization must harness intangible assets (such as human capital) in order to remain at the forefront of its industry.

While many organizational theorists acknowledge and express the import ance of knowledge, most recognize it simply as an object, or as residing in the minds of individuals (Nonaka, 1994; Crossan, Lane, & White, 1999) and do not discuss the importance of dynamic social interactions in the emergence of collective knowledge (Schwandt & Marquardt, 2000). Subsequently, much of the research to date has been focused on knowledge management through the use of information systems, databases, and knowledge portals as a means to collect and capture information (Vincent, 2006). However, this research does not account for the knowledge that is socially constructed through conversations and created by a collective. Thus, there has been relatively little empirical research or scholarly discussion that examines the dynamic nature of the process of creating and managing organizational knowledge. This omission is slowly changing, however.

For example, Nonaka's (1994) original theory of knowledge creation has been refined to encompass a knowledge-based approach to organizations that 'views a firm as a knowledge-creating entity, and argues that knowledge and the capability to create and utilize such knowledge are the most important source of a firm's sustainable and competitive advantage' (Nonaka, Toyama, & Nagata, 2000: 1). Like others (e.g., Schwandt & Marquardt, 2000), Nonaka et al. argue that 'the knowledge-creating view of the firm is different from other theories of the firm in its basic assumptions that humans and organizations are dynamic beings, and in its focus on the process inside the firm' (p. 2).

If one takes the perspective that knowledge is not static and is instead 'context-specific, relational, dynamic and humanistic' (ibid.), then individuals and the relationships and social ties they develop, not organizations themselves, become the key to effective and efficient knowledge management. In other words, social capital becomes the key to knowledge management.

SOCIAL CAPITAL

Researchers have recently positioned social capital as a key factor in understanding knowledge management efforts (e.g., Nahapiet & Ghoshal, 1998). Like knowledge management, social capital has been defined in many ways. Adler and Kwon (2000), for example, list more than 15 different definitions of the term. A forerunner in discussing social capital, Coleman (1998) proposed that social capital is 'a particular kind of resource available to an actor, comprising a variety of entities which contain two elements: they all consist of some aspect of social structures, and they facilitate certain actions of actors—whether persons or corporate actors—within the structure' (p. 98). Coleman elaborated further by stating that social relations 'establish useful capital resources for actors through processes such as establishing obligations, expectations and trustworthiness, creating channels for information, and setting norms backed by efficient sanctions' (pp. 103–104). Putnam (1996: 66) offered a slightly different but similar view by defining social capital as 'features of social life—networks, norms, and trust—that enable participants to act together more effectively to pursue shared objectives.'

McElroy, Jorna, and Van Engelen (2006: 126) summarize one of the basic differences among many of the definitions of social capital, including those by Coleman and Putnam:

> These two orientations to social capital theory differ mainly in terms of who or what they see as the focal actor in action-oriented scenarios. In the case of ego-centric theory, the focal actor is an individual who appropriates resources from social networks or relationships in which he or she is situated, in order to take individual action. In the case of socio-centric theory, the focal actor is a collective, such as an organization or a society, and social capital is found in 'the internal linkages that characterize [their] structures [and which] give them cohesiveness' (Adler and Kwon, 2000, p. 92) and an enhanced capacity for collective action.

A common theme among the definitions of social capital that are focused within an organizational setting is that it can be seen as one way to help firms 'improve their innovative capability and conduct business transactions without much fuss and, therefore, has substantial implications for economic performance' (Maskell, 2000: 111). Social capital is harnessed and developed through processes in which employees interact and learn from one another (thereby building and reinforcing trust, communication networks, and norms). Tempest, McKinlay, and Starkey (2004) state: 'the concept of social capital sharpens the focus upon those features of organization that seem to facilitate collective action in pursuit of shared goals, such as trust, culture, social support, social exchange, psychological contract, informal organization, social and interfirm networks' (p. 1525). These are the same processes and features outlined by Nonaka's theory of knowledge creation, and, ultimately, the same processes that facilitate knowledge management.

Nonaka's Theory of Knowledge Creation

In outlining his theory of organizational knowledge creation, Nonaka (1994) specifies two basic types of knowledge—explicit and tacit. Explicit knowledge is transmittable in formal language and can be expressed in words and numbers. It is easily communicated in the form of hard data, procedures, and practices, and is concretely manageable (Gore & Gore,

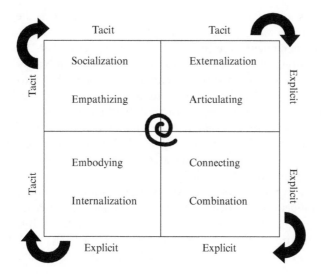

Source: Taken from Nonaka et al. (2000).

Figure 11.1 Nonaka's SECI process

1999). In contrast, knowledge that is tacit begins at the individual level, is context-specific, and is often difficult to communicate (Nonaka & Konno, 1998). It also has a cognitive component, which consists of embedded mental models, beliefs, and perceptions (Gore & Gore, 1999).

The key to Nonaka's model is the social interaction that occurs when each type of knowledge is converted from one stage to the other. Diagramming the process in a cyclical configuration, Nonaka outlined four modes of knowledge creation—socialization, externalization, combination, and internalization (SECI)—that combine to create an amplifying spiral effect. See Figure 11.1.

During the internalization phase, explicit knowledge is converted to tacit knowledge by individuals actively being engaged in a process or procedure that requires them to use new skills. For instance, a college student taking an introductory biology course with no prior experience in the field might refer to a textbook for instructions on how to dissect a frog. After reading the directions, the student would then need to practice what he or she reads in order to internalize the process.

Externalization is the reverse of internalization. During this phase, tacit knowledge is converted to explicit knowledge, i.e., intuitions or images are translated into tangible statements, metaphors, or models (Nonaka & Takeuchi, 1995). In the combination stage, there is an explicit to explicit transfer of knowledge. Here, new data from inside or outside the organization is obtained, shared, and edited or processed into concrete, usable material such as documents or electronic files (Nonaka & Konno, 1998).

Socialization is the fourth and most important stage in Nonaka's model. It is in this phase that individuals communicate openly, begin to share and question their personal beliefs, and attempt to understand the feelings of others (regardless of whether or not an individual agrees with those opinions) in order to develop a shared mental model that will serve as the foundation for future activities (ibid.). While all four modes are important to organizational survival, it is the socialization mode that truly expands and enhances organizational knowledge.

Nonaka isn't the only one who views organizational knowledge creation as being influenced by social factors (e.g., Akgun, Lynn, & Byrne, 2003; Dhanaraj et al., 2004; Lines, 2005; and Senge et al., 2007). But are social relations and interactions the same as social capital? There is little agreement within the literature. According to Bakker et al. (2006: 595):

> two general approaches exist in the social capital literature. One approach considers social relations to be social capital: the more ties one maintains, the larger one's social capital. Alternatively, Gabby and Leenders (1999) make a distinction between the social capital structure itself and its outcomes. Social ties do not necessarily translate into social capital; they only do so if these ties assist an actor in the attainment of particular goals.

Whichever approach one takes (whether it's the number of social ties or their purpose that makes a difference), there is a growing body of literature linking social capital to knowledge management (e.g., Rastogi, 2002; Cross & Sproull, 2004; Hoffman, Hoelscher, & Sherif, 2005; Walker & Christenson, 2005; Wu & Tsai, 2005).

Underlying this link is the realization that 'knowledge creation is the notion that knowledge resides within and is created by individuals' (Nonaka, 1994: 16). The know-how and information that individuals gain over time form their knowledge stocks. Current knowledge stocks shape the scope and direction of the search for new knowledge, so knowledge creation is a path-dependent process (Dosi, 1982) as 'newly acquired inputs are integrated with existing knowledge stocks' (McFadyen & Cannella, 2004: 736). To quote Prieto and Revilla (2006): 'Knowledge stocks in organizations exist at several levels (Nonaka & Takeuchi, 1995; Crossan et al., 1999): the individual, the group and the organizational levels' (p. 173). The key for managers and human resource professionals is how to get individuals and groups to voluntarily contribute their 'knowledge stocks' to benefit the organization as a whole. This is where social capital, fueled by talent management, comes into play.

TALENT MANAGEMENT

Talent is the 'above average giftedness towards a task through which an employee creates added value in his or her work' (Schoemaker & Jonker, 2005: 510), and talent management is 'broadly defined as the implementation of integrated strategies or systems designed to increase workplace productivity by developing improved processes for attracting, developing, retaining and utilizing people with the required skills and aptitude to meet current and future business needs' (Lockwood, 2005). Examples of possible talent management practices and processes include aligning human resource programs with strategic business goals, broadening existing definitions of diversity, developing future leaders, and engaging employees in an effort to increase their emotional and intellectual commitment to the organization. Ultimately, the goal of talent management should be to 'acquire, retain, motivate, and develop the talent needed to keep their organizations operating efficiently and competitively' (Frank & Taylor, 2004: 34). To accomplish this, Frank and Taylor (p. 40) state 'the future of talent management may well be about embracing and leveraging connectedness.' This connectedness takes place between an organization and its employees, and among all staff members, and helps develop and enhance social capital.

As stated by Nonaka et al. (2000):

the theory of organizational knowledge creation is based on the assumption that individuals and organizations have a potential to *grow together* through the process of knowledge creation. . . . When individuals interact with each other at such a place, one transcends one's own boundary, and as a result, changes oneself, others and the place itself. . . . In organizational knowledge creation, one plus one could be more than two. (p. 3)

This belief was echoed by Schoemaker and Jonker (2005) when they wrote:

The organization and the individual have become mutually interdependent. In order to perform, the organization has become dependent on the talents the individuals possess. At the same time the individual needs the organization—a work community—in order to develop and use his or her talents. As a consequence the relationship between an individual and the organization needs to be (re)shaped on the basis of reciprocity. (p. 508)

Schoemaker and Jonker go on to state: 'For service providing organizations the following formula should apply: talents plus social capital equal competitive advantage' (p. 510).

While that formula is logical, the equation should be expanded for all organizations, not just service firms. The formula that should apply is: individual

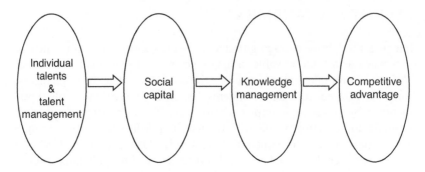

Figure 11.2   Formula for competitive advantage for all organizations

talents plus talent management leads to social capital; social capital enhances knowledge management, which results in competitive advantage. These relationships are illustrated in Figure 11.2.

PRACTICAL APPLICATIONS

Armed with this new equation, as shown in Figure 11.2, what can human resource practitioners and managers do to manage the talent within their organizations to stimulate social capital to enhance knowledge management? Losey, Meisinger, and Ulrich (2005: 170) state:

> Hiring, retaining, and developing people are critical activities in a world in which intellectual capital and organizational capabilities are the key source of competitive advantage, so working on incentive pay plans and improving recruiting and hiring systems are important activities. But there may be a potentially even more important activity for HR—the diagnosing and changing of mind-sets and mental models.

According to the same authors: 'Weick once noted, "Believing is seeing," intervening to affect mental models may be one of the more efficient ways of making the changes that HR so often advocates to build a high performance culture' (ibid.).

To what mental models were Losey et al. referring? What type of philosophy should HR be promoting? One possibility is that talent management doesn't end when a new employee is hired. Instead, managers and HR practitioners must take an active role in the entire talent management process, which includes specific actions before and after an employee is recruited. One must keep in mind that an organization cannot learn or adapt on its own. Instead, the people within the firm must revise their actions (and possibly their belief system) in order to affect meaningful change. To draw from Adler and Kwon (2002), in order for social capital to be activated, it is not enough that individual motivation and ability be present in individuals. There must also be an opportunity for those components to be released in the organization. In addition, the context of the organization, both internal and external, plays a key role in what information comes into the organization from the outside, what is moved through the system in terms of actionable knowledge, and what is ultimately transformed into something that is created or enhanced by the organization and cycled back into the environment.

What makes up this context? Among other things, key components are: the industry and business environment, life cycle of the organization, structure of the firm, core competencies and skills (talent) of the firm's leaders and staff, and established social processes and activities. As stated by Nonaka et al. (2000: 2): 'we view knowledge as context-specific, relational, dynamic and humanistic. Knowledge is essentially related to human action. Without understanding the nature of human beings and the complex nature of human interactions, we cannot understand the theory of organizational knowledge creation.' These words hold true not just for knowledge creation and management, but also for social capital and talent management. All three are: (1) influenced by whether employees choose to interact with one another, form bonds, and share information; and (2) tied to the mission, vision, and business strategy and objectives of the firm. Because of that, an organization must play an active role in developing, maintaining, and enhancing all three through the equation shown in Figure 11.2, beginning with talent management.

Recruitment Strategies

An organization's competitive edge is how it manages the talent within the organization. If a company wants to set itself apart from others in the field, it needs a workforce that is talented and dedicated. As a result, the talent management process should ideally begin before an employee is hired. The first issue that must be addressed is how will staff help the firm accomplish its vision, mission, and strategic goals? The following questions are vital in helping to formulate a plan:

1. What are the key business objectives for the next five to ten years? Every company, public or private, for-profit or not, is in business to achieve its mission and vision. In order to do that, the strategic objectives must be realized. Before management can properly begin the perpetual talent management cycle, it must identify what it is the organization must achieve.

2. What skills and talents will be needed to accomplish the strategic goals? It will be important not to simply accomplish the objectives at a minimal level, but to excel. As a result, the organization's staff will need certain competencies. Are the skills that they need now going to change significantly in the near future? If so, how? Are they skills that can be taught or are they more similar to personality and character traits that are not easily revised? If the competencies can be taught, it's less important that potential and existing employees have the necessary skill sets. If they cannot be easily taught, the organization will have to give considerable thought to how it will effectively and efficiently recruit individuals with the required competencies.

3. Do the current staff within the firm have the skills necessary to help the company achieve its objectives? If so, the organization should make sure it has policies and procedures to retain its employees and encourage their commitment to the firm. If not, the organization will have to develop a plan to educate and train its staff so they can enhance their competencies or contract with individuals who have the needed skills. For example, if an organization specializes in wedding planning and is looking to expand into the event planning business, it would want staff that understand how to interact with corporate clients, who are not the same as engaged couples, and soon-to-be brides. In addition, the firm will need staff who understand the different venues, vendors, and events that will appeal to corporate clients. There are some competencies that might remain the same in the transition from wedding planning to corporate event planning (e.g., project management, time management, multi-tasking, and being customer focused), but there are some that would be very different, such as handling repeat customers over a number of years, delivering formal presentations to large groups of individuals (senior executives), cold calling, and so forth.

Most organizations do an adequate job of detailing the skills required for positions within the firm through the use of classification studies and position descriptions. But how many of those same firms ever take the time and energy to assess and document the competencies their employees possess that go above and beyond what is necessary for their present positions? The tracking of such knowledge and abilities in a skills inventory or database would be of tremendous value by enabling companies to utilize internal talent for just-in-time and unforeseen, urgent tasks and more efficiently forecast the pool of internal candidates who might be qualified for current vacancies and future open positions.

In addition, organizations should strive to hire employees, especially at the mid- and upper levels of management, that have taken steps to enhance their personal and professional development. This could be an indication that such employees actively scan their environment to see how they can remain competitive in the labor market. This same sort of diligence and foresight could translate into large gains for an organization if these employees continue that type of behavior while employed for the firm. Taking college classes, training sessions, and workshops, attending professional conferences, belonging to industry associations, and networking with peers, are all activities that facilitate the acquisition and transmission of new and relevant information. In addition, such actions may indicate that these individuals are already receptive to sharing ideas with others, something that will be vital to establishing and maintaining the type of knowledge creation process that Nonaka (1994) and others have outlined.

As employees complete training, certification, and development sessions and programs (whether company-paid or not) firms should update their skills database with that information. In that way, the inventory of competencies will grow and change as employees enhance their personal and professional development. Once again, the tracking of newly acquired and enhanced skills could aid in filling vacancies with in-house human capital. In turn, such a process could support and facilitate employees' movement through a career-ladder or lateral job progression, thereby strengthening their job satisfaction and commitment to the firm.

Retention Strategies

Once employees are hired, the talent management process should not end. Instead of allowing the talent management cycle to take its own course, organizations must take an active role in harnessing its talent in order to better manage knowledge. This can be accomplished through facilitating and increasing social capital. As discussed in a 2005 article by Hoffman et al., 'social capital helps to facilitate the development of collective intellectual capital by affecting the conditions necessary for exchange and combination [of knowledge] to occur' (p. 98). This sentiment has been echoed by other authors such as Kakabadse, Kouzmin, and Kakabadse (2001), McAdam (2000), and Murray and Blackman (2006). Specific examples of talent management actions that organizations can take to affect social capital include:

1. Establishing knowledge-enabling environments (Nonaka & Konno, 1998) that include a high level of trust, encourage employees to think outside the box, and welcome both teamwork and individual contributions. There should be an opportunity for cross-pollination of ideas between units and departments. This can be accomplished by formal

meetings and events but might be better served by purposefully structuring the work environment so that employees from various departments and with different job duties naturally and regularly interact in an informal way—ways that would logically and over time (McFayden & Canella, 2004) result in the formation of social bonds that strengthen social capital and enhance knowledge transfer.

2. Deliberately utilizing technology, including software and databases, to maximize social interactions among employees. 'The higher the social interaction, the higher the structural dimension of social capital . . . Through interaction, a common frame of reference develops providing a shared language for communication' (Sherif, Hoffman, & Thomas, 2006: 798). Organizations must proceed with caution in this area, however, because research, such as that by Sherif et al. (ibid.) has shown that 'heavy use of electronic networks was negatively associated with [social capital] outcome quality and efficiency' (p. 797) and 'information overloads pose a threat to the development of the cognitive dimension of social capital' (p. 798).

3. Developing and enacting a succession plan to formulate a pool of potential leaders and employees for key positions within the firm. This is critical for the growth and success of all firms and is especially important for 'highly technical, specialized organizations where the learning curve is steep. In such organizations, it is imperative to develop leaders and technical experts at all levels of the organization' (Cotten, 2006: 107).

Some firms, especially federal, state, and local agencies, have an enormous challenge in maintaining vital skill sets due to the large number of middle- and senior-level managers nearing retirement and the added pressure of financial constraints, position cuts, and hiring freezes. The result of such actions is that many organizations could quickly lose valuable experience and corporate knowledge. The only way to prevent a severe brain-drain of corporate talent is to deliberately engage in succession planning to continually recruit, train, and promote existing and new employees so the organization's intellectual and human capital will remain solid.

For succession planning to be effective there must be a well-designed process for selecting appropriate employees and positions, distinguishing the competencies required for these positions, and making those skills known to all employees so those interested in preparing for these positions can have ample time to do so. The skills inventory mentioned earlier in this chapter should also be monitored to guarantee that there 'are no key job skills or knowledge that reside with only one employee, and there should be a comprehensive list of at-risk functions. These are functions that the organization does not perform adequately or is in danger of not performing adequately due to low staffing levels or pending departures' (Cotten, 2006: 109).

As an additional component of succession planning, organizations should establish job shadowing and mentorship programs by which retiring employees and those with key skills who are voluntarily resigning can interact with their potential successor(s) prior to their departure from the firm. This would allow the two groups of employees, each with 'different types and contents of knowledge' (Nonaka et al., 2000: 10) to engage in at least three of the four modes of Nonaka's knowledge creation spiral (externalization, internalization, and socialization; see Figure 11.1) and enable the tacit organizational knowledge of the most tenured employees to be passed to less experienced staff. As stated by Widen-Wulff and Suomi (2007): 'An organization's workforce is not just a collection of expert individuals; emphasize that they must build their intellectual capital, also their skills to adapt and distribute information, in official and unofficial networks. Create an organizational atmosphere that supports and awards knowledge sharing' (p. 64).

CONCLUSION

This chapter has investigated the connections between knowledge management, social capital, and talent management. According to Nonaka et al. (2000): 'knowledge and skills give a firm a competitive advantage because it is through this set of knowledge and skills that a firm is able to innovate new products/processes/services, or improve the existing ones more efficiently and/or effectively' (p. 2). 'Social capital has been shown to enhance a firm's "speed and efficiency in the creation and transfer of knowledge" (Kogut & Zander, 1996) and this can impact an organization's ability to improve performance' (Sherif et al., 2006: 796). In addition, 'organizations with high levels of social capital have more knowledge management capabilities than organizations with low levels of social capital' (Hoffman et al., 2005: 98). To build social capital, organizations must manage the talent within their firms. 'Understanding the value inherent in attracting and keeping excellent employees is the first step toward investing systematically to build the human and social capital in an organization' (Holtom, Mitchell, & Lee, 2006: 316).

Talent management leads to the enhancement of social capital, which is key to knowledge management, which is essential to organizational competitiveness. Stated another way, in order for a firm to remain competitive, it must constantly manage the acquisition, flow, and application of knowledge;

in order to manage knowledge, organizations should maintain and enhance their social capital; and in order to establish social capital, firms must first manage employee talent.

Although empirical research concerning which specific individual talents and skills contribute to social capital and how these competencies can be effectively developed is absent from the literature, there is a growing body of work surrounding various recruitment, retention, and development strategies that can be utilized to enable the exchange, enhancement, and application of social capital in organizations. The most important lessons for managers and human resource practitioners may result from applying these strategies. As stated by Storberg-Walker and Gubbins (2007): 'by identifying the facilitators and inhibitors to knowledge sharing, learning and performance improvement, the HRD [human resource development] practitioner can devise ways to manage the individuals or change the organization, functions, or processes to facilitate individual, team/process, and organizational success' (p. 303).

REFERENCES

Adler, P. and Kwon, S. (2000). Social Capital: The Good, the Bad, and the Ugly. In Lesser, E.L. (ed.), *Knowledge and Social Capital: Foundations and Applications*. Boston: Butterworth-Heinemann, pp. 89–115.

Akgun, A.E., Lynn, G.S., and Byrne, J.C. (2003). Organizational learning: A sociocognitive framework. *Human Relations*, **56**(7): 839.

Bakker, M., Leenders, R.T., Gabbay, S.M., Kratzer, J., and Engelen, J.M. (2006). Is trust really social capital? Knowledge sharing in product development projects. *The Learning Organization*, **13**(6): 594–605.

Coleman, J.C. (1998). Social capital in the creation of human capital. *American Journal of Sociology*, **94**(S1): 95–120.

Cotten, P.A. (2006). *Planning for the Future: A Workforce Needs Assessment for Maryland State Highway Administration*. Maryland, USA: University of Baltimore, Schaefer Center for Public Policy.

Cross, R. and Sproull, L. (2004). More than an answer: Information relationships for actionable knowledge. *Organization Science*, **15**(4): 446–463.

Crossan, M.M., Lane, H.W., and White, R.E. (1999). An organizational learning framework: From intuition to institution. *Academy of Management Review*, **24**(3): 522–537.

De Long, D.W. and Fahey, L. (2000). Diagnosing cultural barriers to knowledge management. *The Academy of Management Executive*, **14**(4): 113–127.

Dhanaraj, C., Lyles, M.A., Steensma, H.K., and Tihanyi, L. (2004). Managing tacit and explicit knowledge transfer in IJVs: the role of relational embeddedness and the impact on performance. *Journal of International Business Studies*, **35**(5): 428–442.

Dosi, G. (1982). Technological paradigms and technological trajectories—A suggested interpretation of the determinants and directions of technical change. *Research Policy*, **11**(3): 147–162.

Farley, C. (2005). HR's role in talent management and driving business results. *Employment Relations Today*, **32**(1): 55–62.

Frank, F.D. and Taylor, C.R. (2004). Talent management: Trends that will shape the future. *Human Resource Planning*, **27**(1): 33–41.

Gore, C. and Gore, E. (1999). Knowledge management: The way forward. *Total Quality Management*, **10**(4/5): S554–S560.

Heinen, J.S. and O'Neill, C. (2004). Managing talent to maximize performance. *Employment Relations Today*, **31**(2): 67.

Hoffman, J.J., Hoelscher, M.L., and Sherif, K. (2005). Social capital, knowledge management, and sustained superior performance. *Journal of Knowledge Management*, **9**(3): 93–101.

Holtom, B., Mitchell, C.J., and Lee, T.R. (2006). Increasing human and social capital by applying job embeddedness theory. *Organizational Dynamics*, **35**(4): 316.

Kakabadse, N.K., Kouzmin, A., and Kakabadse, A. (2001). From tacit knowledge to knowledge management: Leveraging invisible assets. *Knowledge and Process Management*, **8**(3): 137–154.

Kridan, A.B. and Goulding, J.S. (2006). A case study on knowledge management implementation in the banking sector. *VINE: The Journal of Information and Knowledge Management Systems*, **36**(2): 211–222.

Laycock, M. (2005). Collaborating to compete: Achieving effective knowledge sharing in organizations. *The Learning Organization*, **12**(6): 523–539.

Leana, C.R. and Van Buren H.J., III (1999). Organizational social capital and employment practices. *Academy of Management Review*, **24**(3): 538–555.

Lines, R. (2005). How social accounts and participation during change affect organizational learning. *Journal of Workplace Learning*, **17**(3/4): 157–178.

Lockwood, N.R. (2005). Talent management overview. Accessed 9 November, 2006 from http://www.shrm.org/research/briefly_published/Talent%20Management% 20Series%20Part%20I_%20Talent%20Management%20Overview.asp.

Losey, M., Meisinger, S., and Ulrich, D. (2005). *The Future of Human Resource Management: 64 Thought Leaders Explore the Critical HR Issues of Today and Tomorrow*. Hoboken, NJ: Wiley.

Maskell, P. (2000). Social Capital, Innovation and Competitiveness. In Baron, S., Field, J., and Schuller, T. (eds) *Social Capital: Critical Perspectives*. Oxford: Oxford University Press.

McAdam, R. (2000). Knowledge management as a catalyst for innovation within organizations: A qualitative study. *Knowledge and Process Management*, **7**(4): 233–241.

McCauley, C. and Wakefield, M. (2006). Talent management in the 21st century: Help your company find, develop, and keep its strongest workers. *The Journal for Quality and Participation*, **29**(4): 4–9.

McElroy, M.W., Jorna, R.J., and Van Engelen, J. (2006). Rethinking social capital theory: A knowledge management persepctive. *Journal of Knowledge Management*, **10**(5): 124–136.

McFadyen, M.A. and Cannella, A.A. (2004). Social capital and knowledge creation: Diminishing returns of the number and strength of exchange relationships. *Academy of Management Journal*, **47**(5): 735–746.

Murray, P. and Blackman, D. (2006). Managing innovation through social architecture, learning and competencies: A new conceptual approach. *Knowledge and Process Management*, **13**(3): 132–144.

Nahapiet, J. and Ghoshal, S. (1998). Social capital, intellectual capital and the organizational advantage. *Academy of Management Review*, **23**(2): 242–266.

Nakra, P. (2000). Knowledge management: The magic is in the culture. *Competitive Intelligence Review*, **11**(2): 53–60.

Nonaka, I. (1994). A dynamic theory of organizational knowledge creation. *Organization Science*, **5**(1): 14–37.

Nonaka, I. and Konno, N. (1998). The concept of 'Ba': Building a foundation for knowledge creation. *California Management Review*, **40**(3): 40–54.

Nonaka, I. and Takeuchi, H. (1995). *The Knowledge Creation Company: How Japanese Companies Create the Dynamics of Innovation*. Oxford: Oxford University Press.

Nonaka, I., Toyama, R., and Nagata, A. (2000). A firm as a knowledge-creating entity: A new perspective on the theory of the firm. *Industrial and Corporate Change*, **9**(1): 1–20.

Prieto, I.M. and Revilla, E. (2006). Learning capability and business performance: A non-financial and financial assessment. *The Learning Organization*, **13**(2/3): 166–186.

Putnam, R.D. (1996). The strange disappearance of civic America. *The American Prospect*, **7**(24): 66–72.

Rastogi, P.N. (2002). Knowledge management and intellectual capital as a paradigm of value creation. *Human Systems Management*, **21**(4): 229.

Schoemaker, M. and Jonker, J. (2005). Managing intangible assets: An essay on organising contemporary organisations based upon identity, competencies and networks. *The Journal of Management Development*, **24**(5/6): 506–518.

Schwandt, D.R. and Marquardt, M.J. (2000). *Organizational Learning: From World-class Theories to Global Best Practices*. Boca Raton, FL: St. Lucie Press.

Senge, P.M., Lichtenstein, B.B., Kaeufer, K., Bradbury, H., and Carroll, J.S. (2007). Collaborating for systemic change. *MIT Sloan Management Review*, **48**(2): 44.

Sherif, K., Hoffman, J., and Thomas, B. (2006). Can technology build organizational social capital? The case of a global IT consulting firm. *Information & Management*, **43**(7): 795–804.

Silvi, R. and Cuganesan, S. (2006). Investigating the management of knowledge for competitive advantage: A strategic cost management perspective. *Journal of Intellectual Capital*, **7**(3): 309.

Storberg-Walker, J. and Gubbins, C. (2007). Social networks as a conceptual and empirical tool to understand and 'do' HRD. *Advances in Developing Human Resources*, **9**(3): 291–311.

Tempest, S., McKinlay, A., and Starkey, K. (2004). Careering alone: Careers and social capital in the financial services and television industries. *Human Relations*, **57**(12): 1523–1545.

Thomas, K. and Allen, S. (2006). The learning organization: A meta-analysis of themes in literature. *The Learning Organization*, **13**(2/3): 123–139.

Tsai, W. and Ghoshal, S. (1998). Social capital and value creation: The role of intrafirm networks. *Academy of Management Journal*, **41**(4): 464–476.

University of California, Berkeley (1999). Glossary. Accessed 9 November, 2006 from http://www2.sims.berkeley.edu/courses/is213/s99/Projects/P9/web_site/glossary.htm.

Vincent, C. (2006). Leadership in a knowledge society: An examination of the relationship between perceptions of leadership and knowledge management actions using a social action theory approach. *Dissertation Abstracts International*, **67**(5) (AAT 3218612; ProQuest document ID No. 1158518611).

Walker, D.H. and Christenson, D. (2005). Knowledge wisdom and networks: A project management centre of excellence example. *The Learning Organization*, **12**(3): 275–292.

Widen-Wulff, G. and Suomi, R. (2007). Utilization of information resources for business success: The knowledge sharing model. *Information Resources Management Journal*, **20**(1): 46–67.

Wu, W. and Tsai, H. (2005). Impact of social capital and business operation mode on intellectual capital and knowledge management. *International Journal of Technology Management*, **30**(1/2): 147.

12. Certifying knowledge and skills is critical for talent management[1]

Jim M. Graber and William J. Rothwell

INTRODUCTION

Traditional talent management efforts have prioritized recruiting, development, and retention of talent, but don't address how we multiply the impact of talented individuals while they are with the organization, or retain their best practices when they ultimately depart. Knowledge and skill management can address this gap by identification of critical knowledge and skills, followed by systematic transfer of this information.

Organizations use many approaches to capture and transfer knowledge, such as formal training, mentoring, expert networks, best practice databases, and professional gatherings. Although these practices are very valuable, their ability to transfer knowledge *consistently* to other employees is unclear. *Employee certification* is a rigorous, proactive approach to knowledge and skills management. It systematically addresses knowledge/skill acquisition and transfer. This chapter introduces a comprehensive approach to employee certification called CT[5] and provides two contrasting case studies that highlight the manner in which certification can be tailored to organizational needs.

'Our new nurses are stupid. They don't even know the basics.'[2] Mary's comment may sound a bit extreme, but through her lens of 25 years of nursing experience, the new nurses appear ill-prepared. A veteran emergency physician also present during this conversation seconded Mary's comment, noting that when he was on a floor at the hospital where he works, and an emergency occurred, he no longer spoke to new nurses. There was no time. Instead, he directed his instructions to an experienced nurse, who then helped manage the emergency and at the same time instructed less-experienced nurses.

These sentiments are not intended to indict nurses, doctors, or healthcare, but rather to be illustrative of the learning needs of newcomers in many professions. In fact, healthcare is generally far more conscientious than most professions in ensuring that people in critical positions have the training they require. Medical care is regulated by local, state, and federal entities. In the United States, the Joint Commission (JCAHO) provides a rigorous review of healthcare providers at least every three years.

Physician training, although not perfect, far surpasses the training provided in most professions. Here are some of the key elements:

- Careful initial selection. Medical schools look at undergraduate grades, achievements and the MCAT (Medical College Admission Test) exam to help identify individuals with a track record of achievement (grades and activities) as well as appropriate mental capacity to absorb complex material.
- Students are required to build a foundation of required knowledge, primarily science education in the case of physicians. Examinations help assess that they have absorbed what they need.
- Clinical training is also required, with an increase in emphasis as knowledge builds, and time in the program increases. Although medical schools vary in their approach, it is common for them to require a series of experiences (rotations) to give students broad exposure to all aspects of medical practice.
- Medical students receive their doctorate, and become Medical Residents. Residents are productive members of the team, but they continue to develop under the watchful eye of an attending physician. A third-year resident will typically perform more advanced procedures or simpler procedures with less supervision than a first-year resident.
- Individuals that successfully complete their residency become attending physicians.
- Attending physicians may obtain additional experience and pass examinations that qualify them as Board Certified in their specialty, such as Emergency Medicine or Surgery.
- Continuing education is required on a regular basis.

KNOWLEDGE TRANSFER

Knowledge transfer is the process of effectively disseminating, applying, and realizing value from knowledge assets (Knowledge Research Institute, 2000). Formal training is only one of many dissemination approaches. Other knowledge transfer approaches include expert networks, computer-based training, best practice databases, mentoring, and professional gatherings. Knowledge transfer to budding physicians far surpasses that of most other professions, although some others (e.g., airplane pilots) are trained similarly. We believe that most organizations can improve their knowledge transfer through a more systematized approach. Here are the key elements:

- careful identification of the knowledge and skills needed by qualified individuals;
- development of the required technical foundation through formal training and self-study;
- significant hands-on experience accomplished by rotation through a series of important activities;
- exposure to a variety of professionals who accept responsibility for development of new staff;
- knowledge assessments that ensure individuals have gained the information they need to be successful;
- skill assessments that ensure individuals can take the knowledge they have been given and apply it successfully on the job;
- continuing education requirements to preserve continuous improvement of individual competence beyond initial training;
- (optional) accreditation of the training and results by an outside agency.

Admittedly, comprehensive knowledge transfer programs can be expensive and time-consuming to develop and implement and are not justified for every position. It is wise to be selective and employ decision criteria such as ROI (return on investment) forecasting. It may make sense to restrict investment for jobs with low impact or high turnover, but most organizations have critical positions where in-depth knowledge transfer would pay large dividends.

Transfer of Tacit Knowledge

Informal or tacit knowledge (knowledge that is gained through experience, but is usually not expressed or included in training programs) must also be managed. Tacit knowledge is resident in experienced workers in organizations. A knowledge transfer program enables veteran workers to pass tacit knowledge to staff with little or no experience. Additionally, programs to capture tacit knowledge before experienced workers retire or move on to other organizations are advantageous.

Harking back to nurse Mary's comment ('Our new nurses are stupid . . .'), a knowledge transfer plan can go a long way in addressing the deficits that almost all new employees bring. It is no wonder that new workers, despite their fresh academic degrees and credentials, require a significant ramp-up period in order to be effective. Tacit knowledge is usually not taught during academic training because it isn't the priority, it hasn't been clearly identified, and it is often organization-specific. Tacit knowledge transfer is an important element of knowledge management and it has been associated with *technical succession planning*, defined as preserving what has been learned from experience by predecessors, including the reasoning behind previous technical decisions, to avoid repeating mistakes in the future (Rothwell & Poduch, 2004).

How then can such tacit wisdom be identified, captured, distilled, transmitted and assessed? Using experienced workers as subject matter experts, a variety of questions such as the following can be asked:

- What is the most difficult *daily* situation you commonly encounter in your experience? Or, what are the common mistakes?
- What happens in the situation? Can you describe it step by step?
- What makes it so difficult, or so common?
- What do you do in the situation, and what happens as a result of what you do?
- What advice do you have for others who face this situation?

Other variations of these questions may also be used to elicit tacit knowledge.

REVERSING SKEPTICISM ABOUT THE VALUE OF STAFF DEVELOPMENT

Who could logically argue against the benefits of a skilled staff? And yet, the arguments against investing in staff development are abundant. Here is a sample:

- It is easier and more effective to hire the skills we need.
- If we increase our staff's skills, we'll increase the likelihood they will be poached by competitors. In the end, our training investment only increases attrition, which decreases staff skill levels.
- We need the staff producing, not lost to training.
- Contracting is less expensive than hiring.
- Costs need to be reduced, and training is less critical than other functions.

Skepticism runs deep among many organization leaders regarding the effectiveness of training interventions to develop staff and improve performance reliably and cost-effectively, despite decades of rigorous research demonstrating how to structure training (see Bernthal et al., 2004). Even training managers may be unwilling to risk measuring the impact of their training, or unwilling to invest the effort since senior management may not be requesting it (Mirza, 2004). Simply stated, leaders will no longer accept, on faith, that the benefits yielded by training justify the costs, and at the same time their organizations typically are not collecting information that would help them understand better if training is providing a tangible return.

For those that do want to measure the results they are achieving from training and other human resource programs, guidance is readily available (see Phillips & Phillips, 2007). Current metrics for measuring training have evolved far beyond those that were commonly used in the past. Whereas the number of people that received training may have sufficed as a training metric in the past, today the focus is much more on training impact, and many useful metrics have been identified (Fitz-enz, 2000).

What does it take for an organization to buy into comprehensive employee development? A clear business case is always helpful. Forecasting the ROI of various training and non-training alternatives can be very impactful, along with associating employee development to employee retention or succession planning. In an increasing number of cases, employee development is the only viable option for acquiring sufficient numbers of people with the required skills. How must employee development be repositioned to build greater confidence among organization leaders? Here are six guiding principles that are likely to increase commitment and investment:

1. *Employee development should be* tangibly *linked to strategic company objectives, key performance indicators (KPIs), and/or customer needs.* Simply stating that employee development supports organization objectives is not sufficient. Employee development, when used as a performance-enhancing intervention, must have clearly stated performance-related outcomes. Front-end analysis is the key to identifying (a) desired objectives of sponsors and stakeholders, and (b) metrics to measure program success.
2. *Employee development should only occur after a task analysis is in hand, that is, a clear map of the knowledge, expertise, traits, values, and best practices that correlate with success in a role or job.* Job/role profiling, behavioral event interviewing, and/or external research help identify knowledge, skills, values, and attitudes that make a difference.
3. *Employee development should be integrated with work; it is not a separate event.* Given the oft-stated rule of thumb that 90% of learning

comes from experience, why should training be separated from normal work? Much of training can be structured around work and achievement of company objectives. In fact, on-the-job training is one of the most effective ways to get results because trainees are held accountable by their immediate supervisors, not off-the-job instructors (Rothwell & Kazanas, 2004). Further, using extensive on-the-job training helps ensure transfer of training to the job. Employee development should be established as a job expectation that is no less important than accomplishing other critical tasks.

4. *Individuals and training professionals share accountability for process and outcomes.* Rigorous assessment, including documented on-the-job application, demonstrates that individuals have progressed to the desired and measurable levels of development and accomplishment—and also provides a basis for effective coaching and further development.

5. *Employee development will often be more effective when it is blended with other methods, resulting in a holistic approach to performance improvement.* Employee development works better when it is coupled with incentives, be they opportunities for advancement, increased compensation, or simply solutions to handling current challenges. Many other interventions can be effectively combined with employee development, such as improved work tools, more enlightened supervision, or even an enhanced work environment. In fact, in order for training transfer to occur, managers have to set expectations, reward appropriately, and provide opportunities to use new skills. Without managers who are trained to support transfer and development of direct reports, employee development efforts are often frustrated.

6. *Professional knowledge is constantly growing and evolving: individuals must keep pace, as well as contribute to the organization's body of knowledge.* Continuing education requirements and learning reinforcement help create long-term value from the initial training investment. Merely to maintain current knowledge, reinforcement through repetition, practice, or drill may be required. Variations in work context, novel problems, and changing scenarios require that employees continually build upon their previous training, and even create new knowledge themselves, which then should become part of an organization's knowledge management system.

How then can organizations utilize these principles, and be confident that their workforce is capable of achieving the organization mission? Next, we introduce CT[5], a flexible guide for organizations that want to reliably develop critical knowledge and skills.

CT[5]: A COMPREHENSIVE ROADMAP FOR EMPLOYEE CERTIFICATION PROGRAMS[3]

Traditionally, certification has been formulated to demonstrate the individual's ability to perform effectively. Certification has been associated with a wide array of professions (Hale, 2000; Knapp, 2002). There are certified accountants, medical technicians, auto mechanics, and many others.

We believe a broader, more encompassing process and definition is required to meet business needs. We define certification as *a process that prepares individuals and then demonstrates and documents that they meet their employer's requirements. This is accomplished by identifying required knowledge, skills, behaviors, and attitudes, by developing and implementing effective knowledge transfer programs, and by creating and administering a variety of employee feedback and assessment tools.* This approach to certification is consistent with the employee development principles that we enumerated previously. When certification is used in organizational settings, there may be many company-specific requirements. For example, in the two certification case studies described in this chapter, the knowledge and skill needs for General Manager and Salesperson are not profession-wide needs. CT[5] (Certification Track 5) is the acronym for a rigorous, five-track program designed to certify that employees have required knowledge and skills. Organizations select some or all tracks depending on their needs. The five tracks of CT[5] are:

> CT1 = *Organization needs analysis*: confirm organization needs and readiness and plan the certification project
> CT2 = *Job analysis*: analyze role requirements, deliverables, and learning objectives
> CT3 = *Employee development*: identify needed training and learning and design and implement it
> CT4 = *Assess knowledge and skills*: certify and re-certify qualified individuals
> CT5 = *Administer the program*: develop administrative procedures, staffing, and technology and keep certification up to date

Table 12.1 shows the elements included in each track of CT[5].

The CT[5] tracks are arranged in a logical implementation sequence. For example, it generally makes sense to analyze critical job knowledge and skill needs (Track 2) before designing and delivering training (Track 3). However, the tracks may occur in a different order, particularly when an organization implements training, and then moves to some of the other tracks to assess training impact or to increase impact.

Table 12.1   Elements of CT[5]

CT1	CT2	CT3	CT4	CT5
Confirm Organization Needs and Readiness and Plan the Certification Project	Analyze Role Requirements, Deliverables, and Learning Objectives	Identify Needed Training and Learning and Design and Implement It	Certify and Re-certify Qualified individuals	Develop Administrative Procedures, Staffing and Technology and Keep Certification Up To Date
☐ 1. Review organization needs and readiness: • Certification objectives • Business case (justification) • Sponsorship and organization support • Eligibility to participate in the program(s) • What participants need to know and be able to do, at a high level • Learning processes and tools in place	☐ 1. Conduct the selected job analyses: tasks, knowledge, skills, values, and behaviors ☐ 2. Identify detailed learning objectives that define what individuals need to know and what they need to be able to do	☐ 1. Agree on training and development: • Classes • Self-study • Experiences • Job assignments • Mentoring ☐ 2. Design, develop, deliver, and coordinate the needed learning ☐ 3. Track individual learning and proficiency ☐ 4. Provide opportunities for continuing education	☐ 1. Select one or more certification criteria: • General eligibility requirements • Previous education • Work experience • Previous job performance • Completion of training • Knowledge tests • Performance simulations/ role plays • Work samples • On-the-job ratings by boss, team members, customers • On-the-job results • Letters of recommendation • Review Board endorsement • External credentials	☐ 1. Develop administrative policies ☐ 2. Develop incentives and perks for certification ☐ 3. Train staff to manage assessments, coordinate the certification process, etc. ☐ 4. Coordinate marketing and communications of certification ☐ 5. Manage outside accreditation of certification ☐ 6. Implement technology to automate assessments and certification administration

Table 12.1 (continued)

CT1	CT2	CT3	CT4	CT5
Confirm Organization Needs and Readiness and Plan the Certification Project	Analyze Role Requirements, Deliverables, and Learning Objectives	Identify Needed Training and Learning and Design and Implement It	Certify and Re-certify Qualified Individuals	Develop Administrative Procedures, Staffing and Technology and Keep Certification Up To Date
• Learning culture–the organization and individual enablers/barriers • Appropriate metrics and reporting tools • Supporting technology ☐ 2. Document findings and make recommendations ☐ 3. Plan the remaining steps of the project: • Statement of work • Project plan			• Compliance with Code of Ethics ☐ 2. Develop, pilot test, and refine assessment tools ☐ 3. Periodically re-certify individuals ☐ 4. Conduct psychometric analyses of assessments to ensure validity, reliability, and optimal performance as a measurement tool ☐ 5. Periodically review and revise assessments	☐ 7. Report periodically on candidates, certified individuals and those maintaining certification ☐ 8. Evaluate certification program effectiveness

CT^5 is not appropriate for every development situation. It is most useful when employee competence is critical or when an ill-prepared individual may cause a lot of damage. Here are some situations where it might be a fit:

- when developing professionals who have a big impact on organization success;
- the staff need to be consistently good, day after day;
- individuals have complex or many duties;
- when developing a national or international workforce and where workers need to be able to fill gaps;
- for a contract or contingent workforce;
- failures are costly or unacceptable;
- for an initiative that is time-intensive or that involves a large number of individuals;
- there is a requirement to demonstrate ROI on employee development.

The remainder of the chapter provides two detailed case studies of the application of the CT^5 model. The first case study describes a CT^5 implementation where the emphasis was on defining a structured learning program with loosely applied assessments. By contrast, the second case study describes a situation where a formalized structure of knowledge, skill, and business result assessments were developed. The case studies illustrate that CT^5 implementations are likely to vary widely, based on each organization's needs and culture.

CASE STUDY 1: ALR's GENERAL MANAGER DEVELOPMENT PROGRAM

ALR (a pseudonym) is a North American company that owns and manages a commercial real estate portfolio. ALR is in the early stages of developing a comprehensive talent management program that impacts employee selection, on-boarding, training and development, career development, and succession planning.

ALR manages property throughout the United States and internationally. Locations operate semi-independently, but must adhere to many corporate practices, policies, and guidelines. The staffing structure is similar for most ALR locations. There are eight to nine core positions, such as General Manager, Accountant, Marketing Manager, Operations Manager, Leasing Representative, and Security Manager. These are skilled positions that require significant training and experience.

ALR leadership is acutely aware that given their competition, without competent staff at its locations, its business will suffer or even fail. The individuals that fill core positions strongly impact location performance, so the development of pipelines of employees for these positions is a centerpiece of ALR's talent management program. ALR has also estimated that when it must go to the outside to hire skilled staff, the costs associated with hiring managers (recruitment and salary) versus 'growing their own' is easily $40,000–$50,000 higher.

ALR leadership believes in the value of employee development. Its Human Capital Development (HCD) group is ample in size, capable, up to date and active. HCD has innovatively and ably responded to ALR training and development needs for years. And yet, similar to many other companies, ALR leadership has concerns about the effectiveness of its talent management programs. If talent management isn't adding demonstrable value, ALR isn't going to do it. Workloads are heavy, and managers and employees are too busy to spend time on activities that don't provide clear, verifiable value. In sum, the need for talent management is accepted, but skepticism remains on the effectiveness of traditional talent management practices.

Early in 2006, senior leadership met with HCD and expressed uneasiness over the sufficiency of current talent management programs to fill gaps looming due to company growth and normal employee attrition. While there were many needs, ensuring General Manager (GM) bench strength was leadership's number one priority. This feedback was welcomed by the HCD staff, as they too felt that development for critical positions could be elevated. In fact, HCD was waiting for an indication from management that ALR was ready to take the next step forward. HCD engaged the assistance of an external consultant to assist with development of an Assistant General Manager (AGM) program.[4] An AGM Steering Committee was formed of representatives from leadership, operations, and HCD. The Steering Committee met periodically to review the work of a small AGM task force that was responsible for implementing the program.

The CT[5] model was used to guide the design of the project. HCD had a number of specifications it wanted to address:

- The program needed to be very reliable. That is, participants completing the program needed to be consistently highly qualified.
- The program should be very 'hands-on.' AGMs should learn by working with GMs and specialists (e.g., accountants, marketing representatives, etc.).
- AGMs needed to share responsibility for the training. Although the company would provide the path and needed tools, the AGM needed to complete the requirements.

- AGMs would need to demonstrate their competence, although ALR was not ready yet for formal testing.

HCD staff felt that the term 'GM Certification' would not have a positive connotation at ALR, so it was agreed that there would be no references to certification within the program. However, CT^5 was a good match with ALR's needs, and the implementation covered CT1–CT5 in a two-phase process.

- Phase 1: *ALR readiness assessment*. This phase corresponds to CT1.
- Phase 2: *Employee assessment development*. This phase combines CT2–CT5.

Table 12.2 shows the CT^5 program elements that ALR selected and those that it didn't (crossed out).

Phase 1: Gauging Commitment and Designing a GM Development Program (CT1)

Phase 1 at ALR was a seven-step process (see Box 12.1) that evaluated 13 readiness dimensions (Box 12.2). The conclusion from Phase 1 was that ALR had the important elements in place to proceed with Phase 2. No 'red flags' had surfaced.

A variety of helpful program design and implementation recommendations came out of Phase 1. Following is a sample of the recommendations:

- Ensure program has consistent communications, program content, and materials in all regions of the United States.
- Ensure trainees have the opportunity to visit many company locations.
- Ensure trainees have a significant number of interactions with their peers, managers, organization leaders, and corporate staff.
- Tracking of training progress is a priority.
- Current assessments lack rigor and consistency, and this is an important focus for program enhancement.
- Continued mentorship after program completion will assist trainees to be successful.
- Leverage the CT^5 job analysis to also improve the AGM hiring process.

Phase 2: Task Analysis was the First Step

Phase 2 began with job analysis. ALR wanted to identify required *knowledge* and *skills*, but decided that identifying *values* or doing a detailed

Table 12.2   How CT^5 was implemented at ALR

CT1 Confirm Organization Needs and Readiness and Plan the Project	CT2 Analyze Role Requirements, Deliverables, and Learning Objectives	CT3 Identify Needed Training and Learning and Design and Implement It	CT4 Certify and Re-certify Qualified Individuals	CT5 Develop Administrative Procedures, Staffing and Technology and Keep Certification Up To Date
☐ 1. Review organization needs and readiness: ☐ 2. Document findings and make recommendations ☐ 3. Plan the remaining steps of the project	☐ 1. Conduct the selected job analyses: tasks, knowledge, skills, values, and behaviors ☐ 2. Identify detailed learning objectives that define what individuals need to know and what they need to be able to do	☐ 1. Agree on training and development ☐ 2. Design, develop, deliver, and coordinate the needed learning ☐ 3. Track individual learning and proficiency ~~☐ 4. Provide opportunities for continuing education~~	☐ 1. Select one or more certification criteria: ☐ 2. Develop, pilot test, and refine assessment tools ~~☐ 3. Periodically re-certify individuals~~ ~~☐ 4. Conduct psychometric analyses of assessments~~ ~~☐ 5. Periodically review and revise assessments~~	~~☐ 1. Develop program administration policies~~ ~~☐ 2. Develop incentives and perks for certification~~ ~~☐ 3. Train staff to coordinate process~~ ~~☐ 4. Coordinate communications~~ ~~☐ 5. Manage outside accreditation of certification~~ ☐ 6. Implement technology to automate training, tracking, and/or assessments ☐ 7. Report periodically on candidates ~~☐ 8. Evaluate certification program effectiveness~~

246

BOX 12.1   ALR's PHASE 1 STEPS

1. Project kickoff meeting
2. Review of background materials (training materials and job descriptions)
3. Interviews with key sponsors
4. Focus groups with AGMs, GMs, and Group Directors
5. Analysis of interview and focus group results
6. Task force meeting to review and develop consensus on findings
7. Phase 1 report

BOX 12.2   ORGANIZATIONAL READINESS DIMENSIONS ASSESSED AT ALR

1. Clear goals, goal feasibility, and goal agreement of stakeholders
2. Consensus on desired program enhancements
3. Appropriate program metrics identified for monitoring program results
4. General agreement on the knowledge, skills, abilities, values and attitudes that need to be identified and developed by the program
5. General consensus on the targeted levels of learning, from beginner to expert
6. Agreement on the types of criteria that will be used for entry into the program and program completion
7. Stakeholder support for AGM program
8. Sufficient staffing and resources for program
9. Review of competing priorities/timing
10. Cultural and/or other strengths supporting the program
11. Long-term commitment to maintain program
12. Adequate communications strategy, short and long term
13. Sufficient strategies to address likely organization barriers

analysis of *behaviors* of effective performers would be too much and should be put off until a later date. The role of a GM at ALR is a fusion of many different disciplines. Therefore, a task analysis was a critical starting point. Three senior GMs served as subject matter experts and helped identify 12 functional areas critical to their job. For example, Finance & Accounting, Leasing, Operations, and Security were identified. Eleven to 12 essential topics were identified, on average, within each functional area. For example, Finance & Accounting includes topics such as Revenue Forecasting, Accounts Receivable, Expense Recoveries, Income Statements, and the Sarbanes-Oxley Act. A total of approximately 130 important topics were identified at this stage. Later, some topics were merged together and some were dropped, eventually leaving about 100 topics. Each functional area was rated on overall importance compared with the other functional areas. Each topic was rated on importance, how much time should be spent training people on the topic, and how proficient employees needed to be in that area, ranging from familiarity (the low end) up to fluency.

Based on the extensive knowledge and skills required for GMs, it was determined that putting candidates into training positions (Assistant General Manager—AGM) for 12–24 months would be the best approach for developing General Managers. Each AGM would be responsible for accomplishing a variety of job duties, and also responsible for making steady progress on the 12 functional areas and the associated topics required for qualified GMs. Each AGM worked for a GM, and that GM served as the primary mentor. Subsequent experience with the program has demonstrated the attractiveness of the program to program participants. By definition, AGMs are advancing in their careers, and they can look forward to a large increase in salary when they qualify and are placed as a GM. The AGM development requirements take one to two years to complete, but, by comparison to a normal career path, that is short. The program materials are user-friendly and intuitive and the value of the program to candidates and their supervisors is obvious. If the relevance of the program was unclear, or if the complexity was too great, the program would probably not survive very long.

Four Basic Questions at the Heart of ALR's CT⁵ Process

Identification of the important functional areas and related topics is really just a beginning. The build-out of topics is the next step and the heart of the process. A simple data collection template was designed to collect information for each topic (see Figure 12.1). Information was collected on 100 topics over a period of about four months.

Functional Area, Topic #: Topic Name

Introduction and Why This Topic is Important:

Learning Objectives

Know and Explain: Important information that individuals must understand and be able to clearly explain, answer questions on, and make referrals to appropriate resources when necessary.
1.
2.
Do and Show: These are important tasks or skills that an individual must be able to perform and demonstrate to others when necessary.
1.

Available Resources

1.
2.
3.

Development Opportunities

Training and Self-study: Training & development completed individually through classes, study, or observation.	**Date and Comments**
1.	
Observations and Experiences: Tasks or skills that will be demonstrated to you and/or on which you may perform and receive feedback from a subject matter expert or coach.	
1.	

Knowledge and Skill Demonstration

Tasks/skills to Demonstrate: Activities you may lead and or participate in to show your knowledge and to demonstrate your abilities to complete required tasks/skills for this topic area.	**Date and Comments**
1.	

Review Questions

Questions to Answer: Questions you should be able to properly answer prior to completing development on this topic.	**Date and Comments**
1.	

Figure 12.1   ALR data collection template

Four basic yet powerful questions are at the core of program development. The questions are:

1. *Why is this topic important?* This question creates a context for the candidate of why they should bother learning about this area. Impacts on ALR (e.g., ability to satisfy customers or financial or legal impacts) as well as on a GM (e.g., bonus or difficult situations) are covered. If the importance isn't clearly established, the learning will suffer.

2. *What do employees need to know, explain, do and show?* This question breaks out the required knowledge base as well as the most important tasks that the candidate must be able to complete skillfully. Key outputs and deliverables are identified along with the tasks. This is the most fundamental of all the questions; if this question is not answered properly, the development of subsequent elements, such as training, will probably be wrong. This question must be answered specifically and in depth, going beyond identification of needed competencies.

3. *What training, self-study, observations, work assignments, and mentoring will effectively and efficiently provide the needed development?* Internal class offerings, where available, as well as self-study of relevant documents may provide a basic understanding, but a variety of planned experiences such as demonstrations and job assignments under the tutelage of local SMEs (subject matter experts, e.g., the Accountant, the Marketing Manager, etc.) builds skills and provides highly impactful learning.

4. *What questions must employees be able to answer and what tasks must they be able to do in order for us to be confident that they have acquired the necessary knowledge and skills?* This question helps with staff assessment. It drives home the accountability of the candidate for mastering the material, and provides a tool that ALR can use to measure a candidate's readiness. Typically, five to ten questions are developed to assess knowledge, and demonstration by the candidate of three to five tasks is used to show attainment of skills. ALR is not ready to give multiple choice tests or to set up a formal structure for evaluating the accomplishment of the tasks, so the use of the assessment pieces is unstructured for now. However, HCD feels that may well change in a few years.

A structured process was used to collect data for each topic:

- First, to make it easier for SMEs, the HCD and the consultant prepopulated as much of the templates as possible.

- SMEs were identified for each functional area.
- SMEs were asked to review all the topic templates associated with their functional area, and to make additions and corrections.
- The consultant reviewed the templates for content clarity and completeness and highlighted areas needing further discussion.
- The SME and consultant reviewed template content together and made revisions.
- The consultant did final editing and then prepared the template for entry into the Learning Management System.

For example, for the Finance & Accounting functional area, one of the topics is *Payables*. Following are portions of a completed template (Figures 12.2–12.6):

The Future of CT^5 at ALR

SMEs willingly contributed many valuable hours to development of the GM program. Now that the GM program is complete, ALR is leveraging the collected data to build similar programs for its other critical location positions. In comparison to the four to six months required to build the GM CT^5 program, the next critical position CT^5 program was built in just four weeks by modifying the previously collected topic templates to fit for a different critical position. Programs will be built for three more critical positions over the next six months. Additionally, departments that weren't included in the first wave are clamoring to have similar development programs as soon as possible.

Looking ahead one to two years, several enhancements are anticipated. First, the assessment process is expected to become more formalized. Participants are expected to begin to take written tests as well as to be evaluated on task completion by trained observers. New tie-ins to position

---

Section 1: Introduction and Why This Topic is Important:
Payables are the invoices on which we owe money in the near future. If you purchase new tables, there will be a payable. The amount of interest currently due on loans your location has is also a payable. The non-current portion of loans, however, is not a payable. You can imagine that there are a lot of payables that need to be processed daily.   As a GM you need to know how payables are managed, who manages them, and how to recognize irregularities and act to correct them. Proper and timely handling of invoices will foster continuing relationships with vendors. Regular reviewing of invoices can result in opportunities to take discounts provided by vendors, resulting in monetary savings for the location.

Figure 12.2   Introduction section of completed template

Section 2: Learning Objectives
Know and Explain: Important information that AGMs must understand and be able to clearly explain, answer questions on, and make referrals to appropriate resources when necessary.
1. Describe the process that a payable goes through from the point it is received by Accounting to the point at which funds are transferred to the payee.
2. Describe the approval matrix and its use . . .
Do and Show: These are important tasks or skills that an AGM must be able to perform and demonstrate to others when necessary.
1. Examine payable reports and identify any irregularities.
2. Locate a specific payable and communicate information about it to the payee or anyone else with legitimate interest . . .

Figure 12.3   Learning objectives section of template

Section 3: Developmental Opportunities
Training and Self-study: Development you should study and complete yourself.
1. Ordinary capital expenditures course.
2. Review approval matrix policies (online in ALR knowledge base), noting any questions for further discussion with your Accountant . . .
Observations and Experiences: Tasks or skills that will be demonstrated to you and/or on which you may perform and receive feedback from a subject matter expert or coach.
1. Review the following procedures with your Accountant:

a. Vendor files
      b. Invoice coding
      c. Special handling rules . . .

2. Submit re-classes to your mall Accountant monthly.

Figure 12.4   Developmental opportunities section of template

Section 4: Knowledge and Skill Demonstration
Tasks/skills for AGMs to Demonstrate: Activities you may lead and/or participate in to show your knowledge and to demonstrate your abilities to complete required tasks/skills for this topic area.
1. Execute payables process for one week.
2. Identify trends in spending and expenses . . .

Figure 12.5   Knowledge and skill section of template

Section 5: Review Questions
Questions for AGMs to Answer: Questions that AGMs should be able to properly answer prior to completing development on this topic.
1. What are our Sarbanes-Oxley compliance procedures?
2. What is the approval matrix and how is it used?

Figure 12.6   Review questions section of template

placement are also expected. That is, different locations can vary in size, complexity, and focus. Assessment data can be used in the future to make better candidate placements into locations for which they are most qualified. Using employee development assessment data for job placements may require adherence to additional assessment development standards (such as the Equal Employment Guidelines in the United States), but this was anticipated during the initial assessment development. Finally, ALR anticipates being able to use program assessments to quantify the bench strength of candidates (the pipeline) and job incumbents in different functions.

CASE STUDY 2: PDC's SALESPERSON DEVELOPMENT PROGRAM

We now move to a second example of CT^5. In contrast to the first, this case study describes a much more formalized certification program, complete with comprehensive assessment and detailed policies for implementing the certification. Clearly, CT^5 can vary dramatically based on the dictates of the local situation.

PDC (a pseudonym) is a company that distributes commercial goods. PDC services private and public sector clients. Competition is intense, and customers regularly leverage one supplier against another in order to gain the lowest possible price. Discounts are costly, PDC wishes to maintain a reasonable margin on sales, so PDC has decided not to compete by having the lowest price. Instead, PDC has embarked on a strategy of providing greater value to clients. While PDC does not aim to be the low-cost provider for each product, through its value-added services it can cut *overall* costs for a customer and provide the greatest value. For example, a customer has not saved money if they buy an item for $2 less from a competitor of PDC, but it costs $75 to process the extra paperwork and pay the bill.

PDC's sellers are the linchpin of value-based selling. They must be able to demonstrate that PDC is offering higher value despite competition that may be offering identical products at lower per-piece pricing. In order to do this, the sellers need an understanding of business and financial concepts that were not required in the past. Sellers must be able to diagnose where opportunities exist to cut customer costs, and to then make recommendations that will capitalize on those opportunities. Further, the sellers must now be able to have conversations with people that are placed in higher positions at the customer firm and that have different types of knowledge, for example someone in procurement or even a Chief Financial Officer.

PDC has staked its future on the new value strategy. If the salespeople can't implement the strategy, the potential consequences are frightening. PDC has committed to extensive training for all sellers. In addition, it has decided to develop a certification program in order to develop a community of highly skilled, elite sellers that can implement a value strategy with clients.

The key objectives of the certification program are to:

- provide a clear map of the critical knowledge, skills, behaviors, business results and performance outcomes required by an elite seller;
- help guide the development process for leading sellers by outlining the formal training, experiences, coaching and feedback, and other support considered to be important to prepare sellers for certification;
- provide a reliable, valid, and fair method of assessing skills, knowledge, and behaviors of individuals;
- motivate and reinforce outstanding sales performance through compensation, recognition of excellence, and a variety of other rewards.

Table 12.3 shows the CT^5 program elements that are included in PDC's program:

PDC's Program Design—CT1

PDC began its certification process by designating a small task force of sales and training staff to review needs and develop recommendations for the certification program. Key among the recommendations were the following.

- *Proceed with development of the seller certification.* Certification is a sound, valid, and reliable avenue for developing an *elite group* of sellers through skill-building, assessment, and skills maintenance.
- *Require three levels of achievement for certification.* Successful candidates must demonstrate (1) knowledge, (2) performance, and (3) business results.

Table 12.3   How CT^5 was implemented at PDC

CT1 Confirm Organization Needs and Readiness and Plan the Project	CT2 Analyze Role Requirements, Deliverables, and Learning Objectives	CT3 Identify Needed Training and Learning and Design and Implement It	CT4 Certify and Re-certify Qualified Individuals	CT5 Develop Administrative Procedures, Staffing, and Technology and Keep Certification Up To Date
☐ 1. Review organization needs and readiness: ☐ 2. Document findings and make recommendations ☐ 3. Plan the remaining steps of the project	☐ 1. Conduct the selected job analyses: tasks, knowledge, skills, values, and behaviors ☐ 2. Identify detailed learning objectives that define what individuals need to know and what they need to be able to do	☐ 1. Agree on training and development ☐ 2. Design, develop, deliver, and coordinate the needed learning ☐ 3. Track individual learning and proficiency ☐ 4. Provide opportunities for continuing education	☐ 1. Select one or more certification criteria: ☐ 2. Develop, pilot test, and refine assessment tools ☐ 3. Periodically re-certify individuals ☐ 4. Conduct psychometric analyses of assessments ☐ 5. Periodically review and revise assessments	☐ 1. Develop program administration policies ☐ 2. Develop incentives and perks for certification ☐ 3. Train staff to coordinate process ☐ 4. Coordinate communications ☐ 5. Manage outside accreditation of certification ☐ 6. Implement technology to automate training, tracking, and/or assessments ☐ 7. Report periodically on candidates ☐ 8. Evaluate certification program effectiveness

255

- *Certification should be voluntary.* All sellers at PDC are required to demonstrate appropriate knowledge and skills related to value selling. Certification is above and beyond the basic seller requirements.
- *Provide strong incentives for successfully completing certification.* This must be a win–win for PDC and individual sellers. Financial benefits, recognition, and privileges should all be components of the incentives.
- *Anticipate rapid evolution of the certification program.* Pilot test and fine-tune the program, and regularly update it. Let others at PDC know that there will be frequent program improvements.
- *Follow the certification standards of the National Commission for Certifying Agencies (NCCA) to ensure high quality and to enhance program credibility.* Follow guidelines that will qualify the program to be accredited by an outside agency. This will add credibility to the certification, both for customers and sellers.
- *Support the certification with sufficient staff and clear accountability.* Implementing the certification will require significant coordination and overseeing. This should be spelled out in a detailed administrative guide. Careful consideration should be given when assigning responsibility for program administration.

The Job Analysis Process—CT2

Required knowledge, performance, and results were identified through the use of focus groups, SME interviews, a database of seller suggestions on effective behaviors, and job analysis meetings. The approach is described next.

Knowledge
Required knowledge areas had previously been determined when extensive training around the new value strategy was developed for all sellers. To validate those areas, SMEs rated each on a significance scale from 1–4. SMEs were also encouraged to suggest additional knowledge for certified individuals.

Skills
A company database of suggestions on effective seller practices (ESPs) was analyzed. First, the ESPs were sorted according to the seller task to which they most applied. Then, SMEs evaluated whether the suggested practices should be required of persons being certified.

Focus groups were conducted with experienced, effective sellers by telephone to identify effective seller behaviors for each stage of a value sale. Participants were asked to 'tell stories' about customer interactions that went well, and then to identify the critical behaviors and knowledge that led to the success. Participants were also encouraged to relate stories about customer interactions where the results were not positive, and to identify what could have been done differently that would have resulted in success. Approximately 135 unique behaviors were identified.

The behaviors were analyzed for underlying consistent principles because we felt that focusing on 135 behaviors would be impractical for sellers and their managers. For each behavior, we asked the question, 'Why does this behavior work?' Twenty-one underlying performance standards were identified. The 135 behaviors were used as behavioral examples to further define the performance standards.

The 21 performance standards were organized into five higher-level dimensions, for example Communications and Analysis/Recommendations. Then, a new group of SMEs evaluated each of the 21 standards and the 135 practices. All 21 standards were retained, but about one-third of the behavioral examples were eliminated for reasons such as being too basic, insufficiently important, or out of date. SMEs were asked to submit additional standards and practices that were missing from the model. They were also asked to consider whether there were certain negative practices, or knock-outs, that needed to be strongly discouraged.

Business results
Based on their experience, sales operations staff recommended business results requirements as a starting point, and these were submitted to sales leadership for feedback and approval.

Identify Needed Training and Learning and Design and Implement It—CT3

PDC did not design special training for certification candidates. All sellers participate in a series of classes beginning with basic selling skills. The basics are followed by hands-on workshops.

Certify and Re-certify Qualified Individuals—CT4

PDC has built assessments to cover the three levels of requirements— knowledge, performance, and business results. Once a candidate completes a brief application to begin the certification process, he or she has up to 24 months to complete the requirements. Some of the requirements can be met before the 24-month period even begins, and many others can be completed in the normal daily activities of the seller's regular job.

The requirements are extensive and rigorous. It is important to keep in mind that these requirements are for an elite group of sellers and certification is voluntary. Equally important, candidates get feedback at each step of the way and they develop professionally beneficial knowledge and skills while working on their certification. One might overlook the maturation that occurs during certification, but the process is much more than an assessment. Continuous development is an important program objective. In fact, certification provides a structure that has all the pieces needed for rapid and continuous employee development.

The required assessments are listed next, arranged by the three levels of requirements (knowledge, performance, and business results): Participants must complete Level 1 before advancing to Level 2, and Level 2 before advancing to Level 3.

Level 1—knowledge

1. Prerequisite knowledge tests   Passing on-boarding, basic selling, and value selling tests.

2. Knowledge tests   Passing rigorous, 100-item multiple-choice test for certification candidates. The test covers eight areas identified in a job analysis. A test plan was developed, sample questions were written, items were validated in a meeting with SMEs, non-essential questions were eliminated and a passing score was established.

Level 2—performance

3. Role plays   Four challenging role plays were developed. The role plays require candidates to meet with three different officials at a hypothetical company. In order to ensure consistency, the people playing the company officials are given a detailed script that tells them how to behave, what to say, and how to respond to likely questions from the candidate. Similarly, observer/raters of the role play are provided with a detailed assessment form. The role plays are run similarly to assessment centers, a methodology used for hiring new employees or for giving developmental feedback for existing employees.

PDC considered having field observations of candidates by their supervisors instead of role plays, but in the end it was decided that a controlled setting with trained observers would be more effective. However, work samples (described next) provide a view of what the candidate is doing in the field.

4. Work samples   Candidates must provide samples of work completed for two customers. These include:

- general business and financial information that was collected on each customer;

- copies of sales presentations;
- completed customer analysis;
- completed customer recommendations;
- results achieved.

Work samples are evaluated using a consistent set of criteria.

Level 3—business results

5. Experience   Candidates must demonstrate that they are experienced in making value-based sales. They are required to document their experience with ten different customers.

6. Sales results   Candidates must be at 100% of sales plan goal, and they must demonstrate a large dollar amount of customer savings that comes from at least three different customers.

7. Letters of recommendation   Candidates need letters of recommendation from their Manager, their VP, and at least one customer. PDC provides guidelines for writing the letters (what the letter should cover, length, etc.) and a sample letter. Standards for letters of recommendation can greatly increase their value.

8. Effective and innovative practices   Candidates are expected to contribute to continuous improvement at PDC. This can be demonstrated by any of the following methods:

- Submit three effective practices. A written description of three practices the candidate has found to be effective when making a value-based sale.
- Developing an idea that is adopted and rolled out by PDC to other sellers.
- Effective assistance of other PDC sellers. Providing significant assistance to team members that goes beyond the norm expected of all sellers, as judged by the Certification Board. For example, this might include helping other sellers to prepare for presentations, accompanying them on sales calls, sharing tools, reviewing recommendations, and so forth.

9. Certification portfolio   This is the document used to package together all of the seller's credentials for certification. It includes all of the elements described above.

10. Certification Board approval   The candidate is required to make a 15–20-minute presentation of his/her certification portfolio to the Certification Board (a detailed outline has been prepared for the candidate on what is expected in the presentation). The Certification Board then has 20 minutes to ask questions. The Certification Board has also been provided with assessment forms, which will lead to fair and valid candidate reviews.

Certification maintenance
Successful candidates are encouraged to maintain their skills. Beginning one year after certification, individuals must be at 100% of their sales plan goal or greater and continue to document cost savings for their customers. Individuals that maintain their certifications are given a bonus each year and continue to enjoy the prestige and other perks they received when they were initially certified.

Development of Administrative Procedures, Staffing, and Technology—CT5

PDC has prioritized the codification of the certification program. A year earlier PDC had developed a Certification Administrative Guide for another certification, and this has served as the model for the guides of all subsequent certifications. The guide is broken into these major sections, each with their own subsections:

> Section 1: Certification background and summary
> Section 2: Development of certification requirements
> Section 3: Policies on becoming certified
> Section 4: Administration
> Section 5: Certification program description and FAQ for candidates
> Section 6: Methodology used to develop the certification
> Appendices

The Certification Administrative Guide spells out the three key roles for implementing the program, which are Task Force Member, Certification Board Member, and Certification Coordinator. Task Force Members have the following responsibilities:

During program design and development:

- design and develop the certification program;
- recommend administrative guidelines and policies;
- periodically review progress on implementation and provide feedback;
- champion and communicate the benefits of the program.

During program operation:

- champion and communicate the benefits of the program;
- identify when program additions or changes are needed;
- meet regularly to review progress and discuss/solve challenges;
- interface with the Certification Coordinator;
- manage certification incentives;
- interface with the Certification Board for major program changes.

For PDC, working through and completing the Certification Administrative Guide early in the process, rather than toward the end of the certification development, gave confidence that nothing was being missed. Further, it raised difficult questions early enough to develop solutions.

The guide is written primarily for the administrators who implement elements of certification on a regular basis. It is also an excellent resource for the Certification Task Force and Certification Board. However, its lengthy and dry nature makes it unsuitable for broad dissemination. Therefore, an attractive PowerPoint presentation was developed, along with a one-page handout that discusses program highlights.

The Future of Certification at PDC

PDC's seller certification has a high profile. It is serving as a template for other certifications. The sales department has closely partnered with PDC's training and development team (T&D). As a result, T&D have become apostles for much wider application of certification approaches. Their deep involvement in PDC's seller certification has resulted in a much higher level of awareness of how certification can be leveraged to meet many of PDC's talent management needs. Further, T&D has developed the skills to implement certifications and is familiar with the CT^5 approach and how it can be used to tailor future certifications to fit specific needs.

T&D is very involved with administration of the seller certification program. They serve on the Certification Task Force, they manage the multiple-choice test implementation and candidate tracking on PDC's Learning Management System, and they serve as role players in seller assessment centers. The VP of T&D sits on the seller Certification Board.

CONCLUSION

It is very common today to hear or read that, 'People are our competitive advantage.' That people are important to an organization's success is not controversial, but if people are going to be a competitive advantage, they have to be more effective than the talent that staff other organizations, given that those other organizations also have people! Supply chain management and quality management are two examples of disciplines that have been studied, improved, and systematized in the past and subsequently have evolved into significant competitive advantages. In this chapter, we have discussed CT[5], a blueprint for systematizing, managing, and improving the knowledge and skill of an organization's human talent.

NOTES

1. The authors would like to thank the following readers of this chapter for their excellent feedback: John Ceisel, Accenture; Andrew Garman, Rush University Medical Center; and Newton Moore, Abbott Laboratories.
2. From a conversation at a social gathering in Chicago, USA, 2007.
3. CT[5] is a trademarked program developed by Business Decisions, Inc., Chicago, Illinois, USA.
4. The consultant was Jim Graber of Business Decisions, Inc., Chicago, Illinois, USA.

REFERENCES

Bernthal, P., Colteryahn, K., Davis, P., Naughton, J., Rothwell, W., and Wellins, R. (2004). *Mapping the Future: Shaping New Workplace Learning and Performance Competencies*. Alexandria, VA: The American Society for Training and Development.

Fitz-enz, J. (2000). *The ROI of Human Capital: Measuring the Economic Value of Employee Performance*. New York: AMACOM.

Hale, J. (2000). *Performance-based Certification: How to Design a Valid, Defensible, Cost-Effective Program*. San Francisco: Jossey-Bass/Pfeiffer.

Knapp, J.E. (2002). *The Business of Certification: A Comprehensive Guide to Developing a Successful Program*. Washington, DC: American Society of Association Executives.

Knowledge Research Institute, Inc. (2000) *Knowledge Transfer Process Diagram*. http://www.krii.com/downloads/Kn%20Transf%20Process.pdf.

Mirza, P. (2004). Employers say measuring is vital but still don't do it. *HRMagazine*, **49**(4): 18.

Phillips, J. and Phillips, P. (2007). *Show me the Money: How to Determine ROI in People, Projects, and Programs*. San Francisco: Berrett-Koehler.

Rothwell, W. and Kazanas, H. (2004). *Improving On-the-job training: How to Establish and Operate a Comprehensive OJT Program* (2nd edition). San Francisco: Pfeiffer and Company.

Rothwell, W. and Poduch, S. (2004). Introducing technical (not managerial) succession planning. *Public Personnel Management*, **33**(4): 405–420.

Index

360° appraisals 189–90

Abel, D. 139
absorptive capacity 37
accelerated development 139–43
  developing a new story about self
    147–8
  developing/learning to use new
    networks 146–7
  end of program 155
  identity exploration 153–4
  as identity laboratory 151–2
  impostor syndrome 148
  insecure overachievers 148
  and job previews 148–9
  and knowledge work 145–6
  learning to delegate 145
  learning to use the program 152–3
  liminality 150
  new identity development during
    143–4, 150–52
  pre-entry experience 152
  and sharing knowledge 146
  taking on projects 144–5
  transitional space 150–51
  see also development
Acquired Needs Theory 164
acquisitions, gaining knowledge
  through 44
action theories of actors 110–11
actors
  action theories of 110–11
  creation of learning programs 105–6,
    106
  organization of learning networks
    105
  organization of work by 100–101,
    101
  organizations as networks of 96–9,
    98
Adamson, S. 142
adaptation of jobs to employees 42

Adler, P. 219, 225
Alderfer, Clayton 164
Allen, S. 218
alliance partners 46
ALR case study 243–53, 246, 249,
    251–3
appraisals
  and career counseling 127–30
  KM applied to 186–90
  and the TM/PM/KM relationship
    183–6, 186
artificial intelligence 28
assessment of employees 130
attributes of talent management 22
Averbrook, J. 182
Axelrod, B. 196

Bain 51
Bakker, M. 222
Bartel, C. 145
Baruch, Y. 126
Berger, L.A. 199–200
Best, D.L. 70
Best Buy 58
bodies of knowledge 37
Borman, W.C. 47–8
Boselie, P. 178
Boudreau, J.W. 34
British American tobacco 143
Buckingham, M. 196
bureaucratic organizations 97
buying knowledge 44, 46

Campbell, J.P. 47
career counseling
  appraisals as core activity 127–30
  integrated process of 126–30, 127
  integration with other TM practices
    130–32
  as integrative 124–6
  and organizational characteristics
    135

personal development plans
129–30
purpose of 126
responsibilities for 132–4
careers
mobility and organizational
characteristics 134–5
mobility in the internal labor market
121–3
self-management and mobility of
123–4
self-management of 119–20
case-based reasoning 29
case studies
ALR 243–53, 246, 249, 251–3
ODC 253–61, 255
certification of employees
ALR case study 243–53, 246, 249,
251–3
CT⁵ 240, 241–2, 243
ODC case study 253–61, 255
Chaparral Steel 47
CheckPoint 360° 190
chunking 28–9
codification of knowledge 50–51
Coffman, D.O. 196
Coleman, J.C. 219–20
Collins, J. 199–200
combination 36, 221–2
communities of practice 57–8
compensation packages 168–70
competencies of organizations 6–7
competitiveness of organizations
6–7
contracting for talent 44–5, 46
conversion of knowledge 36
*Corporate Training and Development
Advisor* newsletter 23
Corsello, J. 24
creation of knowledge 30, 204–5
creation of learning programs 105–6,
106
critical incident technique of
appraisals 188
CT⁵ 240, 241–2, 243
ALR case study 243–53, 246, 249,
251–3
ODC case study 253–61, 255
culture and knowledge management
27, 43

Darwiportunism 68
data mining 30
Davenport, T.H. 46–7, 145, 146
Davis-Blake, A. 44–5
den Hartog, D. 178
development
accelerated *see* accelerated
development
needs of employees 129–30
reversing skepticism concerning
237–9
diffusion of knowledge 53–8
Doherty, N. 142
Dorsey, D.W. 47–8
Dutton, J. 145

E-MYCIN 28
Eichinger, R. 153
employee certification
ALR case study 243–53, 246, 249,
251–3
CT⁵ 240, 241–2, 243
ODC case study 253–61, 255
employees
adaptation of jobs to 42
assessment of potential 130
development needs of 129–30
flows of 38–40, 39
grouped by strategic value and
uniqueness 45–6
job-based 46
knowledge-based 45–6
learning paths 95–6, 111–13
ranking of 189
recruitment of 21–2, 42, 48–9
retention of 22, 42–3, 227–9
retirement of 51–3
self-management of careers 132
as trainers 55
employment of female graduates
69–70
entrepreneurial organizations 97
Ernst & Young 143
essays from students 84–6
evaluation of performance *see*
performance management
Existence-Relatedness-Growth (ERG)
needs theory 164
expatriate assignments 55–6
Expectancy Theory 165

experience, learning from 204–5
expert systems 28
explicit knowledge 25–6, 35–6, 220–22
externalization 36, 221

female graduates, employment of
    69–70
firm-specific knowledge 37
flows, employee 38–40, 39
Fournies, F.F. 3
Frank, F.D. 223
Frauenheim, E. 24
Frey, R.V. 78
fuzzy logic 28

gathering of knowledge 27, 42
Gazprom, Russia 143
gender
    and graduate employment 69–70
    self-schema and work preferences
        70–71, 81–2
general knowledge 36–7
Generation Y
    attracting 69–78
    boundaryless careers preferred 84
    characteristics of 66–8, 67
    essays from students 84–6
    female graduates employment
        69–70
    organizational attributes preferred
        72–8, 73, 75–7, 81–3
    retention of 78–81, 79, 81, 82
Germany, retention of Generation Y
    78–81, 79, 81, 82
Giddens, A. 114
Gilley, J. 179
Goal-setting Theory 165
graduates, employment of 69–70
Graham, J. 180
Grazier, P. 166–7
Grove, A. 202

Ha, John 22
Hall, D.T. 155
Halogen eAppraisal 190
Hanfield-Jones, H. 196
Hansen, F. 23, 50, 51
Hansen, M.T. 7–8
Hanson, E.M. 99
Heckman, R.J. 6

Herzberg, Frederick 164–5
Hewitt Associates 201–2
Hierarchy of Needs theory 164
hiring of employees
    as function of TM 21–2
    for knowledge 42
    of knowledge workers 48–9
    for social capital 42
Horwitz, F.M. 48, 49
House, Robert 165
Hughes Space Systems Division 205
Hui, P.P. 44–5
human capital 200–202, 201
human dimension of knowledge
        management 7–8
human resource management
    architecture of for knowledge
        45–6
    integration of TM with software
        systems of 24
    interaction of TM and KM in
        planning 26–30
    lack of TM coverage in textbooks
        196
    responsibility for career counseling
        133–4
    as term compared to TM 3–6
    TM and planning 20–25

Ibarra, H. 144, 146, 147
identity
    development of new 143–4, 150–52
    experimentation 154
    exploration 153–4
igus (GmbH of Germany) 9
Illegems, V. 2
implementation
    of KMS in organizations 27
    of TM 23
impostor syndrome 148
incongruence in organizations 31
individuals, motivation of 165–6
industry-specific knowledge 37
information and knowledge 26, 35
information processing systems (IPS)
    26
intangible assets 200–202, 201
integration of TM/PM/KM 183–6,
        184, 185, 186
internalization 36, 221

job assignments, temporary 121
job-based employees 46
job enrichment 122
job matching systems 130–32
job previews 148–9
job rotation 55
jobs, adaptation of to employees 42
Jonker J. 223
Jorna, R.J. 220

Kantor, T. 24
Kets de Vries, M. 142
Kinnie, N. 48
Kirchoff, J. 178, 182
Knez, M. 196
knowledge
  bodies of 37
  capture and storage 50–53, 59, 61
  codification of 50–51
  conversion of 36
  creation of 30, 204–5
  diffusion 36, 53–8, 61, 235–7
  gathering of 27, 42
  general/specific 36–7
  human resource architecture for
    45–6
  and information 26, 35
  from learning from experience 204–5
  making/buying/renting 43–5, 46, 59
  processing 27–30
  saving 205–6
  sharing 146, 206–7
  spillover and loss 43, 61
  as tacit or explicit 25–6, 35–6,
    220–22, 236–7
  teams 56–7
  theory of creation of 220–22, 221
  transfer 36, 53–8, 61, 235–7
  using 207–8
knowledge-based employees 45–6
knowledge management
  applied to appraisals 186–90
  combined with TM 1–2
  competitiveness and competencies of
    organizations 6–7
  cultural problems with
    implementation 27
  definitions 217
  focus on cognitive domain 8–9
  and HR planning 25–6

human dimension of 7–8
integration of with talent staffing
    systems 59, 60, 61
interaction with TM in HR planning
    26–30
as key to survival 218–19
processes of 37
relationship with PM and TM
    176–8, 183–6, 184, 185, 186
and social capital 222
as socially constructed 219
software for integrating PM and TM
    190
knowledge management systems
    (KMS) 26
knowledge spiral 7
knowledge work and accelerated
    development 145–6
knowledge workers
  KSAOs of 46–8, 50–51
  motivators for 48–9
  recruitment of 48–9
Konrad, A.M. 81
Kovach, B. 142, 144
KSAOs of knowledge workers 46–8,
    50–51
Kwon, S. 219, 225

Larsen, H. 142
Lawler, E.E. 201–2
learning
  definition 202
  sources of 204–5
learning-network theory 96–9, 98
  and the structure-agency debate
    114–15
learning networks
  learning-relevant experiences gained
    from 104–11, 106, 107, 111
  organization of 105
  types of 106–10, 111
learning organizations
  global 208–12
  knowledge creation 204–5
  need for 202–3
  saving knowledge 205–6
  sharing knowledge 206–7
  using knowledge 207–8
learning paths, employee's 95–6,
    111–13

learning programs, creation of 105–6,
106
learning-relevant experiences
gained from learning network
104–11, 106, 107
gained from work network 100–104,
104
Leonard, D. 35
Lepak, D.P. 38, 45
Lewis, R.E. 6
Likierman, A. 24
liminality 150
line managers and career counseling
132–3
Lineback, K. 147
Lockwood, N. 20
Lombardo, M. 153
Losey, M. 224
loss of knowledge 43, 52, 61, 205

making knowledge 43–4, 46
Maslow, Abraham 164
Maycunich, A. 179
McCauley, C. 21
McClelland, David 164
McDonalds 205
McElroy, M.W. 220
McGregor, Douglas 165
McKinlay, A. 220
McKinsey and Company survey 23,
197–8
McTernan, J. 22
Meisinger, S. 224
memory, organizational 50
men
preferences in organizational
attributes 78
and work preferences 70–71, 81–2,
83–4
mentoring 54, 229
mergers, gaining knowledge through
44
Michaels, E. 196, 199–200
Microsoft 201
mindset, talent 22
Mintzberg, H. 97–9
mobility in the internal labor market
121–3
Monsanto 53
Morton, L. 20

motivation
of individuals 165–6
for knowledge workers 48–9
and reward and recognition
programs 167–72
of teams 166–7
theories of 163–5
MYCIN 28

NASA 52, 53
needs theories 164–5
Neilson, R.E. 33
networks
of actors, organizations as 96–9,
98
new during accelerated development
146–7
Nohria, N. 7–8
Nonaka, I. 7, 219, 223, 225
Northrop Grumman 57

occupation-specific knowledge 37
ODC case study 253–61, 255
on-the-job training 239
organic unit organizations 97
organization
of learning networks 105
of work by actors 100–101, 101
organizational memory 50
organizations
absorptive capacity of 37
attention to talent and success of
199–200
attributes of 72–8, 73, 75–7,
81–3
characteristics of and career
mobility 134–5
competitiveness and competencies
of 6–7
incongruence in 31
intangible assets 200–202, 201
knowledge creation in 204–5
learning in 204–5
need for reward and recognition
programs 161–3
need to focus on learning 203
as networks of actors 96–9, 98
types of 97–8
O'Toole, J. 201–2
Ouchi, William 165

Paauwe, J. 178
pattern recognition 28–9
Pellant, A. 196
performance management
    KM applied to appraisals 186–90
    in organizations 178–82
    relationship with KM and TM
        176–8, 183–6, 184, 185, 186
    software for integration with TM
        190
perks 170
person-organization fit 71–2
personal development plans 129–30
personalization strategy 51
Prieto, I.M. 222
Procter & Gamble 9–10
professional organizations 97–8
Profiles International 190
Prusak, L. 46–7
public knowledge 36–7
Pulakos, E.D. 47–8
Putnam, R.D. 220
pyramid example 33, 35–6, 40–41

Ramstad, P.M. 34
ranking of employees 189
recognition
    formal 171–2
    for global workforces 172–3
    informal 170–71
    see also reward and recognition
recruitment 225–7
    as function of TM 21–2
    for knowledge 42
    of knowledge workers 48–9
    for social capital 42
reluctance to implement TM 23
renting knowledge 44–5, 46
repatriation 56
replacement planning 57
retention of employees 22, 42–3, 227–9
    Generation Y 78–81, 79, 81, 82
retirement of employees 51–3
Revilla, E. 222
reward and recognition
    in a global organization 172–3
    impact of motivation on programs
        167–72
    motivation of individuals 165–6
    motivation of teams 166–7

and motivation theories 163–5
    organizational need for 161–3
Ruiz, G. 182
rule-based systems 28
Ruse, D.H. 196

Schoemaker, M. 223
Scholz, C. 68
search engines 29–30
SECI model of knowledge creation
    220–22, 221
self-management of careers 119–20
    and career mobility 123–4
self-schema 70–71
Senge, P.M. 207
Sensiper, S. 35
seven attributes of talent management
    22
shadowing 54, 229
smart talent management
    as combination of talent and
        knowledge management 1–2
    value of 9–11
    see also talent; talent management
Snell, S.A. 38, 45
social capital
    definitions 219–20
    expatriate assignments 55–6
    and talent management 223–4, 224
    theory of knowledge creation
        220–22, 221
social networks
    further research 115
    learning networks 104–11, 106, 107,
        111
    and learning paths 96
    relations between 114
    use of framework presented
        115–16
    work network 100–104, 104
socialization 36, 222
software, knowledge management
    190
software agents 29–30
specific knowledge 37
spillover of knowledge 43, 61
staffing systems
    and employee flows 40
    goals and objectives of 41–3
    integration of KM 59, 60, 61

knowledge capture and storage
50–53
knowledge transfer and diffusion
53–8
Starkey, K. 220
Stiffler, M. 180
Stockley, D. 196
strategic value of employees 45–6
structure-agency debate 114–15
Sturges, J. 124
subjectivity of appraisals 187–8,
189
Success Factors survey 23
SuccessFactors 190
succession planning 57, 228–9
Suomi, R. 229
Swart, J. 48

tacit knowledge 25–6, 35–6, 220–22,
236–7
Takeuchi, H. 7
talent
attention to and organizational
success 199–200
contracting for 44–5, 46
definition 34
definitions of 196
war for 197–200
talent management
barriers to 23, 25
combined with KM 1–2
coverage in HRM textbooks
196–7
definitions of 195–7, 217–18
and global learning organizations
210–12
groups referred to 20–22
and HR planning 20–25
integration with HR software
systems 24
interaction with KM in HR
planning 26–30
relationship with KM and PM
176–8, 183–6, 184, 185, 186
reluctance to implement 23
responsibility for 20
seven attributes of 22
and social capital 223–4, 224
software for integration with PM
190

to stimulate social capital 224–9
as term compared to other terms
3–6
talent mindset 22
talent staffing systems
and employee flows 40
goals and objectives of 41–3
integration of KM 59, 60, 61
knowledge capture and storage
50–53
knowledge transfer and diffusion
53–8
Tampoe, M. 48
Taylor, C.R. 223
teams
in knowledge-intensive firms
56–7
motivation of 166–7
Tempest, S. 220
temporary job assignments 121
Tennessee Valley Authority (TVA)
52
textbooks, coverage of talent
management in 196–7
Theory X 165
Theory Y 165
Theory Z 165
Thomas, K. 218
Thorne, K. 196
Tierney, T. 7–8
TM/KM model *see* smart talent
management
Towers Perrin survey 21
trainers, employees as 55
training and development 131–2
needs of employees 129–30
reversing skepticism concerning
237–9
see also accelerated development
transfer of knowledge 36, 53–8, 61,
235–7
transitional space 150–51
Turban, E. 25
Two Factor Theory 164–5

Ulrich, D. 224
undergraduates in UK, organizational
attributes preferred 72–8, 73,
75–7, 81–3
uniqueness of employees 45–6

United Kingdom, organizational
    attributes preferred by students
    72–8, 73, 75–7, 81–3

value of employees, strategic 45–6
Van Engelen, J. 220
Verbeke, A. 2
Viney, C. 142
Vroom, Victor 165

Wakefield, M. 21
Walters, J. 166
Wanous, J.P. 149
war for talent 197–200
Widen-Wulff, G. 229

Williams, J.E. 70
women
    graduates, employment of 69–70
    preferences in orgaizational
        attributes 78
    and work preferences 70–71, 81–2,
        83–4
Wood, A. 21
work, organization of by actors
    100–101, 101
work network, learning-relevant
    experiences gained from 100–104,
    104
work processes, types of 101–3,
    102